Sebastian Labitzke

# Avoiding Unintended Flows of Personally Identifiable Information

Enterprise Identity Management
and Online Social Networks

# Avoiding Unintended Flows of Personally Identifiable Information

Enterprise Identity Management
and Online Social Networks

by
Sebastian Labitzke

Dissertation, Karlsruher Institut für Technologie (KIT)
Fakultät für Informatik
Tag der mündlichen Prüfung: 19. Juli 2013
Referenten:
Prof. Dr. rer.nat. Hannes Hartenstein, Karlsruhe Institute of Technology (KIT)
Prof. Dr. rer.pol. Kai Rannenberg, Goethe-Universität Frankfurt am Main

The cover page illustration is based on empirical data analyzed in
the context of this thesis. The way in which the data is visualized is
inspired by the illustration of Facebook friendships by Paul Butler
(Facebook), Dec. 2010 (cf. Figure 5.8)

**Impressum**

 Scientific
Publishing

Karlsruher Institut für Technologie (KIT)
KIT Scientific Publishing
Straße am Forum 2
D-76131 Karlsruhe

KIT Scientific Publishing is a registered trademark of Karlsruhe
Institute of Technology. Reprint using the book cover is not allowed.

www.ksp.kit.edu

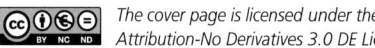
Print on Demand 2013

ISBN 978-3-7315-0094-0

# Avoiding Unintended Flows of Personally Identifiable Information

## Enterprise Identity Management and Online Social Networks

zur Erlangung des akademischen Grades eines

Doktors der Ingenieurwissenschaften

von der Fakultät für Informatik
des Karlsruher Instituts für Technologie (KIT)

**genehmigte**

## Dissertation

von

## Sebastian Labitzke

aus Eschwege

Tag der mündlichen Prüfung:   19. Juli 2013

Erster Gutachter:             Prof. Dr. rer.nat. Hannes Hartenstein
                             Karlsruhe Institute of Technology (KIT)

Zweiter Gutachter:          Prof. Dr. rer.pol. Kai Rannenberg
                             Goethe-Universität Frankfurt am Main

# Zusammenfassung

Online IT-Dienste sind allgegenwärtig, können jedoch oft nur dann verwendet werden, wenn der Nutzer personenbezogene Daten preisgibt, beziehungsweise diese Daten den Diensten zur Verfügung stehen oder gestellt werden. Anbieter von IT-Diensten nutzen personenbezogene Daten, um Zugriffsentscheidungen zu treffen oder um einen Dienst überhaupt anbieten zu können. Zwar können Nutzer bei zahlreichen IT-Diensten sogar selbst Einstellungen vornehmen, die Einfluss auf die Öffentlichkeit oder Weitergabe personenbezogener Daten haben, jedoch mangelt es den Nutzern oft an Bewusstsein für Privatsphäre sowie Verständnis der Prozesse und Implikationen, um mit diesen Einstellungen adäquat umgehen zu können. Insbesondere im Kontext sozialer Medien, wie etwa Sozialen Online-Netzwerken (engl. Online Social Networks, OSNs) entstehen konsequenter Weise (ggf. unerwünschte) Datenflüsse zu Dritten. Können Dritte die offenbarten Daten nutzen, um beispielsweise umfassende digitale Abbilder der Nutzer (auch Profile genannt) zu bilden, kann dies zu einem erheblichen Schaden für die Nutzer selbst führen. Die zentralen Fragen dieser Arbeit sind daher: Wie kann die unerwünschte Ausbreitung personenbezogener Daten quantifiziert werden und wie können Entwickler und Administratoren im Enterprise-Umfeld sowie Nutzer im OSN-Umfeld die Ausbreitung von Daten überwachen, kontrollieren und gegebenenfalls einschränken? Im Fall existierender unerwünschter Datenflüsse interessiert ferner, welche Möglichkeiten sich für Dritte ergeben, diese Daten zu sammeln und zu korrelieren oder gar nicht preisgegebene Daten zu prädizieren. Im Kontext der angeführten Fragestellungen sind die Ziele der hier beschriebenen Arbeit zweigeteilt. Einerseits werden jene Komponenten von IT-Infrastrukturen betrachtet, die eine Basis für die Integration von IT-Diensten darstellen, um einheitliche Zugänge zu diesen anbieten zu können. Diese Komponenten bilden zusammengefasst das sogenannte „Enterprise Identity Management". Andererseits werden OSNs und das darin beobachtbare Nutzerverhalten untersucht, um die resultierende öffentliche Präsenz von personenbezogenen Daten in OSNs zu quantifizieren und Risiken zu identifizieren. In beiden Bereichen galt es zunächst zu bestimmen, welche Daten von Dritten (potenziell ungewollt) eingesehen werden können. Des Weiteren wird untersucht, welche Auswirkungen die Offenlegung der Daten gegenüber Dritten haben kann. Schließlich werden Maßnahmen implementiert, die verhindern, dass Daten unerwünscht an Dritte weitergegeben werden bzw. den Nutzer bei der Aufgabe unterstützen, den Überblick über dessen offen zugänglichen Daten zu bewahren.

# Abstract

Today's online IT services are provided more and more ubiquitously. However, many of these services can only be used if they are provided with personally identifiable information (PII) either by the users themselves or another service that provides the information. IT service providers make use of this PII to perform access control decisions or to provide the service at all. Although users can often adjust certain settings to influence the accessibility or forwarding of PII, a significant number of users are not aware of the risks, e.g., privacy risks, combined with certain possible flows of PII. Hence, we can often identify a lack of understanding of the implications of flows of PII that, in turn, would constitute an essential basis to adjust provided settings adequately. In particular, in the context of Online Social Networks (OSNs), such inappropriately adjusted settings induce unintended flows of PII to third parties. Since those third parties can make use of this PII to, for instance, create comprehensive digital images of a particular user (i.e., profiling), shared PII poses privacy risks and can induce damage. Therefore, in the following, we state the main research questions addressed in this dissertation: How can the unintended proliferation of PII be quantified? How can developers and administrators of an enterprise environment, as well as users within an OSN environment be supported to control and monitor existing unintended data flows and how can they avoid unintended flows of PII before their occurrence? Furthermore, the thesis addresses which pieces of personally identifiable information can how often be gathered, correlated, or even predicted (if not accessible) by third parties to be used for their (possibly illegal) business. In light of the aforementioned research questions, the goals of this dissertation are twofold: On the one hand, we investigate components provided within enterprise environments that constitute a basis to integrate IT services in order to provide uniform service access, i.e., enterprise identity management systems. On the other hand, we focus on OSNs and the users' behavior regarding publicly sharing of information in order to quantify the mass of data available to the public and to identify corresponding privacy risks. For both areas of research, i.e., enterprise identity management and OSNs, we initially identify PII that can potentially be accessed by third parties in an unintended manner. Furthermore, we investigate the implications of publicly shared PII and, finally, we introduce implemented measures to avoid unintended flows of PII and for demonstrating users the potential receivers of their shared information, as well as corresponding privacy risks.

# Vorwort

Auf dem oft steinigen Weg zu einer Dissertation fragt man sich doch des Öfteren, ob das Einschlagen dieses Weges – neben den zahlreichen potentiellen Alternativen nach einem Studium der Informatik – tatsächlich die beste und klügste Entscheidung war. Retrospektiv wird jedoch sehr deutlich, dass die vergangenen Jahre nicht nur unfassbar reich an Erfahrung waren, sondern auch maßgeblich zur eigenen Persönlichkeitsbildung beigetragen haben, was sicher ein starkes Fundament für zukünftige Aufgaben bildet. Am Ende hält man dann dieses Buch als Produkt einer Zeit harter Arbeit sowie intensiver Forschung in den Händen und könnte sich an beliebiger Stelle mit seiner neu erworbenen Würde schmücken. Jedoch muss man feststellen, dass diese Dinge zwar einerseits vielleicht diejenigen sind, wofür man ursprünglich angetreten ist und wofür man all die Jahre gearbeitet hat, dass diese jedoch andererseits lediglich einen winzigen, wenn nicht sogar unbedeutenden Teil des vielschichtigen Gewinns darstellt, den man aus der Zeit als Doktorand mit auf die neu zu beschreitenden Wege nehmen kann. Einen Gewinn auf derart unterschiedlichsten Ebenen erarbeitet man sich definitiv nicht allein, sondern – in meinem Fall – in einem Umfeld äußerst smarter Menschen, denen ich im Folgenden ganz herzlich danken möchte.

Ich möchte mich insbesondere bei meinem Doktorvater Prof. Dr. Hannes Hartenstein bedanken, der mit einer perfekten Mischung aus entgegengebrachtem Vertrauen, forderndem Anspruch, perfekter Führung und überragendem Management den wohl größten Beitrag zu oben genanntem Gewinn geleistet hat. Nicht nur die persönliche Zusammenarbeit, sondern auch der ermöglichte intensive Einblick und Einbezug in die Arbeit als geschäftsführender Direktor eines sehr großen wissenschaftlichen Rechenzentrums hat mir Handwerkzeug und Basis vermittelt, um in Zukunft selbst noch mehr berufliche Verantwortung übernehmen zu können. Lieber Hannes, vielen herzlichen Dank für die Möglichkeit einer Promotion unter Deiner Supervision und die unzähligen lehrreichen Stunden an Deiner Seite.

Des Weiteren möchte ich mich bei Prof. Dr. Kai Rannenberg für die Übernahme des Korreferats und die tolle gemeinsame Zeit voller Ideen und konstruktivem wissenschaftlichen Diskurs bedanken. Dieser Dank gebührt ebenfalls Kais Mitarbeitern, insbesondere Dr. Andreas Albers, die mich als fantastische Forschungsgruppe an der Goethe Universität Frankfurt am Main stets herzlich willkommen geheißen und an vielen Stellen meine Arbeit unfassbar konstruktiv beeinflusst haben. Vielen, vielen Dank.

Ferner möchte ich mich bei Prof. Dr. Tanja Schulz, Prof. Dr. Jürgen Beyerer, Jun.-Prof. Dr. Dennis Hofheinz und Prof. Dr. Peter H. Schmitt für die Begleitung meiner mündlichen Prüfung bedanken.

Ein ganz besonderer Dank gebührt meinen aktuellen und ehemaligen Kollegen der Forschungsgruppe *Dezentrale Systeme und Netzdienste (DSN)* am *Institut für Telematik* des *Karlsruher Instituts für Technologie (KIT)*, in der die vorliegende Arbeit entstanden ist. Kompetenz, Leidenschaft und vielfältiges Talent sind nur einige der Attribute, welche dieses Team auszeichnen. Eine Gruppe von einerseits derart unterschiedlich gearteten und andererseits so exzellenter und smarter Kollegen ist meines Erachtens der wesentliche Schlüssel für erfolgreiche Forschung und die Basis für die Motivation und den Antrieb die eigene Arbeit voran zu bringen. Ein herzlicher Dank geht an Natalya An, Philipp Andelfinger, Tristan Gaugel, Konrad Jünemann, Matthias Keller, Jens Köhler, Holger Kühner und Tessa Tielert sowie die ehemaligen Teammitglieder Dr. Jens Mittag, Dr. Thorsten Höllrigl, Dr. Felix Schmidt-Eisenlohr, Dr. Moritz Killat, Dr. Marc Torrent-Moreno und insbesondere Dr. Jochen Dinger, der mich in der Anfangsphase meiner Promotion perfekt unterstützt hat, um meine Arbeit auf den richtigen Weg zu bringen, sowie Oliver Jetter und Frank Schell. Ich möchte mich auch ganz herzlich bei Astrid Hopprich für die unschätzbar wertvolle Unterstützung in organisatorischen Angelegenheiten sowie bei meinen studentischen Hilfskräften, insbesondere Florian Werling und Irina Taranu, für ihre äußerst wertvollen Beiträge bedanken. Herzlichen Dank Euch allen für eine unvergesslich schöne und zugleich produktive Zeit.

Ich habe während meiner Zeit am KIT ebenfalls intensiv am *Steinbuch Centre for Computing (SCC)*, dem Rechenzentrum des KIT, gearbeitet. Dies war eine wichtige Grundlage dafür, zu keinem Zeitpunkt meiner Dissertation den Blick auf das „Produktivgeschäft" und die Entwicklung, Integration und den Betrieb „wahrer" IT-Dienste zu verlieren. Auch hier war ich stets von tollen Kollegen umgeben, von denen ich nicht nur eine Menge gelernt habe. Allen voran ist hier Dr. Martin Nußbaumer zu nennen, der in meinen Augen einen perfekten Job als Abteilungsleiter der Abteilung *Dienste-Entwicklung und Integration (DEI)* macht und zusätzlich sein Handwerk als Projektmanager vorbildlich versteht. Ferner gebührt mein Dank meinen Identitätsmanagement-Kollegen Patrick von der Hagen, Hans-Peter Hör, Michael Simon und Alvar Wenzel sowie allen weiteren Mitarbeitern der SCC-Abteilung DEI und den Beteiligten des sehr erfolgreichen bwIDM-Projekts, Andreas Lorenz und seinen Mitarbeitern der SCC-Abteilung ISM, Axel Maurer und den Mitarbeitern des erfolgreich abgeschlossenen KIM-Projekts, den weiteren Direktoren des SCC sowie den vielen hier nicht explizit genannten Personen des SCC für die wertvolle, intensive und lehrreiche gemeinsame Zeit.

Ich möchte mich auch ganz, ganz herzlich bei meiner Familie bedanken, die stets hinter meinen Plänen steht und mich so vielfältig unterstützt, dass sie damit eine unumstößliche Säule meines Erfolgs darstellt. Insbesondere bedanke ich mich bei meinen Eltern Regina und Dieter Labitzke sowie meinem Bruder Tobias, bei meiner „Schwiegerfamilie" Claudia und Edgar Bürmann, bei Familie Dres. Ulrike und Norbert Labitzke und bei meinen Großeltern Anneliese und Gerhard Labitzke. Leider blieb meinem Opa – einem großartigen Menschen – sein Wunsch knapp verwehrt, dieses Buch in den Händen halten zu dürfen. Jedoch lebt seine positive und starke

Persönlichkeit in meiner Familie und mir und damit auch in dieser Arbeit in Ehren weiter. Herzlichen Dank Euch allen für Eure bedingungslose Unterstützung.

Ein weiterer Dank gebührt „La mia seconda famiglia", meiner zweiten Familie: Meiner Tanzfamilie. In Zeiten des harten Arbeitens und des vollen Terminkalenders ist es unfassbar wertvoll einen Ort zu haben, an dem man alles um sich herum vergessen kann, um sich als perfekten Ausgleich auf etwas vollkommen anderes zu konzentrieren. Diesen Ort hat mir in den letzten Jahren insbesondere die Tanzschule X-TRA DANCE in Karlsruhe mit den damit verknüpften unvergesslichen Erlebnissen, mit den hunderten tollen Kindern und Jugendlichen, mit denen ich arbeiten durfte, und mit unseren großartigen sportlichen Erfolgen gegeben. Stellvertretend für die vielen Menschen, die diesen Teil meines Lebens zu etwas sehr besonderem machen, möchte ich mich an dieser Stelle ganz herzlich bei Martina Böckmann, Silke Weber und Erika Hoppe bedanken.

Nicht zuletzt darf ich seit vielen Jahren an der Seite einer wunderbaren und liebevollen Person durch alle Bereiche meines Lebens gehen – eine Person, die stets an mich und meine Vorhaben glaubt, meine Arbeit auf unterschiedlichste Weise bereichert und mich in guten und in schwierigen Zeiten fantastisch unterstützt. Julia, vielen lieben Dank!

Sebastian Labitzke
Karlsruhe, Juli 2013

# Contents

# List of Figures

# List of Tables

# 1
# Introduction

*„If people feel like they don't have control over how they're sharing things, then we're failing them"* Facebook founder Mark Zuckerberg

This dissertation addresses the avoidance of potentially unintended flows of personally identifiable information (PII). In particular, we focus on Enterprise Identity Management and Online Social Networks. The risk that third parties can get unintended access to PII is quantified from different perspectives and (technical) measures to avoid these data flows are presented. In this chapter, we motivate the research topic and point out today's challenges of avoiding unintended flows of PII. Afterwards, the vision of a "perfect world" regarding the flows of information is sketched. Furthermore, we state the research questions addressed in this thesis and summarize the main contributions provided in the following chapters. Finally, the structure of the remainder of this dissertation is presented.

## 1.1 The Challenges of Managing PII

During the last decades, information technology (IT) has changed everyday life of millions of people worldwide. In particular, the daily business and even the private life of many people is dominated by an extensive use of IT services – primarily provided and consumed via the Internet. Those IT services are not only provided for the use by professional stakeholders, e.g., employees of a company, students of a university, partners of other organizations, etc., but also a significantly large number of IT services are offered for personal use. Hence, IT services become more and more ubiquitous and increasingly determine peoples' professional *and* private life. Furthermore, most of these IT services rely on identity information, i.e., personally identifiable information (PII) of individual users[1]. In other words, an essential basis for providing IT services is constituted by users' PII that is made available to these services by another service, or even by the users themselves. We refer to IT services that rely on identity information as *identity-related services* in the remainder of this dissertation. PII is required by identity-related services, for instance, to perform authorization decisions or to offer the service at all. It is further necessary that users share PII with certain identity-related services, e.g., social media services, as a basis of, for instance, communication and interaction with other users of these services. However, the other side of the coin is that the PII required by identity-related services might result in a large amount of information that is accessible by entities that are actually not intended to be able to see, or even process the data. This situation poses privacy risks for the owners of the PII, particularly, if the data is unintentionally accessible by third parties as a result of, for instance, users who are not provided with adequate support to overview who can access which piece of their PII. Therefore, (potential) flows of PII from one entity, which can be a service or a user, to another entity represent the main subject of research focused in this dissertation. In this context, an *unintended data flow* constitutes the abstract term for the situation that data could be accessible and processed by third parties in an unintended manner.

As already mentioned, today's users often interact with different and, in fact, hundreds of identity-related services during their everyday life. For instance, the computing center of the Karlsruhe Institute of Technology (KIT) – the Steinbuch Centre for Computing (SCC) – offers about 170[2] individual IT services for their customers, i.e., for more than 9,200 employees, almost 24,000 students, as well as guests and partners of the KIT[3]. Thereby, a large amount of flows of PII is induced by solely providing, for instance, an e-mail service or a portal for students to offer teaching material and insights into their individual course grades. In the context of social media, the situation regarding privacy that is potentially at risk is even more obvious. In particular, Online Social Networks (OSNs) provide IT services, or rather service platforms extensively used by millions of users for interconnecting and communicating with friends and others, as well as for sharing information with a certain (and often broad) audience. Facebook[4] – the currently largest OSN – stated that their services were used by, on average, 655 million *daily active* users in March 2013 and that the OSN has "an increase of 26 % year-over-year" with respect to the number of users[5]. Already in 2011, Facebook revealed that every user shares, on average, 90

---

[1] In this context, PII subsumes the data that characterizes an individual person in a specific context. For instance, identity information reveals users' current location, their hometown, age, relationship state, etc.. However, PII is also a user name and corresponding passwords that are necessary to access an IT service, or just data that results by using an IT service, e.g., the IP address that can be determined by service providers and that can identify the user who has accessed the service (cf. [TLH12]). Krishnamurthy and Wills define PII "as information which can be used to distinguish or trace an individual's identity either alone or when combined with other information that is linkable to a specific individual" [KW10a].

[2] Includes only services described in the Configuration Mgmt. Database (CMDB) of the SCC.

[3] http://www.kit.edu/kit/english/data.php [Last downloaded 2013-05-28].

[4] https://www.facebook.com/ [Last downloaded 2013-05-28].

[5] http://newsroom.fb.com/Key-Facts [Downloaded on 2013-05-28 and 2013-03-14].

pieces of content each month. It is likely that this number is even increasing because of the growing of the network itself and its still rising importance in everyday life of the more than one billion monthly active users[6] ("1.11 billion monthly active users as of March 2013."[7]). However, besides revealing PII on Facebook, users share also a lot of PII with other OSNs, such as Xing[8], LinkedIn[9], MySpace[10], StudiVZ[11], etc.. In this context, Mislove et al. found that also the number of active members of other OSNs is growing [MKG+08]. Therefore, in this dissertation, we do not only focus on the investigation of data flows induced by identity-related services provided within enterprise environments, but also and in particular on Online Social Networks because of the extensive use of these identity-related services.

We started this introduction by quoting Mark Zuckerberg's statement on privacy he gave during an interview by Charlie Rose[12]. In this statement, Mark Zuckerberg said that Facebook would fail their customers if they feel that they cannot control the flows of their own data. In fact, it is likely that most Facebook users do not *feel* that they lost control over their PII and we show in this thesis that, fortunately, not only Facebook, but also most other OSNs actually provide a wide range of features to adjust who can access which piece of information. However, in the context of OSNs, the main challenge is constituted by the issue to provide users with an appropriate chance to understand potential flows of PII as a basis to adjust already provided privacy settings in an appropriate manner. This not only includes the need for novel concepts for privacy enhancing technologies, but also and in particular appropriate quantifications of the risks regarding unintended flows of PII, which also constitutes a major challenge addressed in this dissertation. We tackle the mentioned challenges by presenting empirical investigations of privacy risks and by introducing technical measures to establish appropriate awareness and to avoid unintended data flows. In fact, we address these challenges for both *Enterprise Identity Management* systems and *Online Social Networks*. Therefore, we separately point out the specific challenges regarding flows of PII for both enterprise and OSN environments in the following.

Referring to *Enterprise Identity Management*, developers and administrators often already have the capability to improve the flows of PII to avoid unintentional access. Therefore, in most cases, it is not challenging to implement and provide privacy enhancing technologies in terms of improved processes that handle PII. However, the actual challenge is to implement solutions that are deployable at low effort, as well as operable and maintainable such as the existing infrastructures. Additionally, in enterprise environments, we can observe an increase of service integrations into

---

[6]On October 4th, 2012, Mark Zuckerberg announced – via a Facebook post – that "more than one billion people using Facebook actively each month" Source: https://www.facebook.com/zuck/posts/10100518568346671 [Last downloaded 2013-03-14].

[7]http://newsroom.fb.com/Key-Facts [Last downloaded 2013-05-28].

[8]https://www.xing.com/ [Last downloaded 2013-05-28].

[9]http://www.linkedin.com/ [Last downloaded 2013-05-28].

[10]http://www.myspace.com/ [Last downloaded 2013-05-28].

[11]http://www.studivz.net/ [Last downloaded 2013-05-28].

[12]http://www.youtube.com/watch?v=LFdUEkTzDeI [Last downloaded 2013-05-28].

organizational service infrastructures based on a organization-locally implemented system that handles the identity information, i.e., an *Enterprise Identity and Access Management* (IAM) system. Furthermore, the increase of collaborations between organizations require the federation of IT services and IAM systems across organizational borders. Therefore, IT infrastructures within enterprise environments become more and more complex and data flows are not limited by organizational borders. This situation makes it even more and increasingly difficult to keep any potential flow of PII between the individual services comprehensible. Even developers and administrators are challenged with the task of maintaining an overview of potential data flows, which constitutes a key element for implementing technical measures to adequately monitor, control, and, if necessary, avoid unintended flows of PII. In summary, the key challenge regarding the avoidance of unintended flows of PII constitutes the question whether or not these solutions can be deployed into existing (or even legacy) systems and also operated and maintained at a reasonable effort.

Within OSNs, probably the large amount of accessible PII, as well as the structure of OSNs result in confusions on user side in terms of no comprehensive understanding of who can access which piece of PII. Moreover, in a social media context, no developer or administrator is in charge of the monitoring and control of potential data flows. Instead, the user is responsible to protect his/her PII according to his/her own privacy demands. In combination with a demonstrable lack of privacy awareness (cf. [KW08] and [LTH11]) and potentially existing lacks of the usability of provided features to "adjust privacy" [TLH12], users might be overcharged with the situation or even do not care about possible privacy threats (cf. [KHG+08]). The findings of this thesis show that this is, at least, manifested in the adequacy users adjust privacy settings provided by OSNs to restrict the audience of shared PII. The logical consequence of this situation is that PII – and possibly very sensitive information – can be accessed by third parties that are actually not intended to see the data. Even worse, with a certain amount of information third parties can gain knowledge out of the accessible data that, in turn, leads to a great potential for third parties for making money with this information or even for threatening users' privacy. Hence, in this dissertation, we quantify the risks concerning accessible PII, which empowers users to perform an adequate (personal) risk management regarding privacy. Furthermore, we introduce (technical) measures to make flows of PII comprehensible and to even avoid unintended and potentially threatening flows of PII. In summary, the identification of potential threats, as well as to make those risks clear to users constitute the main challenges with respect to unintended flows of PII due to the use of OSNs that are addressed in this dissertation.

Certainly, also the users can profit from the knowledge third parties can get about themselves in terms of, for instance, interesting product recommendations or IT services provided for free. Therefore, flows of PII to third parties are not per se threatening in any case. Moreover, even not every unintended flow of PII is, at the same time, a privacy threatening data flow and both intended and unintended flows of PII might be significantly beneficial for users. However, some pieces of PII might be very sensitive information, especially if those pieces of information end up in the wrong hands. From the perspective of a user (or in some cases even from the provider's perspective), the unintended access to possibly sensitive information by a third party might pose one of the biggest threats in the area of consuming identity-related services, regardless whether the service is provided via a local network of an organization or via the Internet for a broader target group. In fact, if third parties get access to data in an unintended manner, they might be able to use this data for potentially privacy threatening, or even illegal, but profitable business. In turn, the identification and avoidance of unintended flows of PII constitute the major challenges for consumers and providers of identity-related services.

## 1.2   Managing PII in a Perfect World: an Idealized Vision

The following vision for future use of identity-related IT services forms the basis on top of which the investigations presented in this thesis have been carried out: in a perfect world, everyone would be able to identify any potentially unintended flow of PII as a basis to avoid these data flows, i.e., a situation of full and perfect transparency of data flows. On this basis, not only developers and administrators would be able to detect possible privacy threats within the environments they have to manage, but also users could determine who can access which piece of information forwarded by a service to another service, or even provided (or shared) by the users themselves. Such ability constitutes the basis for a comprehensive understanding of possible privacy threats, which, in turn, is necessary to act in a privacy aware manner when using identity-related services. In order to achieve such a situation, we have to invent features that support developers, administrators, and users in the evaluation of their current situation regarding privacy. In enterprise environments, it is necessary to introduce solutions to avoid unintended flows of PII that can not only just be implemented, for instance, as a prototype, but also can be deployed, operated and maintained at a reasonable effort, i.e., with minimal overhead. In the area of OSNs, users should be provided with the capabilities of developers and administrators of enterprise IAM systems, i.e., features are needed that can put users into the position of being able to monitor and control their PII that potentially can be accessed by third parties in an unintentional manner. In particular, those features should enable users to determine who can get access to information that is about to be shared (i.e., support *before* PII is actually shared) and it is necessary to support users in monitoring data flows and control access to PII *after* sharing pieces of information. Furthermore, quantifying the privacy risks is a must to provide a basis for users to be able to perform an adequate (personal) risk management, i.e., the comparison of the benefits of providing PII, the probability of occurrence regarding privacy leaks, and the potential damage if the PII unintentionally ends up in the hands of third parties.

## 1.3   Today's Situation Regarding Flows of PII

Figure 1.1 illustrates an abstraction of the current situation regarding IT services that are consumed in users' professional and private life. On the left hand side of the

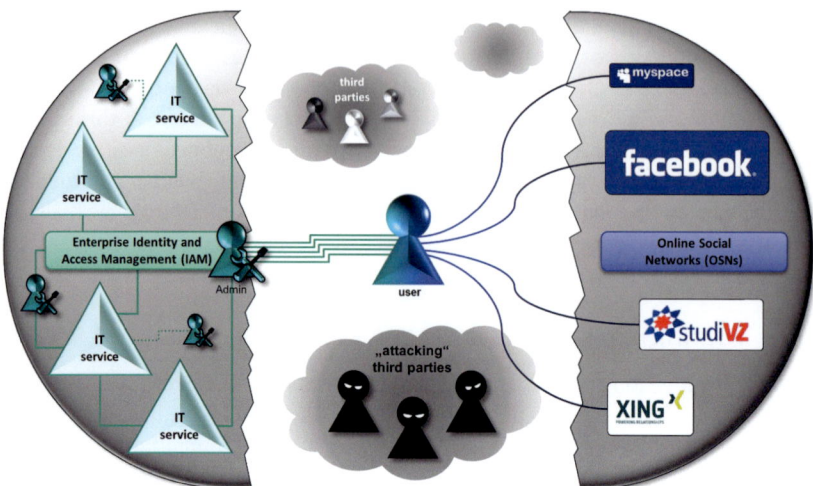

Figure 1.1: Usage of IT services provided, on the one hand, in *Enterprise Environments* and, on the other hand, by *Social Media* providers.

figure, we show exemplary IT services provided within an enterprise environment. In contrast, the right hand side of the figure illustrates the use of Online Social Networks.

In the case of IT services provided within enterprise environments, an infrastructure of identity-related services is often not monitored and controlled by only a single individual person or single team employed by the respective organization for these specific tasks. On the contrary, we have to consider a worse case: several instances are responsible for IT services, or rather are in charge of users' PII processed by these services (illustrated by the green figures on the left side). The services are provided in a more or less integrated manner, i.e., these services are interconnected with each other or, at least, rely on PII not administered by the respective service itself, but rather by one or more centralized instances of IAM components. In the context of such complex infrastructures, it becomes evident that often just a few people – if at all – can overview any potential flow of PII that can occur. Therefore, the situation of progressing integration of services might pose the inherent risk of the existence of unintended data flows despite the fact that access control is mandatory in an enterprise environment.

Referring to the right hand side of Figure 1.1, in OSNs, the user has to care about the management of his/her personal data[13] on his/her own, i.e., access control is a discretionary matter in those environments. No illustrated administrators on this side of the figure indicate that no one other than the users themselves have been imposed with the management of their PII available to these kind of services.

---

[13] Note that the terms *personally identifiable information* and *personal data* are used synonymously in this thesis.

## 1.4 Problem Statement and Research Questions

Unintended flows of PII can occur in enterprise environments, as well as due to the use of *Online Social Networks*. The problem with which privacy stakeholders, i.e., users, developers, and administrators, are confronted is the fact that often not every flow of PII, i.e., every potential third party that can get access to the data, is comprehensible. Regardless of the actual privacy awareness, transparency and a comprehensive understanding of the implications of data flows are *the* issue to solve and *the* essential basis to act in a privacy aware manner. Therefore, it is necessary to provide capabilities to trace the proliferation of PII – or, at least, adequate support to determine who can potentially get access to PII –, and features to control the accessibility of PII in an appropriate – i.e., a privacy preserving – manner. Moreover, a need for adequate risk assessment becomes obvious.

Based on this problem statement, we state the following research questions on top of which we present research findings in this dissertation:

- **PII Management:** *How can potentially unintended flows of PII be identified, quantified, monitored, and – if applicable – avoided by developers, administrators, or by users of identity-related services?*

- **Risk Assessment:** *Which kind of possibilities exist for third parties to correlate and/or infer users' PII by exploiting unintentionally accessible information?*

## 1.5 Main Contributions of this Thesis

As already mentioned, the focus of the presented research is twofold: first, we focus on *Enterprise Identity Management* systems and, second, unintended data flows are investigated in the area of *Online Social Networks*. However, the emphasis is set on contributions in the context of OSNs. In the following, we provide an overview of the main contributions of this thesis that improve the way adequate management of PII and assessments of the privacy risks can be performed by the stakeholders of privacy:

**Deployable, operable, and maintainable solutions to avoid unintended flows of PII in the context of *Enterprise Identity and Access Management* (IAM) systems:** in order to provide cross-organizational access to IT services, IAM systems handle authentications and manage PII of the users. Due to increasingly complex and highly decentralized infrastructures, as well as requirements that have to be fulfilled by an IAM system, some entities within such a system or even third parties can potentially get access to PII in an unintended manner. If such unintended access to PII is possible, the reason can be constituted (1) due to PII that can unintentionally flow to third parties because of inadequately implemented processes in the backend of the IAM systems or (2) due to the frontend implementation that might threaten users' privacy, i.e., due to user names and passwords typed in within insecure environments. For example, such insecure environments are lecture halls where others can spy on the users' keyboard or open terminals on which key loggers can be installed. In this dissertation, we address flows that result from both backend processes and frontend implementations. In particular, referring to (1), today's common IAM systems potentially forward credentials, i.e., user names and passwords, to identity management components that are not intended to get these pieces of PII. For this case, we introduce two solutions that can avoid the unintended forwarding of credentials, i.e., the *JAAS Dispatcher* and the *Extended Login Module*, which can be individually deployed or also in combination. The *JAAS Dispatcher* aims at forwarding credentials just to those components that are in charge of the data. The *Extended Login Module* can interconnect an IAM system with components that only provide proprietary interfaces and can include further characteristics into an authentication decision, e.g., the IP address of a user. The *Extended Login Module* constitutes also the basis for the improvement of frontend implementations to avoid data flows to third parties, i.e., credentials that can be accessed by others due to spying or logging users' inputs (2). To tackle this problem, we introduce a solution that can be deployed in common IAM systems to provide alternative authentications based on, for instance, Quick Response (QR) codes or social media logins. This solution can be deployed instead of or additionally to authentications via combinations of user names and passwords. In the context of enterprise IAM systems, the main research contribution of the solutions presented in this dissertation is constituted by the fact that components implemented on the basis of the introduced approaches can be deployed in already implemented IAM systems without changing much of the existing components and that the IAM system can be operated and maintained just as without the deployment of the introduced components.

**Attribute availability**: in the context of research in the field of OSNs, we initially investigate which pieces of users' PII can in how many OSN profiles actually be accessed by third parties and analyze corresponding privacy risks. Since this contribution is based on the analysis of more than 1.5 million OSN profiles (in total) and because of the large number of individual pieces of PII that have been analyzed, to the best of our knowledge, we provide the so far most extensive study on this topic. Furthermore, the presented results can be compared to previous studies that analyzed the availability of users' PII in OSNs, in order to derive and, particularly, quantify how the users' privacy awareness has been established through the years. Moreover, the results provide a valuable interdisciplinary input for research in the field of social science.

**Linkability of several OSN profiles of a single user**: with this contribution, we demonstrate that it is possible for third parties to link several profiles of a single user registered in different OSNs at low cost. In particular, we show that more than a half of the millions of OSN users publicly provide their list of OSN friends. Based on this available information, it is demonstrated that a user's profiles registered in different OSNs can easily be linked without exploiting sophisticated linking algorithms or high computational power. Instead, just comparisons of the friends' names are sufficient to determine whether or not a profile was registered by the same user who owns another profile. This contribution supports the design of future technical measures for users to identify and avoid unintended flows of PII in terms of a clarification of whether or not their different OSN profiles are linkable (cf. last contribution stated in this section).

**Investigation of the risk that third parties can infer non-provided PII of a user**: if users provide public access to their list of OSN friends, we answer the question whether or not attacking third parties can infer a user's non-provided PII based on information publicly shared by his/her friends. This investigation constitutes a key element of understanding the IT services provided by OSNs. In contrast to, for instance, IAM systems, we demonstrate that flows of PII are not only induced by the implementation of the OSN itself, but also by the possibilities an OSN provides to interact with the services and each other user.

**Investigation of the gaps between technical measures provided for users to control privacy in OSNs and users' mental models of the accessibility of their PII, as well as between privacy settings provided by OSNs and capabilities of developers and administrators working in an enterprise environment**: with this contribution, we identify a gap between today's technical measures provided to adjust who can access which piece of PII shared via an OSN and users' understanding of potential data flows. We investigate the psychological motivation for sharing PII and users' mental models of potentially existing data flows as a basis to identify key requirements for future privacy enhancing technologies. Furthermore, we contrast the capabilities of developers and administrators of *Enterprise Identity Management* systems with current features provided for *Online Social Network* users and demonstrate how developers' and administrators' capabilities can provide a template for the implementation of features that support OSN users in managing their PII.

**A Facebook App that aims at supporting users in matching their mental models to potentially unintended flows of PII**: in particular, a further contribution of this dissertation is constituted by the presentation of a novel concept of implementing privacy support. We show the concept and design, as well as a prototypical implementation of a privacy application that demonstrates a user his/her current situation regarding privacy based on the data he/she *and* his/her friends have publicly shared via the respective OSN.

Parts of the contributions presented in this thesis have been previously published in:

- Sebastian Labitzke, Florian Werling, Jens Mittag, and Hannes Hartenstein. *Do Online Social Network Friends Still Threaten My Privacy?* In Proceedings of the third ACM Conference on Data and Application Security and Privacy (CODASPY'13), San Antonio, TX, USA, February 2013. ACM.

- Irina Taranu, Sebastian Labitzke, and Hannes Hartenstein. *Zwischen Anonymität und Profiling: Ein technischer Blick auf die Privatsphäre in sozialen Netzwerken* (German). In Hannelore Bublitz, Irina Kaldrack, Theo Röhle, and Mirna Zeman, Herausgeber, Automatismen – Selbst-Technologien, Seiten 105–129. Wilhelm Fink, 2012.

- Jens Köhler, Sebastian Labitzke, Michael Simon, Martin Nussbaumer, and Hannes Hartenstein. *FACIUS: An Easy-to-Deploy SAML-based Approach to Federate non Web-based Services.* In Proceedings of the 11th IEEE International Conference on Trust, Security and Privacy in Computing and Communications (TrustCom-2012), Liverpool, UK, June 2012. IEEE.

– Sebastian Labitzke. *Who got All of My Personal Data? Enabling Users to Monitor the Proliferation of Shared Personally Identifiable Information.* In Jan Camenisch, Bruno Crispo, Simone Fischer-Hübner, Ronald Leenes, and Giovanni Russello, editors, Privacy and Identity Management for Life, volume 375 of IFIP Advances in Information and Communication Technology, pages 116–129. Springer Berlin Heidelberg, 2012.

– Sebastian Labitzke, Irina Taranu, and Hannes Hartenstein. *What Your Friends Tell Others About You: Low Cost Linkability of Social Network Profiles.* In Proceedings of the 5th International ACM Workshop on Social Network Mining and Analysis (SNA-KDD), San Diego, CA, USA, August 2011. ACM.

– Sebastian Labitzke, Jochen Dinger, and Hannes Hartenstein. *How I and Others can Link My Various Social Network Profiles as a Basis to Reveal My Virtual Appearance.* In LNI - Proceedings of the 4th DFN Forum Communication Technologies, GI-Edition, Bonn, Germany, May 2011. DFN.

– Sebastian Labitzke, Martin Nussbaumer, Hannes Hartenstein, and Wilfried Juling. *Integriertes Informationsmanagement am KIT: Was bleibt? Was kommt?* (German). In Arndt Bode and Rolf Borgeest, Herausgeber, Informationsmanagement in Hochschulen, pages 35–46. Springer, 2010.

– Sebastian Labitzke, Michael Simon, and Jochen Dinger. *Integrierter Shibboleth Identity Provider auf Basis verteilter Identitätsdaten* (German). In LNI - Proceedings of the third DFN Forum Communication Technologies, GI-Edition, Konstanz, Germany, May 2010. DFN.

– Furthermore, the following publications – in which the author of this dissertation was involved – are also related to the contributions presented in this thesis: [SWS⁺12], [LH11], [HLS⁺09a], and [HLS⁺09b].

## 1.6   Structure of the Thesis

This dissertation is structured as follows. In Chapter 2, we refine the research questions stated in this introduction with a focus on enterprise IAM systems. Beforehand, IAM systems are introduced and fundamentals are presented that constitute the essential basis of research in the field of data flows within enterprise environments. In particular, we define terms and introduce basic concepts of IAM in this chapter. Furthermore, selected related work is presented. Chapter 3 is dedicated to demonstrate the approaches that can improve today's common IAM systems in terms of avoiding unintended data flows. Furthermore, we show statistics of the use of the productive IAM infrastructure of the KIT that has been integrated the *JAAS Dispatcher* and the *Extended Login Module*. Afterwards, we switch the context and present research in the field of OSNs. In Chapter 4, we introduce OSNs, as well as corresponding terms and definitions. Afterwards, we discuss the concept of privacy settings provided by OSNs. Furthermore, we state the specific and refined research questions focused on

OSNs that this dissertation addresses in the following chapters. We complete this chapter by introducing related work. Chapter 5 constitutes the first of two chapters dedicated to present the results in the context of OSNs. In this chapter, we start by discussing requirements for studies in OSNs (mainly) imposed by the German data protection act. Afterwards, the attacker model, on top of which the findings have been gained, is introduced. Furthermore, we give insights into the methodology of the studies presented in this chapter. Finally, we present the results of empirical studies and investigations on privacy risks with respect to PII available due to the use of OSNs and the actual adjustments of privacy settings. In particular, we address how many information can be gathered from OSN profiles, whether or not PII provided in different OSNs can be gathered and linked to each other, and whether or not third parties are able to infer PII that is actually not provided by a user based on other information a third party can gather out of the OSN, e.g., PII of a user's OSN friends. In Chapter 6, we present an application that aims at establishing privacy awareness due to the demonstration of a user's current and actual situation regarding privacy. To introduce the concepts, on top of which this application is build, we discuss the psychological reasons for sharing PII via OSNs, demonstrate that users' mental models of flows of PII are not adequate at this point in time, and transfer the findings from the presented research in enterprise IAM systems to the situation in OSNs to build a basis for implementing privacy enhancing technologies. Chapter 7 concludes this dissertation and provides an outlook on future research. Appendix A provides information on how the solutions presented in Chapter 3 can be deployed. In Appendix B, we show further results on the linkability of different OSN profiles of the same particular user, whereas Appendix C provides further results on the investigation of inferable attributes of OSN users. Figure 1.2 gives a structure overview of the chapters of this dissertation and shows the belonging of each of the chapters with respect to the addressed research areas, i.e., Enterprise Identity Management and Online Social Networks. Additionally, Figure 1.3 (overleaf) provides a content-oriented overview. In particular, the content and structure, as well as an abstract view on the addressed research questions, the contributions and corresponding keywords are illustrated in these two figures.

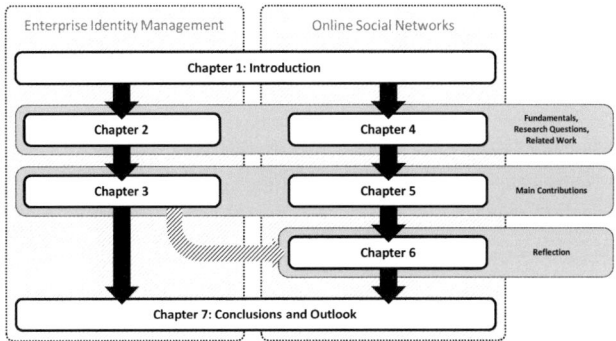

Figure 1.2: Structure overview of this dissertation.

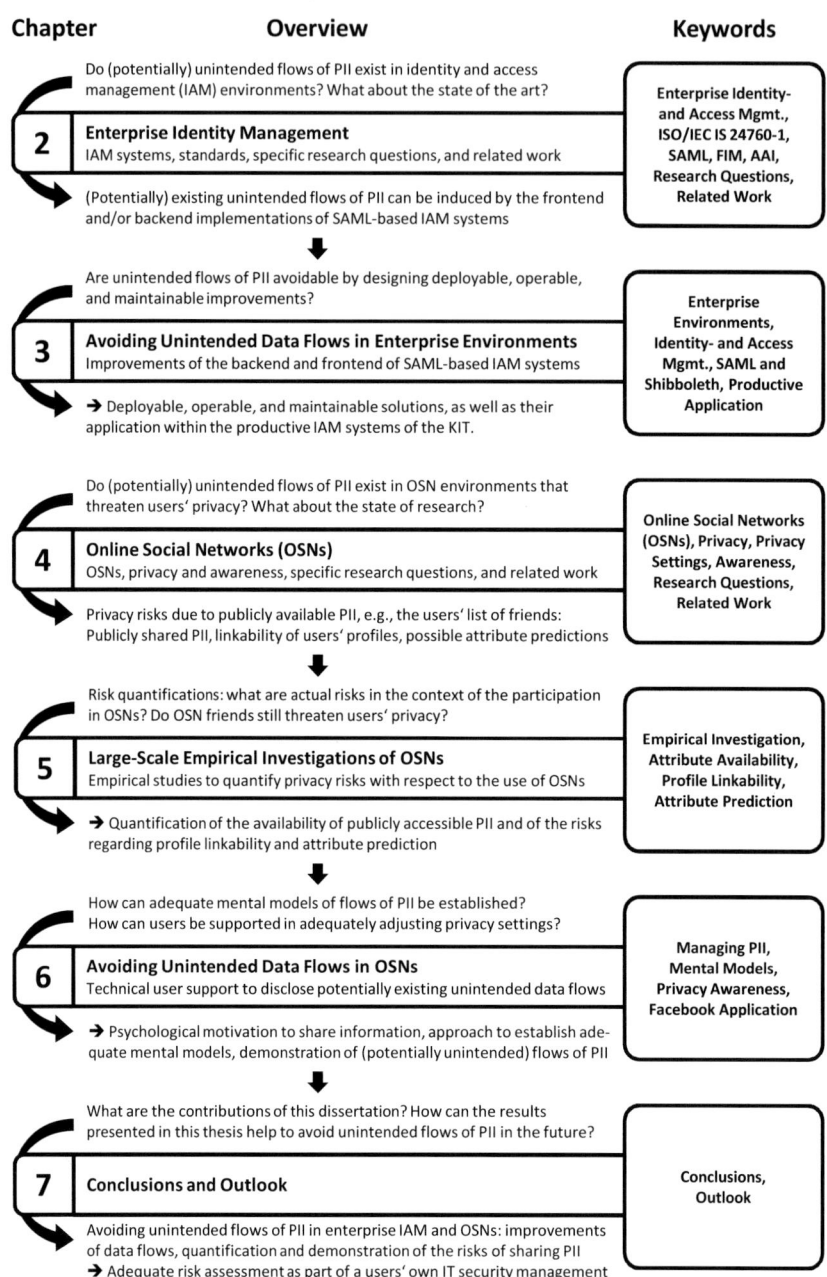

| Chapter | Overview | Keywords |
|---|---|---|

Do (potentially) unintended flows of PII exist in identity and access management (IAM) environments? What about the state of the art?

**2 Enterprise Identity Management**
IAM systems, standards, specific research questions, and related work

(Potentially) existing unintended flows of PII can be induced by the frontend and/or backend implementations of SAML-based IAM systems

Enterprise Identity- and Access Mgmt., ISO/IEC IS 24760-1, SAML, FIM, AAI, Research Questions, Related Work

Are unintended flows of PII avoidable by designing deployable, operable, and maintainable improvements?

**3 Avoiding Unintended Data Flows in Enterprise Environments**
Improvements of the backend and frontend of SAML-based IAM systems

→ Deployable, operable, and maintainable solutions, as well as their application within the productive IAM systems of the KIT.

Enterprise Environments, Identity- and Access Mgmt., SAML and Shibboleth, Productive Application

Do (potentially) unintended flows of PII exist in OSN environments that threaten users' privacy? What about the state of research?

**4 Online Social Networks (OSNs)**
OSNs, privacy and awareness, specific research questions, and related work

Privacy risks due to publicly available PII, e.g., the users' list of friends: Publicly shared PII, linkability of users' profiles, possible attribute predictions

Online Social Networks (OSNs), Privacy, Privacy Settings, Awareness, Research Questions, Related Work

Risk quantifications: what are actual risks in the context of the participation in OSNs? Do OSN friends still threaten users' privacy?

**5 Large-Scale Empirical Investigations of OSNs**
Empirical studies to quantify privacy risks with respect to the use of OSNs

→ Quantification of the availability of publicly accessible PII and of the risks regarding profile linkability and attribute prediction

Empirical Investigation, Attribute Availability, Profile Linkability, Attribute Prediction

How can adequate mental models of flows of PII be established? How can users be supported in adequately adjusting privacy settings?

**6 Avoiding Unintended Data Flows in OSNs**
Technical user support to disclose potentially existing unintended data flows

→ Psychological motivation to share information, approach to establish adequate mental models, demonstration of (potentially unintended) flows of PII

Managing PII, Mental Models, Privacy Awareness, Facebook Application

What are the contributions of this dissertation? How can the results presented in this thesis help to avoid unintended flows of PII in the future?

**7 Conclusions and Outlook**

Avoiding unintended flows of PII in enterprise IAM and OSNs: improvements of data flows, quantification and demonstration of the risks of sharing PII
→ Adequate risk assessment as part of a users' own IT security management

Conclusions, Outlook

Figure 1.3: Content overview of this dissertation.

# 2
# Enterprise Identity Management

In this chapter, we present further motivation on the topic and research questions introduced in chapter 1 with the focus on *Enterprise Identity and Access Management* (IAM) systems[1]. We discuss fundamentals of IAM systems and specify the research questions that form the basis for the contributions presented in this and the following chapter. Furthermore, we present related work with respect to the findings in the area of IAM systems in enterprise environments.

The chapter is structured as follows. We start by introducing common terms, definitions, and processes in the context of IAM systems. Afterwards, we present common architectures of IAM systems. Additionally, we present essential requirements and principles with respect to the implementation of components for today's already existing IAM systems and introduce identity federations, which constitute an essential architectural basis regarding the research questions addressed in this part of the thesis. Next, we refine the research questions stated in Chapter 1 with a focus on enterprise identity management. In particular, we state specific problems we investigate in detail in the following Chapter 3. Finally, in the last section of this chapter, we present and discuss related work. Parts of the contributions presented in this and the following chapter have been previously published in [LNHJ10], [LSD10], and [Lab12].

---

[1] Note that the management of access attempts is inseparable from the processes the term identity management subsumes. Therefore, IAM is just a more specific term for the term identity management and, thus, both "identity management" and "IAM" are used synonymously in this dissertation.

## 2.1   Terms, Definitions, and Processes

In the context of enterprise environments, the implementation of most IT services[2] are commonly based on an organization-internally provided and locally adminis- tered *Identity and Access Management* (IAM) system. In the following, we present fundamentals with respect to IAM systems. We start by presenting several terms and definitions that are common in the field of IAM. The definitions are mainly based on the terminology introduced in the international standard ISO/IEC IS 24760-1:2011(E) that is titled *"Information technology – Security techniques – A framework for iden- tity management – Part 1: Terminology and concepts"* [ISO24760]. Afterwards, we introduce common processes and functions an IAM system provides.

The mentioned international standard starts by defining an **entity**, i.e., an "item inside or outside an information and communication technology system, such as a person, an organization, a device, a subsystem, or a group of such items that has recognizably distinct existence" [ISO24760]. Therefore, an entity constitutes the most atomic structure of the identity-related terms. Based on the term *entity*, the following terms, essential infrastructure components, and processes can be defined:

Terms and Definitions:

– **Context:** we refer to the current situation or process in which a user is acting as a context, i.e., the combination of integrated services that are about to be accessed, possibly interconnected other IAM components, and the user him-/herself.

– **Attribute:** "characteristic or property of an entity (...) that can be used to describe its state, appearance, or other aspects" [ISO24760], i.e., a type of information whose so-called **attribute value** describes an entity from a certain perspective, e.g., a user's date of birth or his/her address, or describes what an entity has, e.g., the right to access a resource or a certain role within an organization.

– **Attribute value:** the value a specific attribute takes in a certain context.

– **Identity:** the "technical" representation of an entity in a certain context is called an *identity* and comprises a comprehensive "set of attributes" [ISO24760] that describes this entity. Usually, an entity, e.g., a user, has not only one single identity, but rather a set of identities that each represents this entity in a certain context. To give an example, a student's identity in the context of his/her uni- versity comprises the set of attributes the university stored about the student necessary to manage his/her accounts and to administer his/her student achieve- ments and course grades. This identity is different from his/her identity in the context of, for instance, his/her Facebook account. Potentially these exemplary identities can have some overlaps with respect to the individual attributes, but

---

[2]In the context of this dissertation, the term *IT service* comprises services that are accessible via the Internet or an Intranet by the use of a computing device. For example, cloud services, OSNs, Apps provided for mobile phones, etc. can be seen as IT services.

also significant differences, e.g., the university might store the student's matriculation number and field of studies and Facebook, on the contrary, knows about the student's hobbies and other information that is not mapped to his/her identity at his/her university, but spans his/her identity at Facebook.

– *Identifier:* On the basis of an identifier an entity can be distinguished from any other entity that is represented in a certain context (derived from [ISO24760]).

– *Identifier space (ID space):* the ID space defines the range of values an identifier can take.

– *Identity information:* describes a "set of values of attributes (...) optionally with any associated metadata in an identity" [ISO24760], i.e. identity information comprises pieces of PII and additional data concerning a specific *identity* and, therefore, a specific *entity*.

– *Credential:* Whereas in [ISO24760] a credential is solely defined as the "representation of an identity", we further particularize a "credential". In this thesis credentials can be constituted by a combination of a user name and a password, as well as by any other attribute with which an entity (e.g., an identity provider, cf. Section 2.2.2) can identify and authenticate another entity (e.g., a user).

IAM Processes:

– *Identification:* The process to check "claimed or observed attributes" for "recognizing an entity" in a certain context[3] (derived from [ISO24760]).

– *Authentication:* an authentication is defined as a "formalized process of verification (...) that, if successful, results in an authenticated identity (...) for an entity" [ISO24760], i.e., the authentication ensures the credibility, or rather the authenticity of an entity, which can be checked based on an unambiguous identity and certain characteristics [Eck08].

– *Authorization:* the process of an authorization is based on an authenticated identity and its attributes and comprises the decision whether or not access can be granted for the respective user, who has been authenticated, for instance, based on his/her credentials. The ISO/IEC IS 24760-1 states that an authorization establishes "entitlements for the entity to access resources and interact with services (...)" [ISO24760].

– *Login:* from the perspective of an entity, the login (aka. log in/Sign-on) describes the process that subsumes the authentication and authorization of an entity, e.g., a user. We refer to a user who has passed the login process as a *logged in* user. A special type of login constitutes the *Single Sign-On (SSO)*. If

---

[3]Note that in [ISO24760] the term "domain" is used to describe a certain context. To avoid confusion between *domains* in terms of separated organizations and *domains* in terms of separated IT services, we refer to a combination of a service and its interconnected IAM components as a "context".

an IAM system provides SSO functionality, a user can access several services by just a single login. A so-called identity provider (cf. Section 2.2.2) remembers the user at the point in time he/she gets forwarded to the identity provider by a service provider for not the first time in a specific period of time. If an identity provider can verify that a user is already authenticated, it redirects back to the service provider, claims the user has passed the authentication, and releases demanded attributes (if necessary and compliant). The ISO/IEC IS 24760-1 also defines an SSO across organizational borders. In this context, an SSO identity constitutes an "identity (...) that includes a single identity assertion (...) that can be verified (...) by a relying party (...) in multiple domains (...)" [ISO24760].

## 2.2    Flows of PII in Identity Management Systems

As already mentioned, many IT services rely on users' PII, e.g., for performing authorization decisions or even to provide the identity-related service itself. If identity-related services are supported by organizational IAM systems, providers of those services do not need to implement service-specific components to administer the users' identity information on their own. Instead, more or less centralized IAM components take over the task of handling PII, i.e., the administration and management of this data, as well as to make the data available for the identity-related services at the point in time it is requested by the service or intended to be forwarded (also known as *provisioning processes*). In this context, an IAM system implements rules, or rather policies on top of which decisions can be made with respect to whether or not it is compliant to make a specific piece of information available in a specific context and time, e.g., for a specific IT service that requested the data. These policies are mainly imposed by the law and, additionally, by data protection officers, the management, and/or the board of directors of an organization, as well as by guidelines and directives established within an organization. Due to the decentralized architectures of IAM systems and the fact that IAM systems forward and, therefore, replicate data within an IT infrastructure, a major challenge with respect to developing and operating IAM systems is the *consistency* of information. In particular, it is an issue to ensure that changes of a piece of information that is present at several different components of the whole IAM system and interconnected IT services are applied to every existing copy of the data (cf. [HDH10]). Furthermore, many organizations already deployed significantly complex IAM systems that provide most of their IT services with PII. Hence, no less challenging than the mentioned issues is the implementation of components for IAM systems that can be deployed into already existing IT infrastructures without the need to change large parts of the IAM system, as well as the IT services that are interconnected with the IAM system to obtain users' PII. Furthermore, it is necessary that the operability and maintainability of the IAM system and interconnected IT services is not negatively affected by newly deployed components (see Section 2.4 for more details on the requirements regarding the implementation of IAM components).

In the following, we refer to identity-related services that are connected to an IAM system as *integrated services*. IT architectures that divide the offering of IT services and

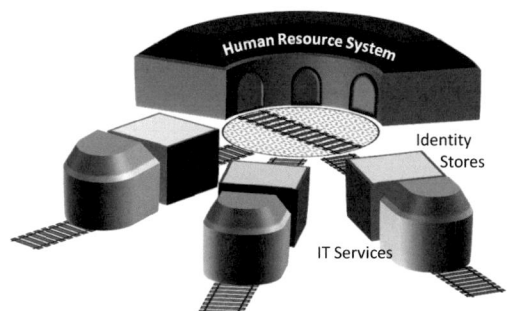

Figure 2.1: Illustration of the hub character of a provisioning system.

the provisioning of PII into separated components are called *integrated information management systems*, where information primarily (but not only) stands for PII. In general, IAM systems can be divided into two categories that utilize different strategies to deliver personal attributes, i.e., up-front provisioning services and IAM services that forward PII on-demand. In the following, we shortly introduce both of these strategies. However, in the remainder of this dissertation, we mainly focus on on-demand provisioning systems.

## 2.2.1   Up-Front Provisioning Services

Up-front provisioning services provide an integrated service with demanded PII by pushing it into a database, or any other (identity) store mostly at the point in time the IAM system obtains the data from the organizational human resource (HR) system or any other authoritative resource[4]. Due to the prompt provisioning of obtained information, the identity information is immediately accessible by one or more dedicated integrated services that are connected to the provisioned store, regardless whether the user has already tried to access the service or not. This push-strategy is common in many organizations (see also [SHH08] and [SHH09]). Up-front strategies for provisioning are implemented by dedicated software that serves as kind of a hub for PII and other information that is necessary for providing the IT services. Figure 2.1 illustrates the hub character of a (up-front) provisioning system. The locomotive hangar – in the background of the figure – represents the authoritative HR system that is deployed to administer human resources, or rather constitutes the authoritative resource for identity information. The hub has access to the HR system and can forward the stored information to several identity stores. In turn, each of the provisioned identity stores is accessible by dedicated IT services.

The processes, or rather flows of PII implemented within up-front provisioning services are "a priori" defined and executed if certain pre-defined events occur. To give an example, if an administration of an exemplary organization employs a new

---

[4]Authoritative resources are those systems that are in charge of (i.e., authoritative for) the *content* of the identity information, or the attribute values, respectively.

member of staff, the IAM processes recognize the new entry with the new employee's PII within the interconnected databases of the administration, take his/her data from this database, convert the information (if necessary), and provide the appropriate identity stores and, therefore, the respective IT services with the demanded pieces of his/her PII as a basis to provide access to the services. Thus, flows of PII are intended by definition, as long as the developers implemented the processes according to the guidelines imposed by the organization and the law.

Up-front strategies of provisioning are necessary and as common as the on-demand strategies introduced in the next section. However, because of the a priori definition and a priori intended character of flows of PII, up-front services play only a minor role in this dissertation. However, we shortly pick up those provisioning strategies in chapter 6 to discuss parallels of IAM systems deployed in enterprise environments and features provided for *Online Social Network* users.

## 2.2.2   On-demand Provisioning Services

In contrast to the introduced up-front provisioning approach, PII can also be provided at the point in time a user accesses a service. This strategy of provisioning is referred to as *on-demand forwarding of PII*, or rather *on-demand provisioning*. Services integrated within an on-demand provisioning system mainly request data at the point in time a user tries to access the service. The IAM system decides whether or not a user's PII can be released and, if this is the case (e.g., if the implemented rules permit the forwarding, if the forwarding is compliant with respect to the law, and/or if the user gave his/her consent), the IAM system provides the demanded information to the requesting service. Additionally, those "on-demanded approaches" often provide an authentication service for users besides the possibility to deliver personal attribute values, or rather pieces of PII to a service that is about to be accessed. The component that authenticates a user and forwards his/her PII and potentially other identity information to a requesting service is referred to as an *identity provider* (see definition below). Identity providers constitute separated components that are interconnected with local databases in which identity information is stored, as well as with identity-related services that have to be provided with identity information. In this dissertation, we mainly focus on these "on-demand" authentication and attribute delivery services, i.e., the identity providers of such systems. In the following, we introduce the four main components of an on-demand provisioning system in detail. In Section 2.3.1, these components are mapped to the specification of the *Security Assertion Markup Language* (SAML) on top of which popular on-demand provisioning IAM systems are built.

Architectural Components of On-demand Provisioning IAM Systems:

- *Identity stores:* identity stores are those databases that contain identity information and are utilized to administer this data.

- *Identity provider (IdP):* an IdP is defined as an "entity (...) that makes available identity information" [ISO24760]. Usually, the identity provider is interconnected with certain identity stores to verify credentials and to obtain identity information that is to be forwarded to another entity, e.g., an IT service.[5]

– **Service provider:** a service provider is the implemented representation of the so-called *relying party*, which is the "entity (...) that relies on the verification (...) of identity information (...) for a particular entity" [ISO24760]. In this context, a service provider has established a trust relationship to, for instance, an identity provider, which, in turn, delivers identity information on which the service provider can dispose whether to grant or deny access for a specific authenticated entity.

– **Discovery service:** a discovery service spans a federation of organizations and/or organizational units and often provides a manual selection possibility for identity providers in a certain federation (see Section 2.3.2 et seq. for a more detailed introduction of federated identity management and common components in such systems).

## 2.3   Identity Federations

Identity federations are interconnected organizations in terms of the interaction of their IAM systems in order to provide cross-organizational access to IT services each provided by one of the participating organization. The advantage of such federations is constituted by the offer of cross-organizational SSO and logins for IT services provided by other organizations by use of the account of the users' credentials managed by their own organization. In the following, we present parts of the *Security Assertion Markup Language* (SAML) specification, which constitutes key elements of on-demand provisioning IAM systems in general and identity federations in particular. Furthermore, we cover the topics *Federated Identity Management* (FIM) and *Authentication and Authorization Infrastructures* (AAIs). Both topics are fundamental for the investigations presented in this part of the thesis. Finally, we address the current popularity of SAML-based AAIs and, based on ongoing research work, we estimate the popularity of SAML in future IAM infrastructures.

### 2.3.1   Security Assertion Markup Language (SAML)

In the context of "on-demand approaches" that provide IT services with users' attributes, popular systems – particularly in the academia – are based on the specification of the *Security Assertion Markup Language (SAML)*[6]. The two most popular

---

[5]Recently, the research community started to make use of the term *Identity **Service** Provider (IdSP)* for this component (cf. [SKR12], [RMN+10] and http://openidentityexchange.org/what-is-a-trust-framework). The fact that IdPs, or rather IdSPs do not provide identities but rather a service related to identity information accessible by the IdP/IdSP led to this change of the term. However, the SAML community still makes extensive use of the term *IdP* so that we also use this term in the following.

[6]http://saml.xml.org/ [Last downloaded 2013-05-28].

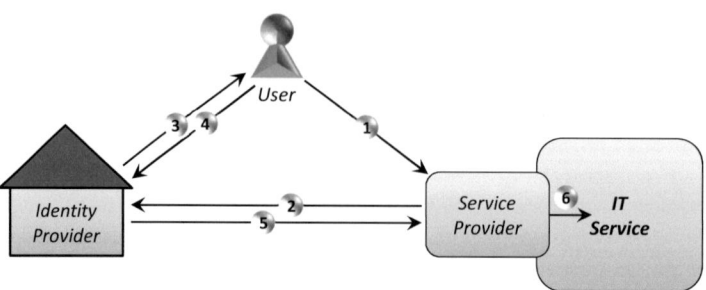

Figure 2.2: Interaction between a SAML identity and service provider.

reference implementations of the SAML specification are *Shibboleth*[7] and *Simple-SAMLphp*[8]. In this dissertation, we mainly focus on Shibboleth as the probably most frequently deployed SAML implementation. However, the SAML specification does not only include definitions of the packages that have to be exchanged between components for authentication and attribute delivery tasks, but also specifies the architecture and design of the interconnected and collaborating components. The two decisive components of a SAML-based infrastructure are the identity providers and the service providers. An identity provider is interconnected with the local IAM system and able to forward users' credentials (for instance, combinations of user name and password) to identity stores for verification. These components can also access users' attributes for forwarding to services, or rather service providers. A service provider represents a facade deployed in front of an IT service and handles requests, the forwarding of users, and the communication with identity providers. The following subsection shows the interaction of these two components, when a user tries to access an IT service.

SAML Components and Workflow

Figure 2.2 shows the interaction of the components specified by the SAML standard, such as it is implemented, for instance, by *Shibboleth* and *SimpleSAMLphp*. The facade that is deployed at an IT service – called *service provider* – interrupts a request from a user (step 1) and forwards the user to an identity provider (step 2). In turn, the identity provider, which is interconnected to local identity stores, presents a login screen to the user (step 3) and can forward users' credentials to the interconnected identity stores for verification. Furthermore, an identity provider has access to users' attributes that can be delivered to a service that is about to be used. At the identity provider side, the user has to provide his/her credentials (step 4). If the verification of these credentials results in a match at an interconnected identity store, the identity provider discloses demanded attributes for the service and redirects the user to the respective service provider (step 5). The service provider evaluates the released attributes and decides whether to grant or deny access to the requested service and can also forward the attributes retrieved from the identity provider to the service itself (step 6). In short, a

---

[7]http://shibboleth.net/ [Last downloaded 2013-05-28].
[8]http://simplesamlphp.org/ [Last downloaded 2013-05-28].

service provider serves as a facade to encapsulate a specific service and the identity provider presents the interface for authentication. Moreover, the service provider handles the forwarding of users to an appropriate identity provider and evaluates attribute values delivered by an identity provider. In turn, an identity provider handles the authentication and release of attribute values according its configuration, i.e., an administrator has to specify what attributes can/must be forwarded to a specific service provider if a user is successfully authenticated, or rather if his/her provided credentials could be positively verified by an interconnected identity store.

Shibboleth and SimpleSAMLphp additionally provide Single Sign-on functionality, i.e., if an identity provider authenticated a user at his/her first attempt to access a service, the user will be automatically authenticated for further service accesses that are handled by this identity provider. As an add-on, administrators can install and activate uApprove[9] that presents a form for getting consent by the user if attributes are going to be forwarded. This add-on is not mandatory, but useful to fulfill the requirements of data protection acts, particularly, requirements imposed by the German law and data protection act.

In summary, from the perspective of a user, the Shibboleth and SimpleSAMLphp login procedure does not look different from common authentication processes. Only the redirect to another website – i.e., the identity provider, or rather its frontend that requests a user's credentials – is unusual and requires instructions, or rather explanations, for users because they might think about a phishing attack when they get redirected to another website for login.

### SAML Messages and Concepts

In the following, we describe how the SAML standard provides information about the communication between the individual components. In particular, the SAML standard defines the content and structure of so-called *assertions*. Assertions are the essential parts of the messages send between identity and service providers. These parts of the messages consist of information about whether or not a user could be authenticated by the identity provider. Furthermore, assertions contain the attribute values that are to be forwarded to the service provider on the basis of which authorization decisions can be disposed. Besides the assertions, the SAML standard defines further terms and structures that are shortly introduced in the following. The SAML *protocol* defines the requests and responses itself, e.g., the forwarding of a user is implemented as an *authentication request* that a service provider sends to an identity provider. The specification of so-called SAML *bindings* contains the mapping of SAML protocols to standard communication protocols. For instance, Shibboleth implemented inter alia POST and REDIRECT bindings via HTTP [RFC2616] and SOAP[10]. In turn, bindings are a sub-category of a *profile*, whereas a profile defines a set of assertions, protocols, and bindings (cf. [Hughes2005]). A comprehensive overview on XML-based security and identity and, particularly, a detailed introduction of SAML can be found in [Mal05].

---

[9]http://www.switch.ch/aai/support/tools/uApprove.html [Last downloaded 2013-05-28].

[10]http://www.w3.org/TR/soap12-part1/ [Last downloaded 2013-05-28].

### 2.3.2  Federated Identity and Access Management (FIM)

In recent years, more and more organizational units, or even multiple organizations work together in terms of sharing services provided by one of the collaborating partners. In this context, IAM systems can not only be deployed for the use within organizational borders but also for cross-organizational collaborations, or rather cross-organizational service access. We refer to those collaborations as *federations* of participating organizations and to the IAM systems that provide cross-organizational service access as *Federated Identity and Access Management (FIM)*. Therefore, FIM provides the basis for cross-organizational integration of IT services, i.e., a user U can access an integrated service provided by an organization A by simply using the account of his own organization (organization B), also known as the *home organization* of user U. In other words, users of organization B can access services provided by organization A by the use of their credentials registered at their home organization B. The basis of such federated service access constitutes a trust relationship between the collaborating organizations on top of which organization A trusts organization B in authenticating a user and forwarding – if necessary – correct information, or rather PII, about the authenticated user U.

An identity that is valid in a cross-organizational manner is called a federated identity. The ISO/IEC IS 24760-1 defines a federated identity as an "identity (...) for use in multiple domains (...), which together form an identity federation (...)". In turn, an identity federation is defined as the "agreement between two or more domains (...) specifying how identity information (...) will be exchanged and managed for cross-domain identification (...) purposes" [ISO24760].

In the context of FIM, it has to be stated that not only cross-organizational federations can be established. The more independent organizational units of a single organization are structured and working, the more worth it might be to apply the concept of a federation onto the inner-organizational structure. An IAM system of such organizations can be seen as an in-house FIM (cf. [SHH08]). The authors of [SHH09] show how this approach is implemented at the KIT.

However, the federation of services or, at least, a federation itself is subject to certain risks, restrictions, and requirements. In a collaborative use of services PII will be forwarded to collaborating organizations and, therefore, potentially leaves the organizational borders if a user tries to access a service that is not provided by his/her home organization. Unintended flows of PII might be the consequence of federation because of the circle of entities that could potentially get access to sensitive information. Additionally, the larger the federations the more the participants have to tackle the problem to prevent the federation from becoming too complex from the perspective of a user. In particular, users often have to choose their home organization (see Section 2.3.3 for further details) out of a list of organizations participating in the federation. If therein not only the organizations are listed, but also several organizational units or if certain individual identity stores are referenced the usability of such a system might be significantly decreased compared to a federation that is spanned carefully with respect to a usable cross-organizational offer of IT services.

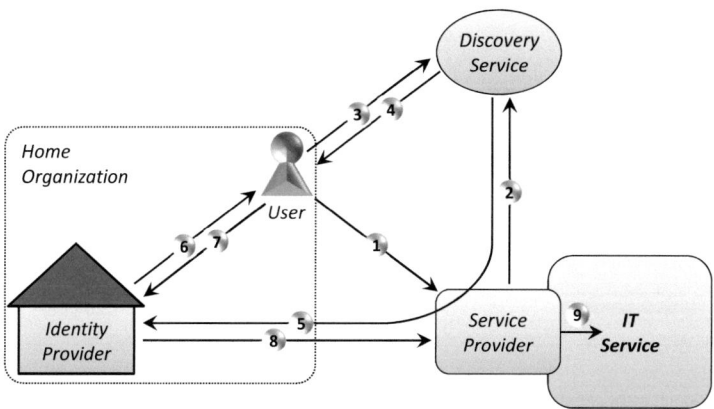

Figure 2.3: Federated IAM with SAML-based components.

### 2.3.3   Authentication and Authorization Infrastructures (AAIs)

Technical infrastructures that provide FIM functionality are known as *Authentication and Authorization Infrastructures (AAI)*. In recent years, many countries built their own AAI, at least, for the academia located in the respective country. In Germany, the German Research Network (German: Deutsches Forschungsnetz, DFN) provides the DFN-AAI for researchers working at German universities, libraries and other institutions of higher education. The DFN-AAI – as well as many other AAIs, particularly, those implemented for the academia – is based on the SAML standard and its implementations.

Figure 2.3 illustrates the basic concept of a SAML-based AAI. Besides the identity and service provider, which have been already introduced in the context of SAML, the AAI components consist of the so-called *discovery service*. In Section 2.3.2, we mentioned that users might have to choose their home organization when trying to access a service provided by a different organization. The discovery service exactly provides this capability and, therefore, spans the federation. In particular, an AAI consists of multiple identity providers, multiple service providers, and a discovery service. If a user tries to access a service (step 1 of the illustration) and several potential identity providers are eligible for authenticating users for this service, the service forwards the user to the discovery service of the federation (step 2). Then, the user gets suggested with a list of potentially eligible identity providers (step 3) and can choose one out of the presented list (4). Afterwards, the workflow is similar to the application of SAML-based authentications in a local environment. The user is forwarded (via the service provider) to the (chosen) identity provider (5). The identity provider presents a login page (6) and the user provides his/her credentials (7). If the credentials can be verified against one of the interconnected identity stores (not considered in this visualization) the user will be redirected to the service provider (8), which can then perform the authorization based on the attributes released by the identity provider and can – if the authorization is successful – permit the access to the service.

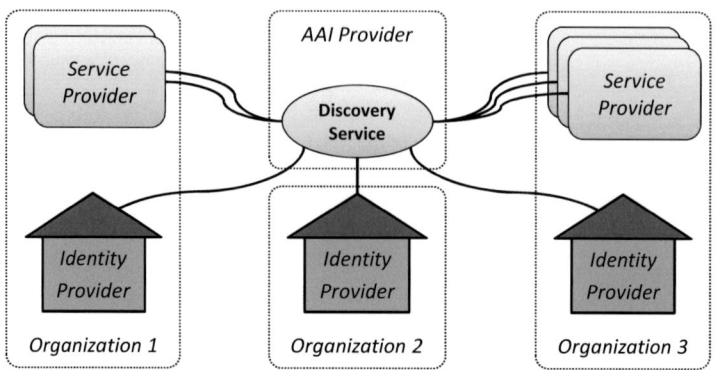

Figure 2.4: Exemplary structure of an AAI and its participating organizations.

Figure 2.4 shows the interaction of an exemplary AAI. In the middle of the figure, we illustrate the Discovery Service, which is operated by the AAI provider, e.g., in the case of Germany's academic AAI, the DFN-AAI. Besides the AAI provider, the figure contains three exemplary participating organizations that operate their own identity provider and/or one or more service providers integrated into the AAI to provide cross-organizational access.

In general, AAIs are essential for the problems stated in the following section. In particular, the restrictions of AAIs imposed for participating organizations mainly induce the problems addressed in the following. However, AAIs are not the core of the solution and the solutions presented in Chapter 3 does not aim at improving the AAI itself, but rather at improving the local components so that unintended data flows can be avoided.

### 2.3.4   Current and Future Popularity of SAML-based AAIs

SAML-based AAIs are commonly deployed at academic institutions, for instance, to provide access for researchers and students to work published by other researchers. Furthermore, many universities already provide SAML-based logins to other IT services provided for researchers and students, e.g., portals, e-mail web interfaces, etc.. Additionally, companies provide software that can be integrated into or interconnected with SAML-based components, e.g., Microsoft's Active Directory Federation Services can be interconnected with Shibboleth identity providers to combine federations that are each built upon one of these technologies. However, not only the academia deployed SAML-based IAM systems, but also companies that provide cross-organizational access to their provided IT services. Furthermore, although SAML-based AAIs are so far primarily designed to integrate *web-based* IT services, researchers spend significant effort into work that enables SAML-based IAM systems for other types of IT services. In particular, AAIs might become increasingly important in the future, not only because of the rising number of organizations participating in one or more AAIs, but also because of the different types of services that can be integrated into those infrastructures. The studies introduced in the following underpin the motivation to investigate SAML-based infrastructures with a focus on potentially existing unintended flows of PII.

Currently, the universities of the state of Baden-Württemberg, Germany, collaborate in the project *bwIDM*[11] that aims at developing a solution to integrate non web-based IT service – such as high-performance computing, cloud, and grid services – into Shibboleth infrastructures (see also [SWS+12] (German) and [KLS+12]). In this project, an innovative improvement of SAML-based infrastructures has been developed so that aforementioned services can be integrated. In particular, a combination of a customized PAM module, a registration service, and an LDAP facade has been invented. This solution is based on the SAML profile Enhanced Client or Proxy (ECP) (see [Hughes2005] for a detailed introduction of SAML profiles). Furthermore, other researchers have integrated specific services into SAML-based infrastructures. For instance, the integration of non web-based services constitutes also the aim of the project *Moonshot* [HNS10]. However, the Moonshot approach for federating non web-based services differs from the bwIDM approach in terms of the fact that Moonshot is mainly based on existing RADIUS infrastructures [RFC2865] and the Generic Security Service Application Program Interface (GSS API) [RFC1508]. Only the release of attributes is planned to be implemented on the basis of SAML, or rather Shibboleth components. The authors of [VTCP12] invented another SAML-based IAM that aims to integrate VISION clouds[12] – a specific type of cloud service – into Shibboleth federations. Shibboleth is also used by the community of grid computing[13] to federate access to the grid infrastructures, e.g., [WBKS05], [SGJ+06], and [GGPW07]. Additionally, the authors of both [BFW10] and [MKMT11] introduced federation approaches for specific grid communities. In these papers, Shibboleth is used to issue so called short-lived X.501 certificates, with which users can access the grid infrastructure. A customized Shibboleth identity provider is also used in the *GridShib* project to issue attributes [BBF+06]. In summary, it is obvious that many inventions have been introduced to enable different kinds of services for SAML and, particularly, Shibboleth. Thus, it is likely that AAIs become more and more important for the collaboration between organizations that share provided IT services – at least, in the academia. Therefore, it is even more important to investigate potentially unintended data flows in such infrastructures. Whereas the collaborative features of SAML-based implementations are based on state-of-the-art cryptographic methods to ensure secure data flows, we identified a lack of studies that investigate data flows – caused by the collaboration of organizations – that occur within the boundaries of a single participating organization.

---

[11]http://www.bw-grid.de/bwservices/bwidm/ [Last downloaded 2013-05-28].

[12]http://www.visioncloud.eu/ [Last downloaded 2013-05-28].

[13]The authors of [FK99] define grid infrastructures as "a hardware and software infrastructure that provides dependable, consistent, pervasive, and inexpensive access to high-end computational capabilities". In particular, a grid integrates several computing resources (independent of the location) to get a large computing cluster. Programs that have to be executed, or rather computing tasks, are called *jobs* (cf. high performance computing) and can travel from one specific grid computing resource to another one.

## 2.4   Principles and Requirements for IAM Components

In this part of the thesis, we introduce terms for the most important principles on top of which the specific research questions – introduced in the next section – are addressed. Before we define requirements closely related to this dissertation, we introduce and discuss some of the general principles regarding IAM systems stated by Kim Cameron (Architect of Identity, Microsoft Corporation). These principles became known as "Kim Cameron's Laws of Identity"[14]. Kim's seven laws are meanwhile referenced in many research and industry publications. In the following, we address only those two laws that are most related to this dissertation. Kim's first law addresses "user control and consent". In particular, he states that "technical identity systems must only reveal information identifying a user with the user's consent" [Cam05]. In principle, this accompanies with the German data protection act (German: Bundesdatenschutzgesetz, BDSG) that states the requirement of user's consent in § 4 et seq. BDSG. However, exceptional cases for the requirement for obtaining the users' consent in the context of data collection and forwarding are also considered by the German law (§ 4 et seq. BDSG). With that, in some circumstances the German law permits the processing of data without users' explicitly stated consent. However, in any case a person has to be informed about the data processing by the responsible institution that gathers his/her PII. Furthermore, this institution has to clarify the purpose on which the processing is based (§ 4a BDSG). See also Section 4.1 for further discussions on the BDSG with the focus on research on Online Social Networks.

Another of Kim Cameron's "Laws of Identity" is titled "Minimal Disclosure for a Constrained Use" and says that "the solution which discloses the least amount of identifying information and best limits its use is the most stable long term solution" [Cam05]. Thus, an IAM system that discloses as minimal information as necessary is probably the system that can be operated for the longest period of time because it will be less susceptible with respect to possibly upcoming restrictions, for instance, regarding data protection. Moreover, the minimality of disclosure of PII is a requirement stated by many laws. For instance, the German data protection act prescribes this minimality in § 3a BDSG.

In the following, we introduce further principles that form essential requirements for implementing components for IAM systems. These requirements form the basis of the research presented in this part of the thesis.

The probably most important requirements are the *deployability*, *operability*, and *maintainability* of modules that are to be integrated into existing IAM systems. Hence, the improved modules for IAM systems presented in the next chapter do not only aim at presenting something very innovative in the sense of the functionality of the modules, but also and in particular the solutions fulfill the mentioned three requirements that are introduced in detail in the following:

- **Deployability:** we define a solution as *deployable* if the effort for integration into existing systems is reasonable and feasible even for an administrator.

---

[14]http://www.identityblog.com/stories/2005/05/13/TheLawsOfIdentity.pdf [Last downloaded 2013-05-28].

- ***Operability:*** we define a solution as *operable* if it fits into existing infrastructures, or even legacy systems, so that the processes implemented in those systems have not to be changed in an unintended manner and the integration does not require unreasonable efforts.

- ***Maintainability:*** a solution is *maintainable* if the changes of the legacy systems, or rather the existing infrastructure, does not induce that updates for the respective system are no more deployable, i.e., if updates provided by the vendor or manufacturer of a system (or infrastructure) can be deployed as before the integration of the new solution, we classify a solution as maintainability preserving.

In summary, a key requirement for designing a deployable, operable, and maintainable solution is constituted by the need that as few changes as possible are necessary to integrate the components into the productive infrastructures, or even into legacy systems, i.e., approaches that, for instance, do not require to change already deployed code. Instead, a solution has to be designed in a modular manner so that – in the best case – it can be integrated by just changing configurations of the existing productive infrastructure. Furthermore, a new IAM component should not induce the need to change existing and established processes of an organization. If a solutions fulfills these requirements and, moreover, an administrator does not need to change the whole configuration to integrate a new component, but just a few lines, we characterize such solution as "minimal invasive" with respect to the infrastructure in which the solutions have to be integrated. However, the three introduced requirements induce that designing a solution for avoiding unintended data flows constitutes a non-trivial task. Whereas the prevention of flows of PII to non-authoritative resources might be trivial in itself, the implementation of solutions that fit into the existing infrastructures in a "minimal invasive" manner sets the basis for the real challenge that is tackled in this part of the dissertation. Note that we sometimes make use of the term "deployability" as a generic term that subsumes the triad "deployability, operability, and maintainability".

In the following, we introduce additional requirements that have to be considered when designing solutions for avoiding unintended flows of PII. A requirement for an improved concept of interconnecting identity providers with identity stores is to not infiltrate the concept that is called "separation of concerns" with respect to the groups of identities and the corresponding responsible departments. Large organizations separate the administration of identities because possibly no organizational unit can be found that could be in the position to represent the authoritative department for any identity information. For instance, at a university it might be problematic for a computing center to administer the accounts of people who are only external customers of the library. In turn, the library staff might be overcharged if the identities of every employee have to be administered and, to give another example, a student account should be administered by the central administration of the university because of the sensitive data – such as course grades – that is attached to the identity information. Therefore, the independence of administrative domains should be maintained by an improved integration method for Shibboleth identity providers.

Furthermore, sensitive data, such as passwords or password hashes, should not be replicated in other identity stores than those that are authoritative for the respective data. Not only security arguments underpin this requirement but also the increased effort of updating data if it is replicated into additional databases.

In the following, we focus on the specific part of a SAML-based, or rather Shibboleth-based identity provider that handles the interconnection with identity stores and state corresponding requirements. Shibboleth implements the modular connection of identity stores via the *JAVA™ Authentication and Authorization Service* (JAAS). JAAS is implemented to be used for two purposes: authentication and authorization for JAVA™-based components. The JAAS reference guide states that JAAS is dedicated "to reliably and securely determine who is currently executing Java code, regardless of whether the code is running as an application, an applet, a bean, or a servlet". Moreover, JAAS can ensure that users "have the access control rights (permissions) required to do the actions performed". Therefore, JAAS constitutes a feature to authenticate and authorize users who are executing JAVA™ code. Since the release of the J2SDK 1.4 it is integrated into the JAVA™ standard edition. In particular, JAAS provides a possibility to interconnect identity stores with JAVA™-based components so that the interconnection has not to be implemented by the JAVA™ component itself. The concept underneath the JAAS feature is a pluggable component that "permits applications to remain independent from underlying authentication techniques", i.e., the interconnected identity stores and, therefore, the mentioned authentication techniques remain transparent from the perspective of the JAVA™ component.[15] As already mentioned, JAAS is integrated in and used by common identity provider implementations, such as Shibboleth, to interconnect with identity stores. JAAS supports interconnections with, for instance, directories based on the Lightweight Directory Access Protocol (LDAP) [RFC4511] or even interfaces based on a Pluggable Authentication Module (PAM) [Sam96]. However, in general, the way of integrating identity stores via JAAS is very common and independent from SAML and Shibboleth, i.e., JAAS is used for SAML components like for any other application that integrates identity stores or any other database via JAAS. Therefore, a requirement for the implementation of an improved integration concept based on JAAS is that the solution can not only be used for Shibboleth but also for any other application that utilizes JAAS. This requirement originates from the demand that we attempt to not breaking already existing and commonly deployed concepts. That means, if we would not target a solution that can be used in any other application that utilizes JAAS, we would fail the requirement for being minimal invasive with respect to the concepts on top of which an implementation of a Shibboleth identity provider is based.

A further challenge constitutes the specification of SAML itself that has to be considered when designing new approaches for avoiding unintended flows of PII, i.e., the compliance with respect to the widely used SAML specification constitutes an additional requirement.

---

[15] http://docs.oracle.com/javase/6/docs/technotes/guides/security/jaas/JAASRefGuide.html [Last downloaded 2013-05-28].

Finally, a last requirement originates from a special circumstance in the academia. The libraries of the universities (particularly, libraries of German universities) have to be open for the public, i.e., every citizen can use the library as a so-called walk-in user. Walk-in users also can use the IT infrastructure to search for books, journals, etc. Otherwise, these users do not have an account like a student or employee. Therefore, it is common to authenticate just the terminals in the library (instead of the user him-/herself) for service requests with respect to, for instance, literature research. Hence, the check of the IP address should be possible with the Shibboleth infrastructures that authenticate users or terminals for access to literature services (see also [ORBL09]).

In summary, the following requirements have to be fulfilled by the concepts presented in the following:

- Design of *deployable* solutions that can be *operated* within existing systems without additional effort and that preserve the *maintainability* of these existing systems.

- "Minimal Disclosure for a Constrained Use" [Cam05].

- Preserving the independence of organizational units or even organizations involved in providing an integrated IT service.

- No change of existing (technical and organizational) processes.

- No replication of passwords or other sensitive information into third databases.

- Automated and configurable identification of the appropriate identity store for each of any user login.

- Maintain common concepts, such as the JAAS concept to interconnect identity stores.

- Compliance with the SAML specification.

- Integration of additional authentication attributes, such as IP addresses.

## 2.5   Specific Research Questions

In the current section, we refine the research questions stated in chapter 1 with the focus on *Enterprise Identity Management* and SAML-based IAM systems.

As early as 2005, Kemp wrote that "a common misconception concerning network security is that the infrastructure is at considerable risk from external attackers" [Kem05]. Furthermore, the author identified, for instance, the "abuse of trust" as a potential attack. In the *Internet Security Threat Report 2011*, the company Symantec state the following prognosis for the analysis of threats in 2012: "While external threats will continue to multiply, the insider threat will also create headlines, as employees act intentionally – and unintentionally – to leak or steal valuable data"[16]. In this

---

[16]http://www.symantec.com/threatreport/ [Last downloaded 2013-05-28].

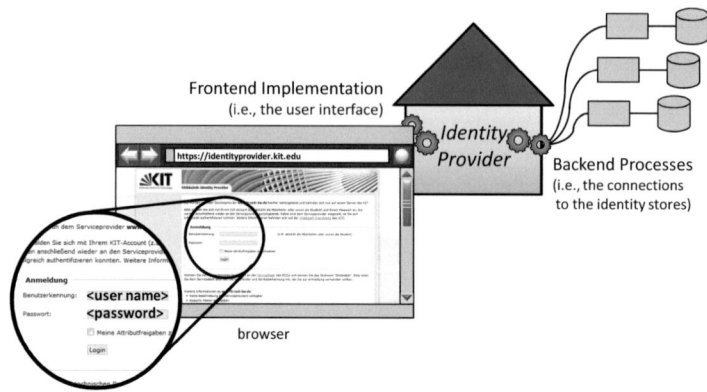

Figure 2.5: Frontend implementation and backend processes of a SAML-based identity provider.

context, the company AlgoSec interviewed 182 IT security and operations experts and state that "the greatest business security risks and challenges come from within the organizational boundaries"[17]. In this whitepaper, AlgoSec also proclaims that "Security is an inside job. As serious as threats may be from hackers and malware, only one out of five respondents see external threats as their #1 risk. IT Security and Operations departments are more focused on gaining visibility into their applications and networks, improving processes that are time-consuming and error-prone, and defending against internal threats". Therefore, we assume that one of the biggest threats come from inside an organization, i.e., from the people working with the respective components or those who can get unintended access to PII processed by these components. In the remainder of this part of the dissertation, we focus on threats coming from inside an organization due to unintended flows of PII in general and focus on the following research question in particular:

– *Who can access what piece of information within a SAML-based IAM system inside the organizational borders?*

In turn, we consciously do not focus on the IT security of the systems in terms of measures to head off external attackers trying to intrude the systems. This IT security perspective is another field of research that is not an essential part of this dissertation. The exclusion of external attacks allows a focus on unintended flows of PII caused by the implementation of *processes* within today's IAM systems in contrast to security leaks that can be exploited by any internal and external attacker. In particular, we focus on SAML-based IAM systems and on the current implementation of processes of SAML-based identity providers connected to individual identity stores as it is implemented in many organizations (cf. for instance, the number of German

---

[17] http://www.algosec.com/resources/files/Specials/Survey files/120404_Survey Report.pdf [Last downloaded 2013-05-28].

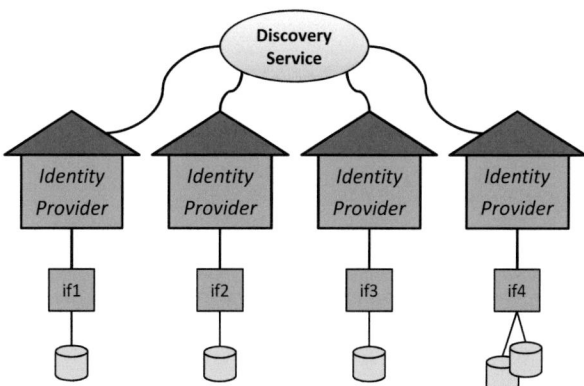

Figure 2.6: Principle approach to federate several identity stores, or rather their interfaces (ifX) via SAML-based identity providers that are federated by a discovery service.

organizations participating in the DFN-AAI[18]). Because of the fact that an identity provider releases requested PII to its integrated services based on rules and policies implemented at the identity provider, an identity provider constitutes one of the most "vulnerable" components in a SAML-based infrastructure with respect to processes whose implementation potentially induces unintended data flows.

As pointed out in Section 1.5, we divide the processes of an identity provider that are focused in this thesis into two categories, i.e., parts implemented for the identity provider *backend* and those implemented to provide a *frontend*. The *backend* of an identity provider connects a SAML component to the local identity stores and ensures the integration into the rest of the IAM infrastructure of the respective organization. In contrast, the *frontend* modules represent the user interface and all corresponding workflows, i.e., providing an interface to the users that is necessary to, for instance, type in their credentials. Figure 2.5 illustrates the partitioning of an identity provider into the backend and frontend implementation. Whereas the backend implementation (right side of the figure) comprises the processes that are based on the interconnection with identity stores, the frontend implementation (left side of the figure) subsumes any process that is related to the user interface and the input of users' credentials.

In the following, we firstly state the specific research questions addressed in this thesis with a focus on the backend processes and, second, we introduce the research direction with respect to the frontend implementations of SAML-based identity providers. However, the main objective of the approaches presented in this thesis applies to both research directions, i.e., we provide simple and, therefore, deployable, operable, and maintainable approaches for implementing IAM components that can be integrated into existing SAML-based IAM infrastructures to avoid unintended data flows.

---

[18] https://www.aai.dfn.de/verzeichnis/teilnehmer/ [Last downloaded 2013-05-28].

## 2.5.1   Unintended Data Flows Within the SAML Backend

In Figure 2.6, we illustrate the principle behind a federation based on identity providers similar as introduced in Section 2.3.3. A discovery service spans a SAML-based identity federation. The identity providers are interconnected with identity stores (illustrated as cans), or rather with interfaces provided by these identity stores (if1, if2, if3, and if4). Note that we abstract from existing service providers in this and the following illustration.

If we now assume a heterogeneous organization, i.e., an organization in which identity information is not stored in a single identity store, several identity providers and a discovery service could span a federation that would constitute a solution to provide access to services integrated in this federation for any user whose identity information is administered by one of the integrated identity stores. In point of fact, organizations tend to implement an identity store for each of any group of users who potentially try to access provided IT services, e.g., a university often implements separated stores for their students, employees, library guests, etc.. Therefore, many organizations are heterogeneously structured with respect to the separation of identity information in different identity stores. However, the users of those organizations could login by just choosing the appropriate identity provider that is interconnected with the identity store responsible for the users' data and by providing their credentials. For instance, a user, who has registered an account at the library of his/her academic institution, can choose the identity provider of the library to perform a federated login. A user with another account – for instance, an account at the computing center – would choose another appropriate identity provider. Thus, such a heterogeneous organization would implement an inner federation of their provided services and identity stores by the use of several identity providers.

Referring back to Figure 2.4 shown in Section 2.3.3, we demonstrated how a cross-organizational AAI is spanned by an AAI provider. Primarily, because of usability reasons, AAI providers strive to keep the number of identity providers listed by the discovery service as small as possible. One of the reasons for this constitutes the fact that users have to pick and choose their identity provider from the website presented by a discovery service. If the number of identity providers listed by this website becomes too large, the usability would significantly decrease. A further reason for allowing only one identity provider per organization is the management overhead that might increase with every additional participating identity provider from the perspective of the AAI provider. Moreover, a single participating identity provider ensures loose coupling of an organization and the AAI provider in the sense that organization-internal processes stay transparent for the AAI provider. Therefore, it is not surprising that a membership of an organization in a cross-organizational AAI often requires that the organization only brings a single identity provider into the federation.

If we again assume a heterogeneously structured organization, which operates several identity stores, an essential issue of implementing SAML-based IAM systems becomes obvious. Because of the fact that hierarchies of identity federations are not intended, not specified by the SAML specification, and, therefore, not implemented, organizations with several identity stores have to interconnect these identity stores

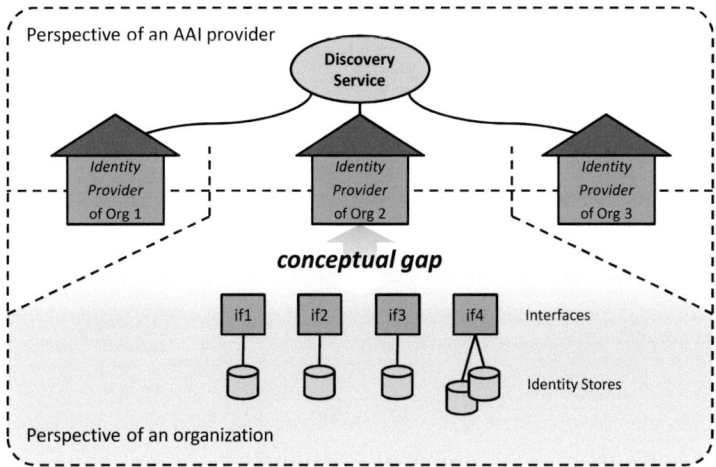

Figure 2.7: Conceptual gap between the perspectives and requirements of AAI providers and individual organizations.

with a single identity provider that participates in the federation to still be able to handle any login attempt by users whose data is administered by one of the existing identity stores. Figure 2.7 demonstrates this conceptual gap. The upper part of the figure shows the perspective of an AAI provider that imposes the requirement of a single identity provider per organization. In contrast, the lower part of the figure illustrates the perspective of a participating organization that is faced with the issue of interconnecting several identity stores to a single identity provider. In summary, the deployment of a single identity provider for an organization is problematic if an organization consists of, for instance, several organizational units that administer and manage "their" identities on their own and do not want to or are not able to delegate the administration into the hands of a central organizational unit, e.g., a computing center. Therefore, a conceptual gap between the requirements for being a member of an AAI (single identity provider per participating organization) and the intents of a SAML-based infrastructure regarding the necessary number of identity providers within the boundaries of an organization is existent.

However, SAML implementations – such as Shibboleth – do provide a solution for connecting more than one identity store to a single identity provider. Therefore, the following research question arise:

– *Does the implementation of IAM processes within SAML-based identity providers for interconnecting several identity stores pose the risk of unintended data flows?*

Figure 2.8 illustrates existing approaches for interconnecting an identity provider with several identity stores. Basically, organizations have two different opportunities for the necessary integration of their identity stores so far.

First, identity stores can be integrated by utilizing the JAVA™ Authentication and Authorization Service. This opportunity constitutes an already built-in feature of

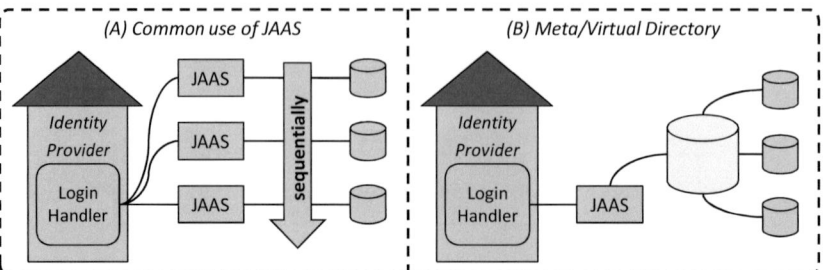

Figure 2.8: Common concepts to interconnect a single Shibboleth identity provider with the identity stores of an organization.

Shibboleth identity providers (see part A of Figure 2.8). With that, for each of every identity store a JAAS module is configured and integrated into the identity provider configuration. At the point in time a user provides his/her credentials at the login page of an identity provider, the JAAS modules are then parsed in a *sequential manner* until a match of user name and password is found in one of the connected identity stores. That implies, the identity provider potentially forwards the user credentials to more than a single interconnected identity store regardless of whether or not the user is known by the provider of an identity store that receives the credentials. This approach poses the risk of unintended data flows if providers of identity stores get notice of the user name and password of a user whose account is not part of their administered identities. In particular, if not the communication to the first configured identity store induces a successful authentication, a user's credentials have been sent to, at least, one identity store that is not in charge of the respective user and the provider of this identity store should not learn anything about this user – neither the password nor the user name. Furthermore, besides the fact that a potential communication to more than a single identity store is not necessary at all, this course of action affects the time needed to decide whether or not a user can be authenticated. Certainly, these are stronger arguments for organizations that consist of remarkably independent organizational units, which, for instance, do not fully trust each other. However, also for organizations with stable trust relationships between the individual organizational units, a sequential processing of identity stores induces unnecessary flows of possibly sensitive information and costs time during authentication, which could, additionally, be annoying for users.

Part (B) of Figure 2.8 illustrates another option for interconnecting more than a single identity store. This concept is based on a Meta or Virtual Directory[19]. With that, the Meta/Virtual Directory constitutes the only identity store that is connected to the identity provider. In turn, this identity store is connected to the "real" identity

---

[19] Meta Directories store data that is originally stored at several other databases that are interconnected with the Meta Directory. The data is replicated within the Meta Directory and, therefore, redundantly stored. In contrast, a Virtual Directory constitutes a facade in front of several databases and provides a single interface to access the data stored in the interconnected resources. In this case, the data is not redundantly replicated but passed on by the Virtual Directory to the requesting service.

stores of the organization and provides an aggregated view on these stores. In other words, a Meta/Virtual Directory serves as a facade for the existing, multiple identity stores. Both the use of multiple JAAS modules and the connection via a Meta or Virtual Directory is common in many organizations. However, also the Meta/Virtual Directory solution has its drawbacks with respect to unintended data flows. Meta and Virtual Directories provide an aggregated view on actually separated stores with sensitive information about users. Such a component constitutes not only a single point of failure but also provides – at least, for the responsible administrators – access to a potentially large number of account information and, therefore, personal data. In light of the assumption stated before that the origination of threats is most likely to be expected from inside an organization, the use of Meta or Virtual Directories also poses potential risks in terms of unintended flows of sensitive information.

In light of the situation that PII might be unintentionally accessible, we introduce approaches that ensure that personal data, such as login credentials, can only be forwarded to dedicated IT services integrated into an organization-internally implemented IAM system so that non-essential and potentially unintended flows of PII can be avoided. These solutions are deployable despite the restrictions AAI providers impose. With these approaches we address the following specific research question:

- *Is it possible to design approaches to implement deployable, operable, and maintainable improvements of interconnections of identity providers and identity stores to avoid potentially unintended flows of PII?*

## 2.5.2   Unintended Data Flows Caused by Frontend Implementations

For those users who have to authenticate at an identity provider, risks regarding unintended data flows do not only exist because of the technical processes on top of which such an IAM component is implemented. Another risk is posed by people who can spy a user who is going to log in for a service. If the user has to type in his/her credentials (e.g., user name and password) the spying person can potentially read the user name and/or can get an idea of, for instance, the length of the corresponding password. In this context, spying on users who are, for instance, typing a password "in order to obtain their personal identification number, password, etc." is the practice that is also known as "*shoulder surfing*" (definition by the Oxford Dictionaries[20]).

Moreover, public computers (public terminals) pose additional risks. These open terminals might be manipulated in certain terms so that an attacker can get access to typed information, particularly, the user name and password. For instance, programs can be installed that can read users' input data for storing and/or forwarding this information to attacking third parties. For instance, so-called key-loggers are programs that can save keyboard input data (and, therefore, also users' credentials). Those programs are acting in a fully transparent manner from the perspective of the user.

Many users often have to authenticate in insecure environments, e.g., students at the lecture hall, and open terminals are extensively used, e.g., at internet cafes on vacation or at the library of a user's university. Therefore, the offer of just the "old fashion"

---

[20]http://oxforddictionaries.com [Last downloaded 2013-05-28].

authentication method, i.e., the use of a combination of user name and password, might be no longer state of the art. Alternative authentication methods can be useful, particularly, if users have to authenticate in such "insecure" environments. Depending on the situation of a user who wants to login to use an IT service, providing alternatives to the login based on credentials that have to be typed in would be preferable. Hence, providers of SAML-based infrastructures – like other providers – have to think about alternative authentication methods and possibilities to provide those features.

In the context of alternative authentication methods, authentications with the help of Quick Response (QR) codes [ISO18004] have been introduced, recently (e.g., [Kim12], [BVDN12]). Additionally, Google spent some effort for evaluating QR codes for authentication[21]. Moreover, the opportunity to use social media logins also became very popular in the last decades. In particular, social media authentication methods are used for services that can work with just uncertain information about a user (see the second part of the next section for further details on alternative login methods). Therefore, in the next chapter, we present modules for SAML-based IAM components that allow the integration of alternative authentication techniques (e.g., QR code-based or social media-based logins) into the frontend implementation.

However, so far, SAML-based identity providers are implemented to support just the user name and password authentication, although the SAML specification would allow alternative authentication methods. Therefore, the following research question arises:

> – *Can existing alternative authentication methods be integrated into SAML-based identity providers to avoid unintended flows of PII due to the login based on credentials that can be spied or logged by thirds?*

Again, the design of improvements that can be implemented and integrated into existing IAM systems aims at providing approaches that are deployable, operable, and maintainable. This aim also constitutes the main issue of designing approaches to integrate alternative login methods, i.e., finding a "minimal invasive" way to bring the new functionality into existing infrastructure.

## 2.6   Related Work

In the first part of this section, we present related work with respect to improvements of data flows of SAML-based components in light of the mentioned issue to operate several identity stores by still fulfilling the requirements imposed by AAI providers. The library of the University of Freiburg (Germany) applied a module named *myLogin*[22], which is implemented as an identity provider extension for Shibboleth. Subsequently of choosing the home organization, or rather the identity provider of the home organization by a user, he/she gets forwarded to another website provided by the identity provider that is installed between the incoming redirect and the form

---

[21]http://www.h-online.com/security/news/item/Google-briefly-experiments-with-Sesame-phone-based-login-1414311.html [Last downloaded 2013-05-28].

[22]https://mylogin.uni-freiburg.de [Last downloaded 2013-05-28].

that asks for the users' credentials. On this additional website, the user can pick and choose his/her appropriate identity store at the university of Freiburg implemented as choosing the corresponding organizational unit, e.g., the library, the computing center, or the university hospital. Therefore, a user is able to choose the identity store that administers the account with which a user wants to login. In particular, this module has advantages for users with several accounts linked with different access rights and registered at more than a single organizational unit. After successfully passing the login the service provider that is about to be accessed retrieves those attributes that are linked to the picked account. Therefore, with *myLogin* an additional hierarchical level was implemented. The main disadvantage of this solution is constituted by the fact that a user has to pick and choose his/her home organization *and*, afterwards, has to pick and choose the appropriate organizational unit, before he/she can login for accessing the service. Furthermore, this invention is only deployable if users can exactly map their accounts to an organizational unit. If users do not know who is in charge of administering their accounts, such an additional interaction with the identity provider would build another barrier, especially for inexpert users. In contrast to *myLogin*, the solutions presented in this thesis can be integrated in a seamless, or rather transparent manner from the perspective of the users, i.e., the introduced modules do not require an additional interaction by the users and, therefore, might constitute a more acceptable add-on for avoiding unintended data flows concerning the demands of users who want to spend as less overhead for logging in as possible. Another approach was taken by the authors of [WS11] to tackle the conceptual gap between a single identity provider and several identity stores. In this paper, a solution is introduced that can be deployed at an identity provider for gathering attribute values from several secondary identity providers. However, the aim of the authors was not to manage accounts separately administered within different identity stores. On the contrary, they aim at introducing a concept of bringing attributes of a single user together that are stored in different identity stores. In contrast, we aim at providing solutions to handle authentications with accounts separately managed by different identity stores. Furthermore, we do not want to install several identity providers. Instead, we implement a single identity provider that interconnects identity stores based on a concept that separates different areas of administration for avoiding unintended data flows in the direction of unauthorized identity stores.

As mentioned in the previous section, providing just the common way to authenticate users, i.e., the authentication by combinations of user name and password, might not be sufficient in the future. Because of the use of open terminals or the use of, for instance, laptops or tablet computers in environments where others can spy on monitors and keyboards require new and more secure ways to authenticate users. In the related work, we can find many different approaches to authenticate users without the use of user name and password combinations. Additionally, some IT service providers provide authentication services, e.g., Facebook provides the Facebook Single Sign-on that can be integrated in web applications due to authenticate users via their Facebook account. However, those mechanisms have not yet been implemented for the widely used SAML-based infrastructures. Accordingly, also no solution has

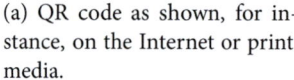

(a) QR code as shown, for instance, on the Internet or print media.

(b) Structure elements highlighted within an exemplary QR code (cf. [ISO18004]).

Figure 2.9: Example of a QR code (Version 9, i.e., a size of 53 modules per row).

been presented that provides a deployable, operable, and maintainable concept. In the following, we present related work on alternative authentication methods that could be useful for authentications in light of the mentioned situations. Furthermore, we point to related papers that introduce concepts and implementations to integrate those authentication methods into existing systems.

The international standard ISO/IEC 18004 specifies QR codes [ISO18004] on top of which several authors have implemented an authentication system. QR codes are 2-dimensional bar codes that can be, for instance, "deciphered" by a smartphone, i.e., a common smartphone can install applications that can read a photo – taken with the smartphone – of the bar code, e.g., the application barcoo[23]. A QR code, such as shown in Figure 2.9a, consists of a 2-dimensional representation of the data and, additionally, areas that structure the QR code itself and provides meta information. In Subfigure 2.9b, we highlighted the structure elements of an exemplary QR code symbol as specified in [ISO18004]. The blue areas highlight the "position detection patterns", whereas the yellow patterns are used for further alignment. The orange patterns are "timing patterns" and appear as alternating black and white modules to determine the coordinates of the symbol in order to be able to parse the single rows of the QR code. The red and green lines are white spaces. The red line is known as the "quiet zone" necessary to detect the borders of the symbol adequately. The green line separates the position detection patterns from the rest of the symbol. Data that is represented underneath the green overlay contains version information, whereas the blue overlay marks areas of information on the format. The largest version of a QR code (Version 40, i.e., a size of 177 modules per row) can represent 3,706 bytes of data [ISO18004]. QR codes are, for instance, utilized by the authors of [BVDN12] to authenticate users. The authors of this paper introduced a login that provides QR codes containing, inter alia, session information instead of a form that requests a user's credentials. A photo of this QR code has to be taken by using the application

---

[23]http://www.barcoo.com/ [Last downloaded 2013-05-28].

the authors implemented for smartphones. The smartphone is equipped with a secure micro SD card[24] that provides a tamperproof storage for key material. Based on this key material (used for securing the communication) the smartphone interacts with a service via the Internet connection of the phone. In turn, this service, which can be seen as an identity provider, interacts with the website/service that a user wants to access. If the identity provider receives valid information about the user of the smartphone and information on the service that is about to be accessed and corresponding session information, the identity provider informs the service about the successful authentication of the user. In the following chapter, we present a solution that aims at integrating this authentication method into a Shibboleth identity provider, i.e., the Shibboleth identity provider serves as a service for which a user has to be authenticated. However, QR codes are used for authentications by several other organizations. Even Google[25] spent some effort to evaluate possibilities to provide QR code logins[26]. The university of Tübingen (Germany) operates a QR code login system for their students, i.e., called Ekaay [27] and founded a spin-off company that sells this partially patented product. In summary, it is obvious that particularly QR codes become popular in the field of novel authentication methods.

Additionally, the authentication via Online Social Network (OSN) accounts constitutes an interesting opportunity for providing alternative login methods. Basically, large OSNs, such as Facebook, provide an authentication service based on a user's credentials, i.e., the user name registered within the OSN and the corresponding password. However, also more sophisticated authentications on top of data out of OSNs are conceivable. To give an example, the authors of [YFB08] introduced a technique to authenticate a user by presenting photos of his/her OSN friends and other people and let him/her choose which of the photos show one or more of his/her friends. Certainly, an authentication by using an OSN cannot completely ensure that a user is no other person than the one he/she claims to be because of the fact that faked accounts can easily be registered within OSNs (cf. Chapter 4). Furthermore, attribute values retrieved from an OSN are mainly provided and managed by the users themselves and, therefore, the correctness of the data cannot be ensured by the OSN. However, for some use cases it might be feasible, or even valuable to integrate OSN authentications into IAM system. For instance, if an authentication does not imply access to potentially sensitive information, a login via an OSN might be also sufficient.

Besides the upcoming of alternatives to user name-password authentications, first studies have been published that aim at integrating novel authentication methods into existing IAM systems. The authors of [ASM13] introduced a concept to integrate Information Cards, i.e., authentications via sets of attributes certified by a trusted party (e.g., Card Space [BSB07][28] and Higgins[29]), into Shibboleth. In particular, a solution is

---

[24] http://www.gd-sfs.com/ [Last downloaded 2013-05-28].

[25] http://google.com [Last downloaded 2013-05-28].

[26] http://www.h-online.com/security/news/item/Google-briefly-experiments-with-Sesame-phone-based-login-1414311.html [Last downloaded 2013-05-28].

[27] http://www.ekaay.com/ [Last downloaded 2013-05-28] and [Kim12].

[28] http://msdn.microsoft.com/en-us/library/aa480189.aspx [Last downloaded 2013-05-28].

[29] http://www.eclipse.org/higgins/ [Last downloaded 2013-05-28].

introduced that enables Shibboleth identity providers to interact with an "Information Card-enabled relying party", i.e., a service provider. The authors implemented a browser extension that works with the mentioned Information Card approaches and does not require (major) changes of the corresponding Information Card components and the identity provider. However, we present solutions that can be integrated into SAML identity providers so that users are not involved in the deployment process, for instance, due to the need to install components at the local client. Furthermore, the aim of the solutions presented in this dissertation is mainly at avoiding unintended flows of PII and focus, inter alia, on integrating emerging technologies, whereas the development of Information Card approaches are rather retrogressive or, in the case of Microsoft's Card Space even discontinued. Another work that aims at integrating novel authentication methods into common IAM systems is presented by the author of [Bec11]. In his master's thesis, he introduced a proof-of-concept that integrates QR code-based authentications via smartphones into an OpenID[30] environment. In contrast to this work, we, inter alia, aim at integrating QR code-based authentication into SAML-based environments that are more commonly deployed in enterprise environments, whereas OpenID is often used for services provided for personal use.

In summary, we showed that SAML-based IAM systems become increasingly popular, at least, because of the progressive integration of several types of IT services. Furthermore, we showed that alternative authentication methods are emerging, so that providers of IAM systems should be prepared for future demands of their users. Finally, we presented first studies that aim at integrating novel authentication technologies into existing IAM systems. In the following chapter, we present improvements of Shibboleth identity providers that, at first, aim at avoiding the mentioned kinds of unintended flows of PII. Furthermore, the presented approaches provide future-oriented solutions in terms of possibly emerging demands of users. Therefore, we provide essential contributions for operating SAML-based IAM systems in a privacy aware manner in the future.

---

[30] http://openid.net/ [Last downloaded 2013-05-28].

# 3

# Avoiding Unintended Data Flows in Enterprise Environments

Referring to the specific research questions and related work introduced in the previous chapter, the current chapter presents the main contributions in the area of avoiding unintended flows of personally identifiable information (PII) within enterprise identity and access management (IAM) systems. We demonstrated that implementations of SAML-based identity providers can induce flows of users' credentials to non-authoritative resources or third parties (1) if more than a single identity store is interconnected with an identity provider (potentially unintended flows of PII in the *backend* of SAML-based identity providers) and (2) if third parties can spy on or log the input of users' credentials (potentially unintended flows of PII induced by the current implementation of an identity provider *frontend*). In the following, we separately present the approaches with respect to backend and frontend improvements. First, we show the components that can be integrated into SAML-based identity providers to improve the flows of data within the backend of an identity provider. Additionally, we show how these approaches have been deployed in a productive environment and present key indicators for the actual usage of the components. Second, we introduce concepts and a respective implementation – as a proof-of-concept – that allows to suggest users of SAML-based identity providers with alternative authentication methods, such as QR code or social media logins. Afterwards, we evaluate both the backend and frontend approaches with respect to the principles and requirements regarding the implementation of IAM components stated in Section 2.4. Finally, we discuss and conclude the enterprise IAM part of this dissertation. Parts of the contributions presented in this chapter have been previously published in [LSD10].

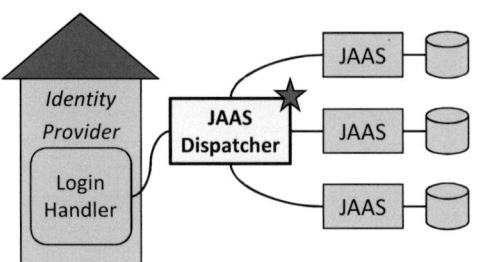

Figure 3.1: The concept of the *JAAS Dispatcher*.

## 3.1 Approaches for Improving Backend Processes

In the current section, we introduce solutions to improve the data flows in the backend of a Shibboleth identity provider (cf. the research questions stated in Section 2.5.1). First, we introduce two different approaches to avoid unintended data flows in the backend of a SAML-based identity provider. Afterwards, it is demonstrated how the contributions are deployed within the productive IAM systems of the Karlsruhe Institute of Technology (KIT). We give insights into the experiences we gained from the productive application of the introduced IAM modules and present key performance indicators to demonstrate that the deployed modules are intensively used by employees, students, guests, and partners of the KIT.

### 3.1.1 The JAAS Dispatcher Approach

In this part of the results section, we present an IAM component that we call the *JAAS Dispatcher*[1], i.e., an additional JAAS module that is integrated between the identity provider and the existing JAAS modules. The *JAAS Dispatcher* itself can be implemented as just another JAAS module, i.e., the *JAAS Dispatcher* adopts the concept and design of JAAS modules regarding class structures, interfaces, etc.. However, in contrast to usual JAAS modules, the *JAAS Dispatcher* does not encapsulate identity stores, but rather several other JAAS modules that, in turn, encapsulate the identity stores. Thus, we propose an additional hierarchical level for the interconnection of identity stores via a cascade of JAAS modules. The advantage of such a solution is that – from the perspective of both the module of the identity provider that connects the identity stores and the interconnected identity stores – no code and nothing of the principle infrastructure has to be changed. Just the configuration of the identity provider has to be adjusted to integrate the *JAAS Dispatcher* instead of directly integrating several identity stores.

Figure 3.1 shows the concept of the *JAAS Dispatcher*. The figure illustrates the adaptation of the concept of integrating identity stores by configuring JAAS modules for each of every identity store that is to be integrated. As mentioned above, we retain the concept of configuring JAAS modules for the implementation of the additional

---

[1] *JAAS Dispatcher* download: https://dsn.tm.kit.edu/3050.php [Last downloaded 2013-05-28].

JAAS module, i.e., the *JAAS Dispatcher*. However, the *JAAS Dispatcher* encapsulates the other (regular) JAAS modules and serves as kind of a hub for requests dedicated for a specific identity store. In comparison to up-front provisioning systems introduced in the previous chapter, the *JAAS Dispatcher* constitutes an equivalent component to the provisioning software that decides which databases have to be provisioned with which piece of PII, with the difference that the *JAAS Dispatcher* decides which identity store is to be used to verify a user's credentials at this point in time the credentials are provided by the user via the authentication frontend. In contrast to the existing concepts of interconnections introduced in Figure 2.8, the application of the *JAAS Dispatcher* makes it possible that identity providers do not have to request identity stores in a sequential manner (cf. part (A) of Figure 2.8). Furthermore, it is not necessary to implement a redundant identity store that can be (ab-)used to get a comprehensive view on actually distributed data in terms of a Meta or Virtual Directory, which suggests an identity provider with just a single access point to every identity store that is to be integrated (cf. part (B) of Figure 2.8).

However, the *JAAS Dispatcher* can decide which identity stores might be in charge of the identity that is registered by the entity that provided the credentials. On the basis of regular expressions this module limits the number of identity stores that have to be requested with a user name and password a user provided. In the best case, based on these regular expressions, which have to be configured by, for instance, an administrator, the *JAAS Dispatcher* can explicitly determine the appropriate identity store. At the KIT, this decision process is based on the range of the ID space and the structure of the identifiers that are, fortunately, completely disjoint, i.e., no over-lapping identifiers. For example, the identifier assigned by the Steinbuch Centre for Computing (SCC) consists of two letters and four digits, which is distinguishable from, for instance, the identifiers assigned by the library that consist of twelve digits and no letters. However, if more than a single regular expression matches a provided user name, the administrator can decide between two options: (1) the regular expres-sion that matches at first determines the identity store that is requested and (2) every identity store whose regular expression matches the user name will be requested by the *JAAS Dispatcher* via the respective JAAS modules in a sequential manner.

If the *JAAS Dispatcher* can determine a JAAS module that is connected to the appropriate identity store, a new so-called *JAAS Context* is built. This is a necessary step to delegate the authentication to the JAAS module that is configured for the appropriate identity store. For each of every JAAS module placed downstream from the *JAAS Dispatcher*, a specific name space have to be defined and configured in the file (*login.config*). The essential part of this configuration file is exemplary shown in the following code listing:

```
ShibUserPassAuth {
    edu.kit.scc.dei.JAAS.dispatcher.Dispatcher sufficient
        regExp.0=".*@kit.edu"          JAASContext.0="mail.kit.edu"
        regExp.1="[a-zA-Z]{2}[0-9]{4}" JAASContext.1="scc.kit.edu"
        regExp.2="[0-9]{12}"           JAASContext.2="bib.kit.edu"
        ;
};
```

After the "preamble" of the configuration snippet, the second line references the namespace of the *JAAS Dispatcher* and tags the configuration with the command *"sufficient"*, which is important to ensure that this part of the configuration is read and executed. Each of the next lines consists of an identifier, a regular expression and a namespace. The latter two values are read by the method `initialize()` of the *JAAS Dispatcher*. The method `login()` builds the mentioned *LoginContext* and delegates the login to this context and, therefore, to the appropriate JAAS module, which is directly connected to an identity store. The invocation of the chosen JAAS module is proceeded exactly as the invocation of the *JAAS Dispatcher*. Hence, the identity provider invokes the dispatcher module and, in turn, the dispatcher module invokes the appropriate JAAS module.

In the context of identity providers deployed within enterprise environments, the *JAAS Dispatcher* avoids unintended flows of credentials to identity stores that are not in charge of the corresponding identity. Moreover, the application of this improvement reduces the overhead induced by sequential communications between an identity provider and identity stores. Furthermore, the *JAAS Dispatcher* approach maintains the independence of configured identity stores that administer just a subset of identities that can use the identity provider for authentications. Moreover, providers of identity stores do not have to change their infrastructure as a basis to deploy the *JAAS Dispatcher* at the identity provider. Additionally, it is not necessary to replicate any of the identity information into another data base (cf. the Meta Directory approach), e.g., no passwords have to be copied to another identity store. In this context, a solution that requires to replicate passwords would, per se, not be deployable in some of the current systems, because most identity stores archive only hash values of the passwords to not provide a clear text view on this sensitive information for, e.g., attacking third parties or their own administrators. Therefore, some of the identity stores are not even able to replicate a password into another database, particularly, if this database requires another algorithm used for hashing the passwords than the one that is utilized by the identity store.

In general, the *JAAS Dispatcher* is implemented without breaking the principle JAAS concept. It provides a JAAS interface for interconnecting an identity provider and an interface to be connected to JAAS modules that, in turn, encapsulate identity stores. Therefore, this solution for dispatching JAAS modules provides just an additional hierarchical level between identity providers and identity stores and, hence, it is not only applicable for Shibboleth identity providers, but also deployable within any infrastructure that utilizes JAAS. Appendix A provides further information on how easily the *JAAS Dispatcher* can be integrated into Shibboleth identity providers and other components that are based on JAAS.

Since 2010, the *JAAS Dispatcher* is also integrated in and can be downloaded from the official website of the DFN-AAI[2].

---

[2]https://www.aai.dfn.de/dokumentation/identity-provider/tools/ [Last downloaded 2013-05-28].

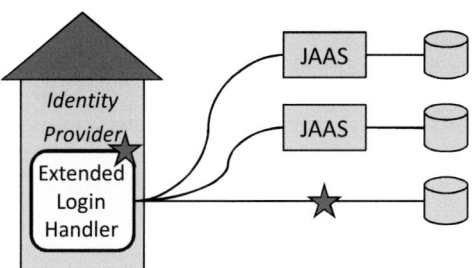

Figure 3.2: The concept of the *Extended Login Handler*.

## 3.1.2   The Extended Login Handler Approach

The second concept that we present in this thesis is called the *Extended Login Handler* and aims also at improving interconnections between an identity provider and identity stores. However, in contrast to the *JAAS Dispatcher*, the *Extended Login Handler* approach enables an identity provider to interconnect identity stores that provide only proprietary interfaces that cannot be integrated with common JAAS modules. Furthermore, this approach makes it possible to include further (identity) information in the decision on whether or not a user can be authenticated, i.e., with this approach not only the user names and passwords can be used for authentication, but also, for instance, the IP address or further attributes (cf. the requirements stated in Section 2.4).

The *Extended Login Handler* is a customized module that can be integrated into the Shibboleth code itself in a modular manner (see the stars within Figure 3.2). In particular, the *Extended Login Handler* replaces the common LoginHandler used in Shibboleth infrastructures. Thus, the *Extended Login Handler* constitutes a modular part of the identity provider itself (whereas the *JAAS Dispatcher* is an additional, previously non-existent module).

However, the common implementation of the Shibboleth identity provider suggests the JAAS modules only with user names and passwords typed in by a user. For this, the LoginHandler of the identity provider utilizes the concept of a so-called *Callback Handler*. By utilizing the common LoginHandler approach, further attributes cannot be forwarded to the JAAS modules to become part of the authentication process. In contrast, the (individually) implemented *Extended Login Handler* can provide JAAS modules with any information that is known by the identity provider, e.g., a user's IP address. The inclusion of further attributes such as the IP address is an important extension for identity stores that have to ensure that a user fulfills further requirements, e.g., that he/she is located at a certain computer. As already mentioned, for a specific group of library users (i.e., the guests of the library) it is obligatory to check whether they are sitting at a computer at the library or elsewhere, e.g., at home. The reason for this is constituted by the fact that the publishers admit the availability of publications for those guest users only if they are using a library computer, i.e., a computer provided inside the library (cf. Section 2.6 and, in particular, the referenced paper [ORBL09]). Therefore, the *Extended Login Handler* allows not only to check whether credentials that a user has entered are valid or not, but also can involve constraints into the decision process to answer the question whether or not to let the user pass the authentication. Moreover, the *Extended Login Handler* can not only pass additional attributes to interconnected JAAS modules but also can integrate further identity stores that only provide proprietary interfaces.

From a technical perspective, the *Extended Login Handler* is implemented as a replication and extension of the *usernamePasswordLoginHandler*[3], which is the most frequently implemented LoginHandler for Shibboleth identity providers. Then, we put all replicated classes into the name space of the *Extended Login Handler*. Additionally, we expanded the method *authenticateUser* of the class *usernamePasswordLoginServlet* in order to fulfill the requirement regarding further attributes that have to be included into the Callback Handler of a JAAS request. In particular, the method *authenticateUser* extracts the IP address of the user by the command *request.getRemoteAddr*. If the appropriate identity store requires this information, or rather if the identity provider detected that a guest of a library tries to get authenticated, the value returned by this command is integrated into the following authentication process. Thereby, the access of an identity store can be implemented by a JAAS module or, alternatively, directly from the identity provider, or rather the *Extended Login Handler*. However, the latter would compromise the modular character of the Shibboleth implementation that is intended to encapsulate an identity store via a JAAS module.

Both the *JAAS Dispatcher* and the *Extended Login Handler* are compatible solutions that can be integrated in parallel into the same Shibboleth identity provider. Therefore, it is possible to keep the necessary changes of the common LoginHandler very small, i.e., only the forwarding of, for instance, the IP address is included. The part of selecting an appropriate identity store is then handled by a *JAAS Dispatcher* or, alternatively, a consecutive processing of the identity stores via the configured JAAS modules as it is the originally implemented way. However, whereas the *JAAS Dispatcher* can be used for any application that utilizes JAAS to interconnect identity stores, the *Extended Login Handler* can only be implemented in Shibboleth.

### 3.1.3   Productive Application of the Contributions

The main objectives of the introduced improvements were to design components that are deployable, operable, and maintainable. Deployability is an essential requirement because most organizations are already operating IAM systems that cannot completely be changed in a short period of time. Therefore, new components that have to be implemented in the existing systems have to fit in these architectures without the need of changing the whole infrastructure and its existing components. In other words, the most essential requirement is that the new modules do not induce more than just minimal changes of the existing components. Furthermore, if the new modules are deployed, it is essential that the administrators can handle the system not worse

---

[3]Replicated classes: usernamePasswordLoginHandler, usernamePasswordLoginServlet, usernamePasswordLoginHandlerBeanDefinitionParser, usernamePasswordLoginHandlerFactoryBean, and BaseSpringNamespaceHandler.

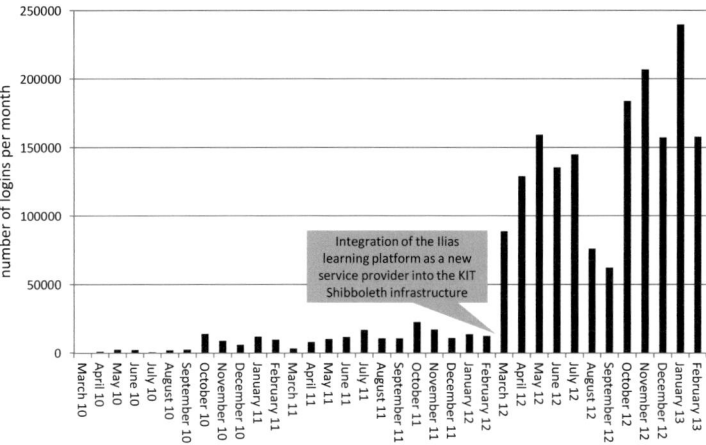

Figure 3.3: Monthly logins via the Shibboleth identity provider of the KIT.

than before and that they are still able to deploy updates without any restrictions caused by the newly integrated components. In summary, we aimed at designing modules that fulfill not only the demands of the specifications and standard on top of which the existing components were build, but also the requirements constituted by the deployed systems and components themselves. In the following, we show that the introduced concepts are valuable in terms of their deployability, operability, and maintainability. In particular, we show how we implemented them into the on-demand provisioning systems of the KIT.

The operative infrastructure for "on-demand provisioning" of the KIT, i.e., a Shibboleth infrastructure, utilizes both the *JAAS Dispatcher* and the *Extended Login Handler*. In particular, the KIT identity provider has integrated a *JAAS Dispatcher* module, as well as an *Extended Login Handler*. For deploying one of the presented modules, administrators only have to adapt the existing configuration of the SAML-based identity provider of their organization, which constitutes a low overhead that might be acceptable for avoiding unintended flows of PII. In fact, for integrating the introduced modules only a single line of configuration has to be changed in each case. For a productive use of the *JAAS Dispatcher*, an administrator must also configure the regular expressions to decide which identity store, or rather JAAS module is to be used for which type of identifier.

In the following, we show plots that demonstrate the amount of logins that are handled by the KIT identity provider and, therefore, also by the *JAAS Dispatcher*, as well as the *Extended Login Handler*[4]. Figure 3.3 shows the overall number of logins for each month between March 2010 and February 2013. In January 2013, we detected the so far largest number of logins, i.e., 239,949 logins per month. The increase of

---

[4]The statistics were gathered by and the plots were built in collaboration with Michael Simon. He is in the role of the main administrator of the KIT Shibboleth infrastructure at the Steinbuch Centre for Computing (SCC).

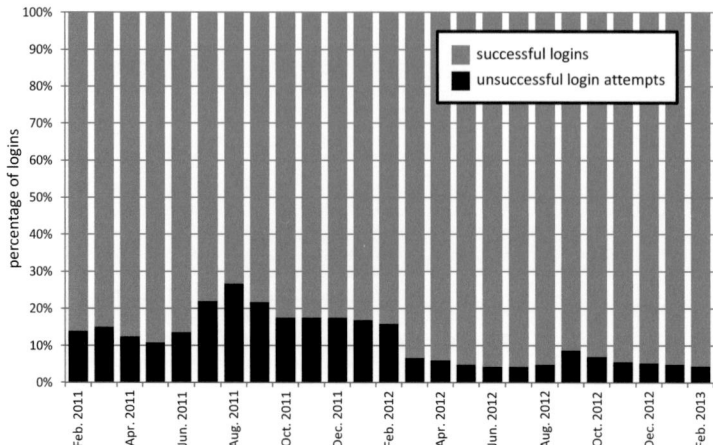

Figure 3.4: Ratio of successful and unsuccessful logins.

the number of logins since March 2012 is caused by the integration of the ILIAS[5]
learning platform of the KIT into the Shibboleth infrastructure to authenticate users
by the KIT identity provider.

Figure 3.4 shows the success rate (gray/upper part of the bars) of logins, i.e., the
ratio of user credentials that could be assigned to an appropriated JAAS module by
the *JAAS Dispatcher* and resulted in a successful login, i.e., the combination of user
name and password could be verified by the chosen identity store. The black part of
the bars show the ratio of login attempts in which the respective user did a mistake
and typed in an incorrect or unknown user name or he/she typed in a non-valid
combination of user name and password. Obviously, the integration of the student
platform ILIAS induced a drop of unsuccessful logins. This might be explainable
because students have less accounts at the KIT because services the KIT provides
for students have an higher degree of integration, i.e., almost all of these IT service
can be accessed by utilizing just a single account. In contrast, KIT employees often
have registered several additional accounts in (not yet or consciously not integrated)
legacy systems that administer their own identity store, so that it is more probable
that employees choose the wrong account for a login attempt. However, the latter is
only speculative and the influence of other factors cannot be ruled out. For instance,
students' (eventually better) error rate during typing in combinations of user name
and password could also be a reason for the decrease of unsuccessful logins.

However, in Figure 3.5, we demonstrate details on the number of logins in November
2012. In particular, we provide information on how often which JAAS module was
depicted by the JAAS Dispatcher. A *user principal name* (upn) is represented by an
e-mail address, whereas a sAMAccountName (sam) is a short login name provided
by the computing center of the KIT. Note that the name is only a dependence to the
attribute sAMAccountName that constitutes an obligatory attribute within Microsoft

---

[5]https://ilias.studium.kit.edu [Last downloaded 2013-05-28].

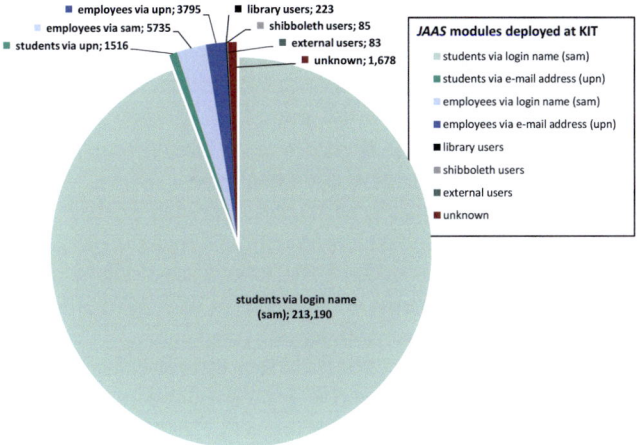

Figure 3.5: Number of login attempts via the Shibboleth identity provider of the KIT w.r.t. the JAAS module chosen by the *JAAS Dispatcher* (Nov. 2012).

Active Directories (AD). In the case of the KIT infrastructure, the sam-attribute is mapped to the AD-attribute sAMAccountName, but this is not a necessity in general. The JAAS module *library users* indicates the mentioned connection to the identity store for library guests, which is based on the *Extended Login Handler* that provides the JAAS modules with the IP address of the entity that attempts to log in. The module *shibboleth users* encapsulates an identity store in which separated Shibboleth accounts are administered, and the module *external users* encapsulates an identity store that contains mostly employees of a company who implement services for the

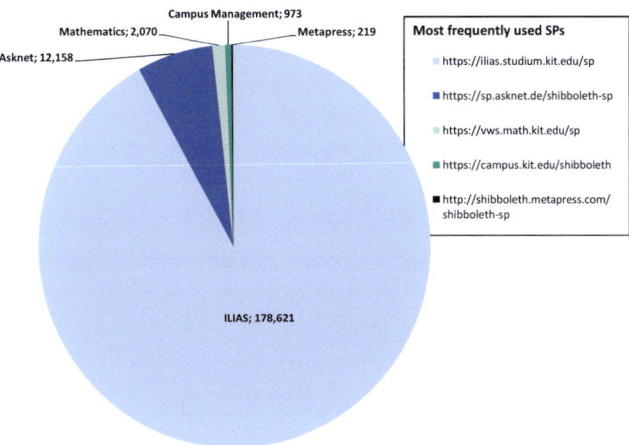

Figure 3.6: Number of logins for the most frequently used service providers via the Shibboleth identity provider of the KIT (Nov. 2012).

KIT. The category *unknown* indicates the number of login attempts that could not be assigned to one of the configured JAAS modules. These faulty assignments are caused by incorrectly entered user names and/or passwords, i.e., a user input contained non-valid credentials. In contrast, at this point in time, faulty assignments caused by the *JAAS Dispatcher* and/or the *Extended Login Handler* could not be found in the log files since these modules have been deployed.

Figure 3.6 shows the most frequently used service providers of the KIT in November 2012. In this plot, the reason for the aforementioned increase of logins per month becomes apparent. The service provider URL "https://ilias.studium.kit.edu/sp" represents the mentioned ILIAS platform for students. In November 2012, 178,621 logins were performed by users to access this service provider.

In summary, we can state that the contributions introduced in this chapter of the dissertation constitute not only deployable, but also operable solutions for avoiding unintended flows of PII in enterprise environments. Furthermore, the longstanding character of the infrastructure that has integrated the *JAAS Dispatcher* and the *Extended Login Handler* indicates that the infrastructure is as maintainable as before, which is not very surprising in light of the fact that only a single line of configuration has to be changed to integrate the modules. In point of fact, the administrators deployed several individual updates for the identity provider since the deployment of the *JAAS Dispatcher* and *Extended Login Handler* without the need to change anything of both deployed modules.

## 3.2   Approaches for Extending Frontend Implementations

In light of the disadvantages regarding the frontend of SAML-based identity providers (analyzed in Section 2.5.2), we discuss whether or not the SAML standard and its implementations are able to apply novel authentication methods, which constitute alternatives compared to common logins based on combinations of user names and passwords. First, we analyze the login process of the probably most popular SAML implementation, i.e., Shibboleth. Afterwards, we present the concept and implementation of a flexible integration of alternative authentication methods into SAML-based implementations of IAM systems – particularly, Shibboleth.

### 3.2.1   Analysis of Common Identity Provider Logins

For deploying alternative authentication methods without giving up the SAML specification, it is necessary to analyze the authentication process currently implemented by Shibboleth and the guidelines imposed by the SAML standard. Figure 3.7 shows an UML-like representation of the Shibboleth login process. Basically, the interface *LoginHandler* is implemented by the abstract class *LoginHandler*, which in turn is extended by the specific LoginHandler, i.e., the *UsernamePasswordLoginHandler*. The dedicated LoginHandler invokes a servlet, i.e., in this case the *UsernamePasswordLoginServlet*, which extends the HttpServlet and invokes the user interface (*login.jsp*) that provides the user with an input form – or rather login screen – for obtaining a

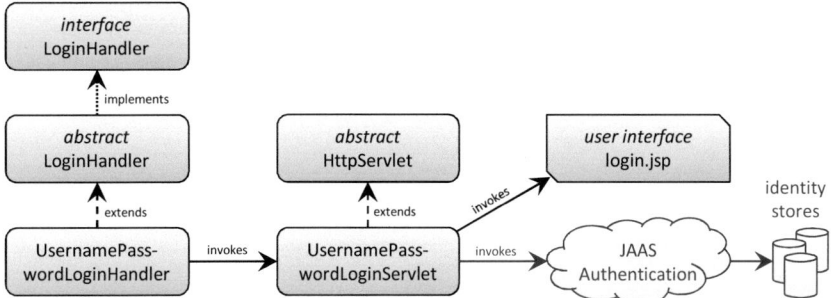

Figure 3.7: UML-like illustration of the login procedure as it is implemented within the Shibboleth identity provider.

user name and the corresponding password. The user interface is implemented as a JAVA™ Server Page[6]. With a user's name and password the servlet can invoke the JAAS modules integrated into the identity provider. The JAAS part handles the connection to configured identity stores, such as shown in Section 3.1. In general, it is obvious that the Shibboleth part that is in charge of the user authentication is implemented in a very modular manner – like the other parts of the Shibboleth implementation that also follows a very modular approach to implement the SAML standard.

In the following sections, we show the conceptual design of the integration of alternative authentication mechanisms into the introduced login procedure of Shibboleth. Again, we aim at introducing a deployable, operable, and maintainable solution. Therefore, the key requirement constitutes the seamless and modular integration of the solutions into Shibboleth (minimal invasive integration), as well as the compliance with the SAML standard. Furthermore, the solution itself has to be designed as modular as possible and service providers should not be affected by the changes because the processes that pose the risk of unintended data flows are solely operated by the identity provider. An involvement of service providers, or rather the need to change those components would lead to an inappropriate effort for integration.

## 3.2.2 Design and Implementation of the Integration Solution

Shibboleth provides the possibility to change the LoginHandler that is to be used during authentication processes by changing just a single line of its configuration. As introduced in the previous section, Shibboleth implements two dedicated classes that handle the login processes, namely the classes UsernamePasswordLoginHandler and the UsernamePasswordLoginServlet. Furthermore, the mentioned JAVA™ Server Page is involved in the authentication process. It suggests the user with an interface for submitting his/her credentials. Obviously, for a solution that aims at integrating alternative authentication methods, it is necessary to adapt this user interface because of the fact that no longer just the opportunity of an input of credentials has to be

---

[6]http://www.oracle.com/technetwork/java/javaee/jsp/index.html [Last downloaded 2013-05-28].

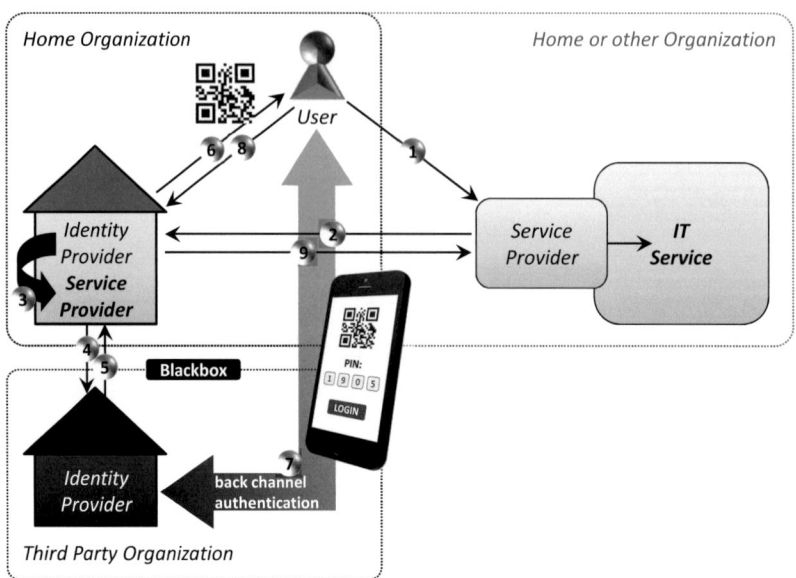

Figure 3.8: Third party authentication via direct back channel communication.

provided by the interface, but also the necessary information for utilizing alternative authentication methods. However, the user interface is implemented in just a single file (*login.jsp*) that is simply interchangeable with another file that undertakes the task of the communication with the user. Even without restarting the whole identity provider this file can be changed by the administrator of a Shibboleth identity provider. Therefore, user interfaces of alternative authentication methods are easily deployable by just changing the file *login.jsp*.

On this basis, the question remains whether or not further classes have to be adapted for providing alternative authentication methods. In fact, it is necessary to adapt the LoginServlet to support other authentication methods instead or besides the authentication via user name and password. Therefore, it has to be considered whether or not customized LoginServlets can be integrated in a similar "minimal invasive" manner compared to the integration of an adapted user interface. Certainly, this is true because – as mentioned above – the authentication part is implemented in a very modular manner and the modules that are to be used by the identity provider are configured in a single configuration file.

### Resulting Architecture of the Integration

So far, we provided an analysis of the common login process implemented by SAML-based identity providers and presented necessary changes to integrate alternative authentication methods at all. In the following, we present the architecture that results from integrating alternative third party authentication methods based on the technical concepts presented in the previous section. Figure 3.8 and Figure 3.9

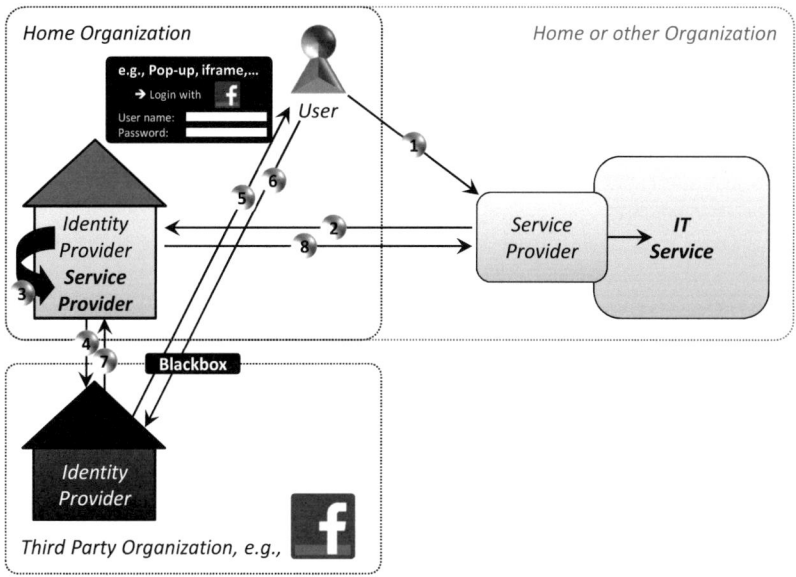

Figure 3.9: Third party authentication via indirect communication.

provide an abstract overview of the resulting architecture and, additionally, in each of both figures, a process of login that can be implemented depending on the type of authentication method.

In principle, the basic components, i.e., the service provider and the identity provider, are still in place and the beginning of the workflow presented in Section 2.3.1 is unchanged, i.e., the user tries to access a service that is encapsulated by a service provider (step 1 of Figures 3.8 and 3.9), which forwards the user directly or via a discovery service to an appropriate identity provider (step 2). However, at this point in time the user is forwarded to the identity provider, this component switches its role towards another service provider (step 3) that again hands over to another identity provider, i.e., the third party identity provider (step 4). If the user can be successfully authenticated by the third party identity provider the identity provider of the home organization (i.e., the one that switched its role) receives a positive authentication statement by the third party identity provider and – based on a trust relationship – it handles this authentication statement just as the user would have been authenticated by itself. Again, the rest of the workflow is unchanged, i.e., the user gets redirected by the identity provider to the service provider where it is to be decided whether or not to grant access to the actual service (step 9 of Figure 3.8 and step 8 of Figure 3.9.

The integration concept allows two different types of interaction between the third party identity provider and the user him-/herself. First, the user can be authenticated by the third party by the use of a back channel communication (see step 7 of Figure 3.8). In this case, the identity provider of the home organization presents some data to the user, e.g., a QR code containing, for instance, session identifiers. Then, the user can use this data to start a back channel authentication, for instance, via his/her smartphone (see next section for an example of such a back channel authentication that is also utilized for the proof-of-concept implementation presented later in this chapter). If this back channel authentication is successful, the third party can inform the home organization with a positive authentication statement. The second option is to enable the user to directly communicate with the third party identity provider, i.e., a communication integrated into the browser the user uses for accessing the service (see Figure 3.9). In this case, the third party provider suggests the identity provider of the home organization with a Pop-up, iframe, or something similar that can be shown to the user by the home identity provider and be used to, for instance, type in the authentication credentials.

### Integration of Specific Alternative Authentication Methods

In the following, we go into detail how the Shibboleth authentication modules can be adapted to provide specific alternative authentication methods. Recently, QR code-based approaches for user authentications became popular – as shown in Section 2.6. Those QR code-based mechanisms are mostly externalized back channel authentications, i.e., an instance that can communicate with the user's smartphone can tell, for instance, an identity provider whether or not a user has successfully passed the login process (cf. Figure 3.8). For instance, in the case of the solution presented in [BVDN12], a Web Service[7] is provided by the implementation of this QR code authentication. The identity provider obtains the QR code by this web service and, then, can present this QR code to a user. The user takes a picture of it by utilizing his/her smartphone that, in turn, runs an application that can communicate with the instance of the QR code authentication service, i.e., the Web Service, based on a secured channel. After the presentation of the QR code, the identity provider has to request the web service periodically to check whether or not a user has been authenticated and which user has been identified. Therefore, this solution is based on a kind of "black box" approach in which a trust relationship between the identity provider and the instance of the QR code authentication has to be established. Obviously, such a black box approach can be integrated without changing much of the already existing code of a LoginServlet. In fact, just the communication with the web service has to be integrated. The JAAS part and, therefore, the interaction with several identity stores, is no more necessary for performing QR code logins implemented in such a way.

However, it is likely that an organization does not want to establish further trust relationships between its identity provider and third parties, such as third party providers of QR code authentications. In the following, we discuss whether it is feasible to integrate the whole process of the QR code authentication into the identity provider.

---

[7] The W3C defines a web service as "a software system designed to support interoperable machine-to-machine interaction over a network. It has an interface described in a machine-processable format (specifically WSDL). Other systems interact with the Web service in a manner prescribed by its description using SOAP messages, typically conveyed using HTTP with an XML serialization in conjunction with other Web-related standards." (http://www.w3.org/TR/ws-arch/#whatis [Last downloaded 2013-05-28]).

The identity provider runs in the context of an application server, such as Apache Tomcat[8] or Jetty 7[9]. An application server is designed to provide interfaces that can be accessed by users via a URL [RFC1738] and a port. Therefore, the application server can be configured to establish communication channels between a smartphone and the identity provider, which is running on this server. Thus, it is feasible to integrate this logic into the identity provider itself.

Besides authentication methods based on QR codes, the login via social media accounts became very popular in recent years. The main advantage of social media logins constitutes the fact that it also provides Single Sign-on and it is probably more likely that users are already authenticated at their favorite social media service than, for instance, at the Shibboleth-based SSO login of the service platform of their home organization (probably less often used and shorter periods of valid authentications). Once logged in into a social media site, such as Facebook, a user can use any service that relies on the Facebook authentication without typing in user name and password again. Since users are more likely still logged in into Facebook – because of the extensive use of the social media platforms (see Chapter 4 et seq.) –, such an authentication might be more secure if a user is located in an insecure environment just because it is more likely that a user do not has to type in his/her credentials because he/she is still authenticated.

However, such possibility of authentication might be interesting for providers of services that do not require to identify a user exactly as the person he/she pretends to be. For instance, a more relaxed authentication might be feasible for forums where users can only post some comments or communities that provide chats and other services. In other words, for IT services that do not require the traceability of actions of their users and a reliable mapping of accounts to particular persons a less reliable authentication might be feasible. However, for integrating social media logins, such as a Facebook login, into a Shibboleth identity provider, we show that also only the *login.jsp* and the LoginServlet have to be changed. In particular, in the case of the integration of a Facebook login, the authentication screen has to show a button that links to a pop-up window provided by Facebook (cf. Figure 3.9). In turn, this Facebook pop-up window suggests the user with a login screen for the input of user name and password if the user is not already logged in. If a user is still logged in the pop-up window does not show up, or rather disappears immediately because of the already logged in user and Facebook informs the identity provider about the successful login and (optionally) releases certain attributes about the user who has been authenticated.

---

[8]http://tomcat.apache.org/ [Last downloaded 2013-05-28].
[9]http://jetty.codehaus.org [Last downloaded 2013-05-28].

## Proof-of-Concept Implementation

For proofing the introduced concepts, we implemented two specific integrations of alternative authentication methods into Shibboleth. Furthermore, we show that these solutions can be integrated without changing code or changing large parts of the configurations. First, we integrated the QR-Code authentication introduced by Boukayoua et al. [BVDN12]. Second, we integrated a Facebook login mechanism into a Shibboleth identity provider.

For integrating the authentication via QR codes, we firstly adapted the frontend implementation of the Shibboleth identity provider, i.e., the *login.jsp*. In particular, we added the presentation of the QR code itself to this JavaScript-based file. Furthermore, we implemented an automated refreshing of the login page of the identity provider. This is necessary to check whether or not a user has been authenticated by the use of his smartphone, with which he/she took a photo of the presented QR code. By reloading the login page the identity provider triggers a request to the Web Service to get a status response whether or not a user has already successfully passed the authentication. This request is implemented within the LoginHandler, the part of the identity provider that is also adapted for implementing the *Extended Login Handler*. However, when the Web Service responds with an indication of a successful authentication the adapted LoginHandler hands over to the authorization part of the identity provider just like it is implemented for the case that a user has successfully passed an authentication via configured JAAS modules.

As it can be seen, we just had to customize the *login.jsp* that can be deployed by just replacing the originally deployed *login.jsp*, which can even be done during runtime of the identity provider. Furthermore, an administrator has to replace the existing UsernamePasswordLoginHandler with the customized LoginHandler prepared for QR code authentication via communications with a Web Service. This replacement can, as already mentioned in the context of the backend improvements, be done by changing just a single line of configuration of the identity provider. Due to the fact that the configuration is retained during an update of the identity provider this solution is not only easily deployable, but also the maintainability of the system is kept. Its operability is given by the fact that no established processes (instead of the authentication process itself) have to be changed for the integration of alternative authentications via QR code-based IAM systems.

For integrating a social media login, in particular, a Facebook-based login, we just had to adapt the same classes or files compared to the integration of QR code-based authentications, i.e., the *login.jsp* and the existing LoginHandler. However, in contrast to the QR code solution, the Facebook login does not require to implement Web Service requests within the LoginHandler. Instead, the communication with Facebook is handled by the JavaScript part of the identity provider, i.e., the *login.jsp*. After integrating the Facebook login into this file, a user can click on the Button labeled "Login with Facebook". Afterwards, a pop-up window appears and, if the user is not already logged in into Facebook, the user is suggested with an input form for providing his/her Facebook credentials. If he/she is already logged in, the pop-up window closes immediately after appearing. If the authentication was successful, the *login.jsp* hands over to the LoginHandler that is adapted due to receive the user name of the user who has logged in via his/her Facebook account. The LoginHandler hands this user name over to the authorization part of the identity provider, which has not to be changed for integrating this alternative authentication method.

Because of the fact that no other component of an identity provider has to be changed as for the *Extended Login Handler* presented in Section 3.1.2, the arguments regarding the deployability, operability, and maintainability stated before apply also for the proof-of-concept integration of QR code-based and Facebook-based logins. Further details on the implementation of the concepts introduced in this thesis can be found in [Wer12].

### Limitations and Security Concerns

Besides the advantages of alternative authentication methods, a lot of drawbacks have to be considered if it has to be decided whether or not to deploy such login mechanism into an operative IAM infrastructure. The website of eKaay provides a comparison of traditional credential-based logins with QR code logins[10]. In particular, the inventors of eKaay state that a QR code-based authentication has advantages in light of the risk of, for instance, shoulder surfing. Furthermore, attacks, such as "dictionary attacks" or "social engineering", pose less risks than induced by traditional logins via credentials. However, the eKaay vendors also identified certain risks posed due to the fact that a smartphone can be stolen by third parties that would be able to login by the use of this stolen device if no further security mechanism, such as a PIN code, is required to login. Moreover, a trojan can be installed on such a device, so that the authentication can be manipulated to steal, for instance, the users session established by the use of the QR code authentication. The potential attack that was also discussed at the KIT and that constitutes the reason for not deploying QR code-based logins into the productive IAM systems of the KIT is a potential man-in-the-middle attack, i.e., an attacker could go to the login page, extract the presented QR code, put exactly this QR code on his/her own page, and get users to try to authenticate via the attacker's page by the use of their smartphone QR code application. The authentication via such a faked page would result in a successful login for the attacker if the user establishes the backend channel to the Web Service, successfully passes the authentication process, and, therefore, grants the access for the attacker who has originally been provided with the particular QR code, which he/she foisted on the user.

A login via credentials that correspond to an organizational account is also often preferable compared to a social media login. The reason for this constitutes the fact that anybody can register for an Online Social Network (OSN) and, thus, the pieces of information about the user, which are forwarded to a service, or rather an identity provider by the OSN, is "insecure", i.e., the data could be faked by the user because OSN providers do not check the validity of any attribute provided by the users themselves.

In summary, although alternative authentication methods are deployable into today's SAML-based IAM systems under the requirements stated in Section 2.4 (see Section 3.3 for a detailed discussion on how the introduced approaches fulfill the

---

[10] http://www.ekaay.com/security [Last downloaded 2013-05-28].

stated requirements), the deployment of some types of alternative authentication methods might imply certain drawbacks so that the classical authentication via user names and passwords might be still preferable today. However, with the approaches presented in this thesis, providers of SAML-based IAM systems are prepared for future authentication methods that can now be integrated in an operative infrastructure at low effort and cost.

## 3.3 Evaluation of the Approaches

In this part of the thesis, we firstly introduced the approaches of the *JAAS Dispatcher* and the *Extended Login Handler*. Both concepts aim at avoiding unintended data flows within the backend of SAML-based identity providers. Furthermore, the *JAAS Dispatcher* can be implemented within any identity services that connects identity stores via JAAS modules. Additionally, we presented approaches to integrate alternative authentication mechanisms into SAML-based identity providers based on the concept of the Extended Login Handler that has been introduced in the context of backend improvements of data flows. However, in general, with these approaches, we have shown that it is possible to implement improved authentication processes (1) without changing much of the existing infrastructure, (2) without changing the identity provider code, (3) without the need of a developer, i.e., an administrator is able to add the improved modules due to configuration, and (4) without limiting the maintainability of the systems, i.e., it needs no more effort to be operable compared to the "native" implementation and updates can be installed despite the integrated customized and, therefore, non-standard authentication modules. On the basis of the presented proof-of-concepts, we provide evidence that the SAML standard can deal with new authentication modules and the systems in which those modules have been implemented can be deployed in productive environments without reducing the maintainability of the whole system. In the following, we check whether or not the list of requirements stated in Section 2.4 can be fulfilled by the introduced approaches. Afterwards, we argue that the approaches constitute valuable findings for further research.

### 3.3.1 Fulfillment of the Requirements

Table 3.1 shows an overview of the requirements stated in Section 2.4 and an indication regarding whether or not the individual components fulfill these requirements. We have shown that the *JAAS Dispatcher*, as well as the *Extended Login Handler* are deployed at the productive infrastructure of the KIT. Furthermore, we argued that both modules have not hindered the deployment of updates or any other operational process since the deployment of the components in 2010. Because of the fact that both introduced integrations of alternative authentication methods are also based on the concept of the *Extended Login Handler*, we take their deployability, operability, and maintainability also for granted.

Referring to the remaining requirements, we can state that every approach follows the principle of "minimal disclosure" of PII, i.e., the backend improvements avoid

| Requirement | JAAS Dispatcher | Extended Login Handler | QR code integration | Social Media Module |
|---|---|---|---|---|
| Deployability | YES | YES | YES | YES |
| Operability | YES | YES | YES | YES |
| Maintainability | YES | YES | YES | YES |
| Minimal disclosure | YES | YES | YES | YES |
| Independence of org. units | YES | YES | –[1] | –[1] |
| No change of processes | YES | YES | YES | YES |
| No replication of passwords | YES | YES | –[1] | –[1] |
| Automated/configurable identity store determination | YES | YES | –[1] | –[1] |
| Retain JAAS concepts | YES | NO[2] | –[1] | –[1] |
| Compliance with SAML | YES | YES | YES | YES |
| Integration of additional authentication attributes | NO[3] | YES | YES | YES |

[1] These requirements are not relevant for the respective approach.
[2] If identity stores are directly connected.
[3] If deployed without the *Extended Login Handler*.

Table 3.1: Evaluation of the introduced approaches w.r.t. the principles and requirements for the implementation SAML-based IAM components stated in Section 2.4.

potentially unintended flows of PII and, additionally, retain the common concepts of existing modules for interconnecting identity stores. The frontend extensions allow to provide alternative authentication methods in order to avoid spying and logging of users' credentials and, thus, also less PII will be disclosed by applying these modules. Furthermore, the backend improvements preserve the independence of organizational units, i.e., any organizational unit that operates an identity store has not to hand over responsibilities with respect to identity information to, for instance, centralized components. Note that these requirements are not relevant in the context of providing alternative authentication methods. Additionally, all approaches fulfill the requirement that established processes do not have to be changed for deploying the introduced modules. Moreover, the *JAAS Dispatcher* and the *Extended Login Handler* do not replicate or require to replicate passwords and determine appropriate identity stores in an automated and configurable manner. The *JAAS Dispatcher* also retains the principle JAAS concepts, i.e., since the *JAAS Dispatcher* is just an additional JAAS module neither the identity provider nor the other JAAS modules have to be changed to integrate the dispatching component. However, this requirement is not fulfilled by the *Extended Login Handler* because it can directly connect interfaces of identity stores and, therefore, would not integrate identity stores in a modular manner. The requirements regarding the replication of passwords, the automated determination of identity stores, and the retaining of JAAS concepts are also not relevant in the context of alternative authentication methods. However, every introduced approach is compliant with respect to the SAML specification, i.e., the approaches do not bring concepts into the SAML-based IAM system that are not already included and defined by the specification. Furthermore, three out of the four approaches support alternative or additional attributes to authenticate users. The *Extended Login Handler* can include, for instance, the users' IP addresses. The approaches to integrate alternative authentication methods are per se able to perform authentications based on alternatives to the classical combination of user name password. However, only the *JAAS Dispatcher* is not able to evaluate further attributes, at least, if it is installed solely, i.e., without the *Extended Login Handler*. In combination with this module, it is possible to hand over additional attributes to a JAAS module for including this attribute into the authentication decision.

### 3.3.2  Valuableness of the Findings for Further Research

From a research point of view, the findings presented in this chapter are demonstrably valuable. In particular, the discussions on the topic itself, as well as the results significantly influenced the ongoing research in this field. The universities of the state of Baden-Württemberg started the project *bwIDM* that aims at providing SAML-based access to non web-based services. So far, SAML-based infrastructures are almost only be used for web-based IT services. However, the demand for similar solutions with respect to non web-based services, such as cloud, grid, and high performance computing infrastructures has been significantly grown in recent years. The experiences with Shibboleth and, particularly, the knowledge on how to improve such systems without violating the guidelines of the respective standards induced the mentioned project *bwIDM* in which researcher try to adapt the existing SAML components for the non web-based use case. Thereby, again the requirements deployability, operability, and maintainability play a major role and the work presented in this thesis serves as a fundamental basis to design components that fulfill these requirements.

## 3.4  Summary and Conclusions

In this chapter, we discussed Identity and Access Management systems in enterprise environments and possibly existing unintended data flows. We introduced several improved modules that are deployable for IAM systems based on (particularly, but not only) the SAML implementation Shibboleth. First, we presented the *JAAS Dispatcher* that avoids unintended flows of credentials within an organization and provides a comfortable solution to fulfill the requirement of a single identity provider claimed by providers of *Authentication and Authorization Infrastructures*, such as the Deutsches Forschungsnetz (DFN) for the DFN AAI. Furthermore, this module reduces overhead during authentication processes and, therefore, ensures less delay from the perspective of users who have to be authenticated. Second, we presented the *Extended Login Handler* that constitutes a SAML standard-compliant and also deployable module to interconnect identity providers with proprietary interfaces of identity stores and to implement more sophisticated authentication processes than just checking a user name and password combination, e.g., considering users' current location in terms of their IP address. Third, we introduced a methodology to implement alternative authentication methods so that users do not have to type in their credentials while located in an "insecure" environment where others can spy on the display and/or keyboard that is used. Finally, we gave an overview on how we implemented two of the three modules into the productive systems of the KIT and how frequently they are used by the employees, students, guests, and partners of the KIT.

In general, we have shown that it is possible to improve the flows of data within on-demand provisioning systems without violating the specifications of the corresponding and accepted standards. We showed that (1) improvements are possible and sometimes easy to reach, and (2) that corresponding implementations are deployable with respect to the effort that has to be expended to integrate the modules into the productive (legacy) systems. We have shown that the solutions are also operable and maintainable with respect to the effort that have to be expended to keep the modules up and running and to maintain the interaction of the new modules and the existing infrastructure components.

# 4
# Online Social Networks

In the previous chapters, we analyzed specific and widely deployed enterprise IAM systems due to identify and avoid unintended flows of personally identifiable information (PII). However, users commonly consume a lot more services in their everyday life than those provided by their (or any collaborating) organization. These services are not intended to, for instance, ease the work of an employee, but rather are utilized to keep in touch with other people, to express oneself, and to share and consume content that might be of interest for others, e.g., messages, posts, comments, photos, videos and more. We refer to the entirety of identity-related IT services that are provided via the Internet for supporting the satisfaction of social needs as *Social Media*. In this context, *Social Media* services that primarily provide a platform for creating so-called *user profiles* for sharing information constitute a specific type of *Social Media* services and are referred to as Online Social Networks (OSNs).

With the advent of *Social Media* and, in particular, OSNs, users got the opportunity to easily communicate and share content with a large amount of others. Thereby, the benefits for users accompany with certain potential risks regarding privacy. In this part of the dissertation, we focus on OSNs and potentially existing unintended flows of PII caused by the combination of shared information via OSN user profiles and (possibly) inadequately adjusted privacy settings, i.e., measures to define the "audience" of shared information. In particular, we investigate how much of today's shared information can be accessed by the public, or rather by any logged in member of an OSN. Furthermore, we analyze how all these members and, therefore, also attacking third parties can potentially *link* information shared by a single user via different OSNs. Additionally, we study *correlations of information* shared by users and their OSN friends. OSN friends are users who are linked to another user as a representation of a whatever kind of relationship, e.g., friendships, professional relationships, such as colleagues, online acquaintances, etc.. Based on the study on the correlation of PII, we quantify the risk that third parties can infer users' non-provided information based on the information shared by their friends. Finally, we introduce *concepts for avoiding unintended flows of PII* with respect to information shared via OSNs and third parties that can potentially get access to this information, or even can infer PII.

In this chapter, we provide an introduction to OSNs and refinements of the research questions stated in chapter 1. Furthermore, we present and discuss related work as a basis for the results presented in the following chapters. This chapter is structured as follows. First, we introduce OSNs in general and define corresponding terms. Afterwards, we introduce the term *privacy* and demonstrate how members can adjust their privacy settings within OSNs, i.e., users' capability to decide who can access which type and piece of shared information. Afterwards, we present the mentioned refinements of the research questions and a selection of related work with respect to the research findings presented in the following chapters. Parts of the contributions presented in this and the following two chapters have been previously published in [LDH11], [LTH11], [LH11], [Lab12], [TLH12], and [LWMH13].

## 4.1   Terms and Definitions

Before we present the specific research questions and related work, we introduce OSNs in general, as well as essential terms and definitions. In the following, we introduce and discuss definitions of OSNs. Subsequently, we present fundamental terms regarding OSNs. Since we are discussing and investigating the interaction of users with the IT system "OSN", finally, we show how users setup "their part" of an OSN.

The authors of [BE07] define OSNs as follows: "*We define social network sites as web-based services that allow individuals to (1) construct a public or semi-public profile within a bounded system, (2) articulate a list of other users with whom they share a connection, and (3) view and traverse their list of connections and those made by others within the system*". The Oxford Dictionary defines OSNs as "*(1) a network of social interactions and personal relationships*" and "*(2) a dedicated website or other application that enables users to communicate with each other by posting information, comments, messages, images, etc..*"[1]. Thereby, the first definition tries to reflect the users' perspective and the latter focuses on the *social graph*[2] that is constructed by an OSN. However, both of these definitions have in common that they address a direct connection to the Internet (particularly, the Web) and that OSNs are primarily provided to share information.

However, before a user can share information, he/she has to register for the OSN that is about to be used. With this registration process users set up a so-called *OSN profile*. These OSN profiles constitute key elements of an OSN and are also referred to as *profile pages* or *user profiles*. A profile page can be used to share information (e.g., PII) for any other member of the network or for a dedicated audience. Profile pages

---

[1] http://oxforddictionaries.com [Last downloaded 2013-05-28].

[2] The graph that results due to OSN friendships is called the *social graph*. The users are represented by the nodes of the social graph and the edges represent the friendship relations. See [MMG+07] for a detailed analysis of the structure of social graphs.

are provided for sharing content elements, such as posts, comments, photos, videos, etc.. These pieces of information can not only be shared via a user's own profile page, but also via profile pages of others. Additionally, other users' profile pages can be linked to a user profile in order to indicate a so-called OSN friendship. Therefore, user profiles contain a list of other profiles. Whereas these lists of friends (also known as *friends lists*) are often accessible by default for any logged in member, in most OSNs users are provided with privacy settings with which the group of users who can see the friends list can be restricted. Such restrictions can also be adjusted by users with respect to the accessibility of content they share via their profile pages. An additional feature provided by OSNs is the opportunity to discuss the content that is shared by others and themselves. OSN users can comment on it or, for instance, can link users, or rather profile pages, within shared photos and other content. In general, in many OSNs – particularly in the most popular OSN Facebook – a user profile consists of, at least, an information page, a favorites page, a friends list, a wall, a news feed, a messaging area, and sometimes a chat. In the following, we introduce these and further essential terms, or rather features provided by OSNs, in detail:

– **User profile:** a user profile represents a user within the OSN community, i.e., the profile consists of information that a user has shared. Furthermore, others, such as OSN friends, can generate content in the context of a user's profile in terms of posts, comments, photos, etc.

– **Information page:** the information page is part of a user profile and can be used to publish certain information about oneself, mostly in terms of PII that discloses, for instance, where the user lives, his/her date of birth, or other (possibly sensitive) information. Hence, on this page, users disclose PII that often characterizes themselves in a more or less detailed manner.

– **Friends list:** a list of so-called friends (OSN friends) constitutes an essential part of every OSN user profile. This list contains any other OSN member that stands in a certain relation to the owner of the user profile, i.e., members who are friends with the profile owner in real life, his/her family members, or just other users he/she met via the Internet, or even via the OSN itself. We refer to the profiles of a user's OSN friends as *friend profiles*.

– **Wall:** the wall is a feature that is part of a user profile. Users, as well as their OSN friends, or – depending on the users' privacy settings – even any member of the network can post comments, photos, videos, etc. on their wall. Information that is shared via the users' wall appears also on the news feed (see next item). In Facebook, the wall is referred to as the *timeline* because of its chronological order of shared content.

– **News feed:** the news feed aggregates information posted on users' profiles and, in particular, via their walls. Some OSNs weight any shared information according to an often mostly unknown algorithm to predict its importance. For instance, Facebook makes use of the so-called *Edgerank Algorithm*[3] that filters content to show, for instance, information that initiated a lot of reaction by other users on a higher position within a news feed than content that is more or less unnoticed by others. Furthermore, OSNs offer companies an option to pay for a more popular news feed position of *their* shared content. Cf. [DA12] for an interview-based study on "what factors determine the attractiveness of content shared via" OSNs that (potentially) appears on a user's news feed.

– **Likes (Google+[4] analogue: 1+):** Likes are provided to react on content shared by another user without commenting on it on a textual basis. If a user is, for instance, pleased by a user's shared photo, appreciates a statement, or enjoyed watching a shared video he/she can *like* the shared content to show others his/her positive opinion on it.

– **Like-Button (German analogue: „Gefällt mir"-Button):** the Like-Button is the feature that enables users to *like* shared content as introduced before. For instance, Facebook integrated this button underneath any content shared within the OSN and, additionally, shows the number of users, as well as a list containing those users' profile names, who *liked* the content already.

– **Apps:** the most popular OSNs, such as Facebook, provide the opportunity for third parties – e.g., companies – to implement their own applications based on the OSN, i.e., a third party application (App) can be integrated into the OSN and information shared by users can be forwarded to the App provider from this point in time a user installs/uses an App for the first time. In turn, via Apps third parties can not only provide additional OSN features, but also can, for instance, get access to shared content or even users' walls in order to advertise their products. Apps are the features further addressed in Chapter 6. See [NRG+09] for a detailed investigation of the network level interaction of Facebook and integrated Apps, as well as corresponding flows of information.

– **Editorial content:** another type of content implemented by some OSNs is constituted by a feature that, for instance, Facebook calls *pages*, i.e., more or less commercial representations of companies, associations, clubs, or even famous persons, such as musicians, actors, and moderators. In the case of Facebook, those pages can be *liked* by users, which induces that information shared via these pages appears on their news feed.

– **Favorites page:** a favorites page shows the pages, i.e., editorial content, a user *liked*. In some OSNs, the favorites page is implemented as just a part of the main profile page. Other OSNs structure this part of a profile within a separated page that is linked by the main profile page (e.g., Facebook).

---

[3]Cf. http://blog.getpostrocket.com/2013/04/infographic-facebook-edgerank-102-understanding-how-news-feed-stories-are-filtered/ [Last downloaded 2013-05-28].
[4]https://plus.google.com/ [Last downloaded 2013-05-28].

– **Messaging area:** the messaging area constitutes kind of an e-mail service that can be utilized to write a message to one or more other users. It differs from a classical e-mail service in terms of the fact that only members of the network can be reached. However, Facebook offers also the possibility to send a message to a user's Facebook e-mail service, i.e., they provide users with a classical e-mail address in the form of their user name and the suffix "@facebook.com".

– **Chat:** the chat provides users with an instant messaging service similar to other chats provided via the Internet. In the chatting environment, a user can see who of his/her OSN friends is currently also logged in to the OSN.

## 4.2 Flows of PII in Online Social Networks (OSNs)

Today, OSNs provide everyone an opportunity to "implement" a virtual self-projection without any knowledge with respect to developing, hosting, and operating websites. Layouts of profiles and their appearance are usually standardized to the greatest possible extent. From the users' perspective, publishing information about themselves satisfies an individually distinctive urge for self-representation and OSNs provide an easy-to-use opportunity to share data, particularly PII. However, resulting potentially unintended flows of PII lead to privacy risks for the users.

OSNs are platforms mostly provided by a single company in a centralized manner[5]. In this context, other researchers focus on the avoidance of flows of PII to an OSN provider (cf. [BH11]). However, this dissertation primarily focuses on flows of PII to *attacking third parties* in order to provide an adequate quantification of the privacy risks regarding PII that can unintentionally flow to third parties and in order to provide measures to avoid these data flows. Whereas the investigation of flows of PII to OSN providers constitutes very important research, these data flows are more obvious for the users of an OSN, i.e., most users might be aware of the fact that their shared information is also accessible by the provider of the OSN. However, flows of PII to third parties might be more often underestimated by the users because of the fact that they are just simply not aware of the existence of these potential data flows. The reason for this is that users cannot determine who has accessed their shared PII. Instead, it is only possible to determine who could potentially access the information, which makes it hard to consider any potentially accessing third party.

These privacy risks are further increased by the fact that any third party, even a "casual attacker", e.g., a (potential) boss, an insurance agent, a headhunter, etc., can register for a user profile in order to get access to publicly shared information. Moreover, in most cases, the OSN provider does not check whether the user is "real" or whether a user registered a profile with faked information. Also the registration of profiles to get access to information by a software occurs, i.e., crawlers and scrapers (see Section 5.1

---

[5]Decentralized, or rather user-centric OSNs are also existent (e.g., Diaspora, http://diasporaproject.org/ [Last downloaded 2013-05-28]). However, the number of users is significantly lower than those registered in commercial OSNs provided by a single company. Furthermore, some decentralized OSNs are even in a preliminary stadium of development.

for more details on crawlers and measures OSNs take to avoid automated access to information shared by their users). However, the fact that potentially any third party can register a profile and, therefore, can get access to users' PII and other information shared with any member of the network indicates that those pieces of PII are almost public information. Moreover, the standardized layouts of today's OSNs make it even more easy to gather publicly shared information in an automated manner and the often not sufficiently effective measures OSN providers take to avoid automated extraction of users' data by third parties form the basis for unintended flows of PII. Hence, the following question is the basis of the investigations presented in this part of the thesis:

*How extensive can shared PII be accessed in an unintended fashion and possibly be (ab-)used by third parties so that it constitutes a privacy risk for OSN users?*

## 4.3  Privacy and Privacy Protection

In the following, we address the term *privacy* and discuss implications of potentially existing unintended flows of PII. Furthermore, we introduce and discuss current settings OSN users can adjust to define who can access which type and piece of information shared via OSNs, i.e., features that are called *privacy settings*.

The Oxford Dictionary defines privacy as *"the state or condition of being free from being observed or disturbed by other people"*[6]. Therefore, particularly in the context of OSNs, privacy designates a user's right that his/her information (in particular, PII) is kept in secret by users, as well as third parties that are provided with the information. Furthermore, privacy means that information is only accessible by a *comprehensible* group of users/third parties and that confidential information is not forwarded by third parties without the user's consent. If users are not able to determine who can potentially get access to their PII, privacy is threatened.

In the early 90's, privacy threats were still merely a problem with respect to the potential leakage of credit card and social security numbers, as well as address information and telephone numbers that were of interest to, for instance, send spam or call a person (cf. [Rot92]). However, with the advent of OSNs third parties recognized the monetary potential of PII shared by OSN users and new markets have been developed, primarily in the area of advertisement. Furthermore, other third parties, such as insurance companies, potential employers, or even ex-partners might be interested in users' PII. Therefore, any user's privacy might be threatened today if he/she shares PII or other information, for instance, via OSNs and cannot fully understand who can actually access the data. Hence, an adequate awareness of these risks has to be established if it is not already existent.

In the context of privacy, the ISO/IEC IS 24760-1 defines privacy-related terms. We shortly introduce these terms in the following. The right of any user to determine whether or not information is allowed to be forwarded to a third party, for instance, by an OSN provider, is referred to as "selective disclosure" and defined as the "principle of identity management (...) that gives a person a measure of con-

---

[6]http://oxforddictionaries.com [Last downloaded 2013-05-28].

trol over the identity information (...) that may be transferred to a third party, e.g., during authentication" [ISO24760]. In this context, the term "minimal disclosure" subsumes the principle that only a minimum of PII is released to a requesting third party, i.e., only those pieces of information that are "strictly required for a particular purpose" [ISO24760]. Additionally, the standard introduces the terms "pseudonym" and "anonymity". A pseudonym contains sufficient identity information to bring a certain entity into the position to link this information to a "known identity". In contrast, anonymity requires that a link to a known identity cannot be established by any entity. However, this does not prevent that the anonymous identities are distinguishable from each other (derived from [ISO24760]). These two terms are important in the context of the empirical studies presented in the following chapter. In particular, an automated investigation of user profiles – such as it is performed for the empirical investigations of this dissertation – requires to permanently store only anonymous information that does not bring someone into the position of being able to determine the "real" identity that corresponds to the statistical data. In the context of storing data in an anonymous manner further terms have been established that describe specific degrees of anonymity, e.g., *k-anonymity* [Swe02], *l-diversity* [MKGV06], and *t-closeness* [LL07]. However, these terms are not significantly relevant for and used in light of the research findings presented in the remainder of this thesis (see [FWCY10] for a detailed introduction to these specific degrees of privacy). In the following, we address the term privacy awareness and show how today's OSN users can actually adjust their privacy by the configuration of so-called privacy settings provided by the OSN.

## 4.3.1  Privacy Awareness

In this dissertation, we refer to privacy awareness as the term that describes the state of education users reached with respect to the awareness that privacy constitutes an important influential factor when it is to be decided whether or not to share a piece of content. Furthermore, a fully privacy aware user knows about any potential flow of shared information to third parties and behaves according to the potential risks, i.e., he/she adjusts privacy settings adequately according his/her privacy demands.

## 4.3.2  Privacy Settings

Privacy settings designate features provided by OSNs in order to enable users to manage the audience of shared information, i.e., choosing who can get access to which type and piece of shared information. At this point in time a user registers a profile within an OSN, the privacy settings are adjusted to the *default* configuration. Depending on the OSN, this default privacy settings can vary from a very restrictive configuration with which shared information is only accessible by a user's OSN friends – or even only by the user him-/herself – to a very barely restrictive configuration with which any user of the OSN – or even any Internet user – can access the information a user shares. However, we can observe that privacy settings of the largest OSNs are not very restrictive by default, i.e., if users do not adjust the privacy settings according their privacy demands a lot of shared information can be accessed by a broad audience.

| Default Privacy Settings | | Can third party Apps used by OSN friends potentially get access to the attribute by default?[1] |
| --- | --- | --- |
| Attribute | Attribute Accessibility *Default Configuration* | |
| friends list | public[2] | YES |
| e-mail address | friends | NO |
| mobile phone number | friends | NO |
| other phone numbers | friends | NO |
| instant messaging | friends | NO |
| address | friends | NO |
| religious views | friends *and* friends of friends | NO |
| political views | friends *and* friends of friends | NO |
| date of birth | friends *and* friends of friends | YES |
| interested in/sexual orientation | public[2] | NO |
| gender | public[2] | _[3] |
| languages | public[2] | _[3] |
| work/employer/company | public[2] | YES |
| college | public[2] | YES |
| high school | public[2] | YES |
| relationship status | public[2] | YES |
| family members | public[2] | YES |
| current city | public[2] | YES |
| hometown | public[2] | YES |
| website | public[2] | YES |
| likes | public[2] | YES |
| posts/status updates[4] | public[2] | YES |
| posts by others[5] | friends | _[3] |
| view posts by others[6] | friends and friends of friends | _[3] |
| view posts with tag[7] | friends and friends of friends | _[3] |
| photos/photo albums | public[2] | YES |
| videos | public[2] | YES |
| online status | friends | YES |
| search-ability[8] | everyone | – |

[1] "People on Facebook who can see your info can bring it with them when they use apps. This makes their experience better and more social. (...) control the categories of information that people can bring with them when they use apps, games and websites." [facebook.com]
[2] At least, accessible for any logged in Facebook member.
[3] Probably not.
[4] "Who can see future posts?" [facebook.com]
[5] "Who can add things to my timeline? Who can post on your timeline?" [facebook.com]
[6] "Who can see what others post on your timeline?" [facebook.com]
[7] "Who can see posts you've been tagged in on your timeline?" [facebook.com]
[8] "Who can look you up using the e-mail address or phone number you provided?" [facebook.com]

Table 4.1: Facebook default privacy settings (Status: 2013-04-16).

In particular, even sensitive PII is often not protected if users do not change the default privacy settings. To give an example, we review the current default privacy settings of Facebook[7]. Table 4.1 shows which pieces of information will be available to which group of others if the information is provided by a user *and* if the default privacy

---

[7] See http://mattmckeon.com/facebook-privacy/ for an overview of the "evolution" of Facebook's default privacy settings [Last downloaded 2013-05-28].

settings remain untouched by the user. It can be seen that some sensitive pieces of PII can only be accessed by a user's OSN friends, such as the e-mail or physical address, as well as a user's telephone numbers and further contact information. However, users religious and political views, as well as their date of birth are accessible by their OSN friends *and* the OSN friends of their friends if the default privacy settings have been retained unchanged (with an average number of about 200 OSN friends in Facebook, this configuration implies an average audience of up to 40,200 Facebook members, depending on the overlap of the friends lists). Moreover, a lot of other pieces of PII are publicly accessible by default, such as the users' sexual orientation, relationship status, and their current city to name just a few. Furthermore, posts and comments a user and other users write on his/her timeline are publicly available by default. Not least, the fact that users can be found within the OSN by any other member constitutes also a default configuration of the Facebook privacy settings. In addition to the availability of users' PII to a possibly broad audience, also third parties can get access to PII shared by an OSN user. In particular, not only third parties that provide additional services (Apps) used by the users themselves can get access to their PII, but also third party providers of Apps used by the users' OSN friends. The last column of Table 4.1 indicates which pieces of a user's PII can be accessed by third party providers of Apps used by his/her OSN friends if the user retains the default privacy settings (in Chapter 6, we pick up the problem regarding information flows from users via their friends to providers of Apps). However, not only Facebook provides non-restrictive default privacy settings. OSNs like Google+ or Xing provide very similar default settings, e.g., Google+ provides public access by default for information on, for instance, the users' jobs, education, and current city and Xing makes cv information of their users available for a large group of members. Furthermore, the participation in some OSNs, such as Google+ and StudiVZ, requires to give consent that the OSN provider is allowed to use (some of) the users' PII for purposes with respect to marketing and advertising. Whereas other privacy settings are adjustable according users' demands, the consent regarding advertising and marketing often is a must for participation.

In summary, privacy settings suggest users with the capability to intervene in potential flows of information. Some OSNs even provide very fine-grained measures to restrict the audience of shared information. However, the partially barely restrictive default privacy settings pre-configured by the OSNs accompanied with users' current motivation to adjust those settings might explain the mass of information still shared publicly (cf. Section 5.2). In this context, Thaler and Sunstein discuss peoples' attitude to adhere to default settings [TS08]. The authors refer to [SZ88], in which the "status quo bias of decision making" is investigated, and provide the following example: most people retain the default settings of their mobile phone, i.e., the background picture, the ring tone, the volume and frequency of the ring tone, etc., because of a certain power of sluggishness induced by several reasons. Probably, this "status quo bias" can also be transferred to the adjustments of default privacy settings within OSNs and, therefore, users are lazy in adjusting these settings appropriately.

## 4.4  Specific Research Questions

The authors of [ACF12] state that an essential contribution for developing new kinds of privacy enhancing technologies is the concept and measure of risk. Therefore, risk quantification constitutes the basis on top of which potentially effective privacy tools can be designed. Hence, we analyze publicly shared PII, demonstrate how many pieces of PII can actually be accessed by third parties (on average), and quantify corresponding privacy risks. Furthermore, as another essential part of this dissertation, we discuss whether or not and how it would be possible to bring users into the position to understand potential flows of PII as a basis for adjusting privacy settings in an adequate manner. Finally, we present a Facebook App that demonstrate users their current situation regarding possibly unintended flows of PII. Initially, in the current section, we start by further motivating the research on privacy risks induced by publicly available PII in OSNs. Afterwards, we state the specific research questions this part of the dissertation focuses on. As already mentioned, these specific research questions are refinements of the research questions stated in Chapter 1.

On the one hand, in Section 1, we argued that users share a lot of PII via their OSN profiles with an often broad audience[8]. However, on the other hand, in recent time, privacy in OSNs has attracted a remarkable attention of the media, which is probably one of the most influencing factors of the increase of users' privacy awareness. To give examples, "the daily press reported that several companies are crawling OSNs, such as Facebook, to learn more about the private life of users in general, or of their customers and job applicants, in particular. Some of these reports state that even insurance companies try to gather accessible data of OSNs for risk assessments with respect to specific customers or to acquire new customers[9]" [LWMH13]. The increased privacy awareness is also confirmed by a German survey among teenagers that are between twelve and 19 years old. This study is carried out on a yearly basis. In the 2012 survey, already 87 % of the respondents stated that they make use of privacy settings [JIM2012]. In the year 2010, only two thirds of the interviewed teenagers stated that parts of their profiles and published information is only accessible for users on their friends list [JIM2010]. In 2009, only 47 % of the respondents stated that they make use of privacy settings [JIM2009]. Krishnamurthy et al. showed that only a quarter of Facebook users made use of privacy settings in 2008 [KW08]. Compared to the situation in 2005, when only about 1.2 % of OSN users restricted the search-ability of their profiles and only 0.06 % restricted the profile's visibility [GA05], it becomes obvious that privacy awareness has been increased since then. A further demonstration of the change of user's behavior in adjusting privacy settings is presented by the authors of [DJR12]. In 2010, they crawled a large sample of Facebook users living in New York City and again analyzed the same sample of users 15 months later. The results show that, for instance, 17.2 % of users out of the first sample did not provide public access to their friends list, whereas in 2011 already about 50 %

---

[8] In Section 5.2 we quantify today's amount of PII publicly available in OSNs.

[9] E.g., http://socialbarrel.com/insurance-companies-watching-you-on-facebook/ [last downloaded 2013-05-28].

of users configured the privacy settings so that their OSN friends or even no other users can see the friends list (see Section 4.5.1 and, in particular, Table 4.2 for more details on this and other studies). However, in light of the grown privacy awareness, the question arise whether or not third parties are *still* able to gain information by analyzing the public part of users' OSN profiles.

Obviously, the adjustment of some privacy settings does not imply a consistently adequate usage of these settings in any case. An indication of a still existing large amount of PII that is publicly available is provided by the authors of [LGKM11]. They demonstrated that de facto adjusted privacy settings are not congruent compared to users' expectations concerning privacy. In particular, the authors found a match of users' expectations and the actual behavior regarding the configuration of privacy settings in only 37 % of the analyzed cases. Additionally, we show that a significantly large number of OSN members do not hide all of their shared information from strangers, e.g., in 2011, more than 78 % and, in 2012, still almost 62 % of Facebook members publicly shared, at least, one piece of PII that would be actually concealable. Moreover, although Facebook acquired a remarkable market share in recent time, many users are (still) member of one or more other OSNs despite the fact that they might not actively participate in these OSNs. In turn, multiple OSN memberships increase the number of communities in which PII is potentially (still) publicly provided and could be accessed by third parties. Even worse, publicly shared PII can easily be gathered in an automated manner because of the standardized layouts of OSN user profiles (cf. [CPWF07]), i.e., third parties can easily develop software that is able to parse a large amount of OSN profiles in a short period of time. Hence, accessible PII might still pose remarkable privacy risks for users.

Therefore, in this part of the dissertation, we quantify privacy risks and discuss measures to enforce privacy aware acting in OSNs. Thereby, we address the question whether or not still sufficient PII is publicly shared so that users' privacy might be threatened by attacking third parties. We investigate this question from four different perspectives, or rather in light of four fields of specific research questions, introduced in the following.

## 4.4.1   Attribute Availability

The first part of the investigations in the area of OSNs focuses on the amount of PII that is shared via OSN profiles and that is, additionally, made publicly accessible. Therefore, we investigate whether or not OSN members are (still) unduly generous in adjusting privacy settings and in sharing PII that can be accessed by any member of the network, regardless whether or not an OSN friendship exists. Hence, we address the following research question:

– *Which pieces of PII are publicly accessible in how many user profiles of an OSN?*

In this context, we provide extensive statistical data gathered by multiple individual samplings. The corresponding findings provide evidence that still a lot of PII can be accessed by the public, i.e., any third party who is able to register an account

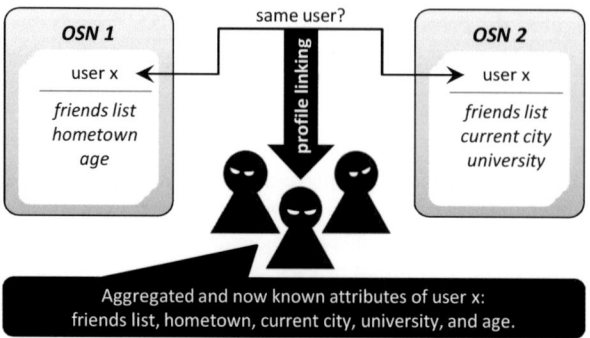

Figure 4.1: Illustration of the linkability of two profiles registered in different OSNs by a single user and the potential gain in information for attacking third parties.

at the respective OSN. Furthermore, we show that some pieces of PII are publicly provided by many users and some are rarely provided publicly. Moreover, we show that the results differ from one OSN to another, so that the diversity of specific pieces of PII that are accessible in many user profiles varies. The findings are presented in Section 5.2 and the results constitute the statistical basis for the research questions focused in the two following parts of OSN research.

### 4.4.2 Linkability

As mentioned, the specific pieces of PII that are publicly provided in many user profiles of an OSN are not congruent to the most frequently provided pieces of PII of another OSN. Therefore, we can observe a remarkable diversity of specific pieces of PII that are often publicly shared. Based on this finding, we investigate whether or not third parties can aggregate the different pieces of PII publicly provided by a single user in different OSNs. In particular, we delve how third parties can assemble a comprehensive digital image of an OSN member, despite the fact that he/she potentially has hidden, or not even shared, some pieces of PII in one OSN, but made it publicly available in another OSN. Thus, the focus is set on the possibilities to link PII published via several OSNs. We refer to this potential threat as the "*linkability*" of a user's OSN profiles[10].

Figure 4.1 illustrates the linkability of two exemplary profiles out of different OSNs registered by a single user x. In this figure, we illustrate third parties that can potentially aggregate publicly available PII of both of an exemplary user's profiles and are able to build a more comprehensive digital image of the user than possible by just analyzing one of his/her OSN profiles. If this constitutes a possible threat even if third parties do not have to utilize large resources in terms of high computational power or have to exploit sufficient linking algorithms (cf. the introduction of the assumed attacker model in Section 5.1.2), linkability poses a remarkable risk for users who registered profiles in several OSNs and publicly provide different pieces of PII depending on the OSN.

---

[10] Besides linking information, third parties could exploit the knowledge about whether or not a user has several OSN profiles, for instance, to clone his/her identity [BSBK09].

We are fully aware of the fact that linking of OSN profiles can not only pose a risk, but also can be utilized to support users, i.e., "linking of profiles could also be used to reveal and demonstrate users their virtual appearance across social networks. Bold and simple revealing of their linkability to users might help to motivate a more careful and adequate adjustment of privacy settings" [LDH11] (cf. the discussions in Chapter 6). Moreover, linking shared PII can be intended by users, e.g., "if users linked their profiles on their own by use of services such as https://about.me/, the linkability is implicitly given and intended by users" [LTH11]. However, an investigation of the linkability quantifies the risk that different pieces of PII publicly shared by a single user via different OSNs can be gathered and correlated. For those cases users' profiles are not per se linked by themselves, we investigate the risk with respect to the linkability of users' several OSN profiles in light of the following research questions. The results of this particular investigation are presented in Section 5.3.

- *Based on the observation that friends lists are often made public by OSN members, we ask whether or not this or other publicly shared information is sufficient to successfully link OSN user profiles. In other words, can third parties aggregate information that has been shared via different OSNs by a single user?*

- *Is it possible to link profiles at low costs, i.e., can profiles be linked by third parties without investing high computational effort or complex linking algorithms?*

## 4.4.3  Attribute Prediction

In the following chapter, another potential privacy threat is investigated, i.e., the risk that third parties can infer PII that a user has not even publicly provided via his/her OSN profiles. In particular, if a user provides a public friends list (in fact, more than 52 % of Facebook users publicly share their list of friends[11]), we ask whether or not third parties can infer the user's non-provided PII based on the PII publicly provided by his/her friends.

Figure 4.2 illustrates a very restrictive user with respect to publicly shared PII. However, this exemplary user publicly provides his/her friends list and, in turn, his/her OSN friends publicly provide some pieces of their PII. In such a situation, an attacking third party could analyze the user's friends list and the PII provided by the OSN friends in order to predict pieces of PII of the owner of the friends list. We refer to the threat regarding third parties that can infer users' non-provided PII as *attribute prediction*.

However, attribute prediction only poses a privacy risk if the PII provided by users' OSN friends strongly correlate with the users' PII. In order to quantify the risk regarding attribute prediction, we investigate the degree of correlation between PII shared by OSN users and their friends. In general, a "phenomenon called *homophily* is the basic reason for the fact that attribute values of OSN friends correlate. *Homophily*

---

[11]Besides the fact that more than a half of the members of the most popular OSNs provide public access to their friends list, according to [JKJ13], a non-provided friends list can even be reconstructed by, for instance, exploiting the posts on a user's wall saying that the user is now friends with a certain other user.

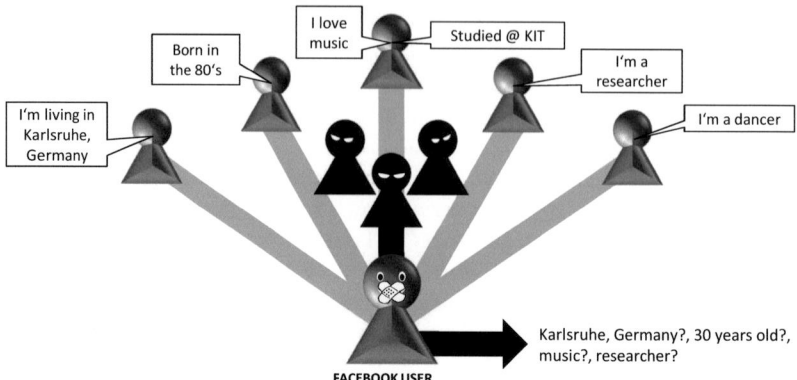

Figure 4.2: Illustration of the privacy threat that PII can potentially be inferred by attacking third parties.

means that people who are similar in interests and personal attributes more likely become friends than those with different characteristics [MSLCo1]. Recent studies have shown that it is possible to predict, for instance, the gender (2008: [XZL08], 2009: [JM09]). Lewis et al. found correlations of provided favored books, movies, and music [LGK11]. Some others introduced algorithms that can be (ab-)used to infer PII (e.g., [GA11]). However, recent studies have also shown that the user awareness regarding privacy significantly increased within the past years and users are more restrictive in adjusting privacy settings (...). Hence, the risk regarding privacy leakage *might be* decreased and it is unclear whether third parties are still able to predict the value of *any* type of attribute in an OSN" [LWMH13]. Therefore, we quantify the accuracies of predictions that can be reached by attacking third parties with respect to individual pieces of PII. For this investigation, we assume again an attacker that do not utilize high computational power or sophisticated algorithms to attack users' privacy. On the contrary, we assume a more or less casual attacker who just takes a peak on a user's OSN friends, or rather their shared PII to predict, for instance, where the user lives, his/her age, or other attributes.

In light of investigating the risk regarding attribute prediction and the mentioned attacker model, we define the following specific research questions that are addressed by the investigations presented in Section 5.4 of the next chapter:

- *Which kind of PII can be inferred by third parties in the case the user has not provided the respective information?*

- *Is it possible to infer users' PII at low costs, i.e., can third parties predict attributes without investing high computational effort or complex prediction algorithms?*

### 4.4.4   User Support for Avoiding Unintended Data Flows

The three previously addressed areas of research mainly focus on the quantification of privacy risks regarding OSNs. In the following, the forth part of addressed research questions in the field of OSNs is introduced.

In the following chapter, we show that privacy is at risk, in particular, if OSN users publicly provide their list of friends. In particular, we show that (1) a lot of PII is still publicly shared despite a demonstrably increased privacy awareness, (2) several OSN profiles of a single user are linkable at low cost, and (3) attribute prediction poses a risk if third parties analyze pieces of PII shared by a user's OSN friends. In light of these findings, we ask whether or not and how it would be possible to bring OSN users into the position of being able to identify unintended flows of PII in terms of determining any third party that can potentially get access to individual pieces of PII. In particular, we introduce concepts to design a novel type of technical measures to establish adequate mental models of the actual (potential) flows of PII and to support users in performing their individual identity management, i.e., the management of their PII in the context of OSNs. For proofing the concept of such a novel measure of user support, we also introduce an implemented Facebook App that is based on this concept (see Chapter 6). The underlying research questions are stated in the following:

– *How can users be supported in identifying possibly unintended flows of PII and in adjusting privacy settings in a more adequate manner than today?*

– *Would it be feasible to exploit a user's linkability and his/her actual risk regarding attribute predictions to show his/her current situation regarding privacy?*

## 4.5   Related Work

In the following, we present and discuss related work with respect to the presented four areas of OSN research this thesis focuses on. We start by introducing work that is generally related to the studies presented in this dissertation. Subsequently, we individually present specific related work regarding each of the four mentioned areas of research questions.

The authors of [KHG+08] discuss that many users do not care about privacy, even if OSNs provide privacy settings that can be adjusted and despite the fact that the privacy awareness has demonstrably been increased during recent years. Probably, users are reluctant regarding privacy aware behavior concerning OSNs because of the urge for "satisfaction of the needs for belongingness and the esteem needs through self-presentation, together with peer pressure" [KHG+08]. In this context, it is common that OSN users often state the "I've got nothing to hide"-argument. However, Daniel J. Solove impressively discuss the weakness of this and related phrases [Sol07]. We argued that some OSN users might be overcharged in determining the actual audience of PII that is to be shared. In 2010, Krishnamurthy pointed out the ignorance of users regarding the adjustment of privacy settings in an appropriate manner and stated: "From an awareness point of view, the situation is pretty bad" [Kri10]. Even worse, some users might even have difficulties to decide whether or not it is appropriate – concerning their own privacy demands – to share a specific piece of content with their OSN friends. In this context, *Dunbar's number* implies that humans are cognitively able to keep in touch – in terms of stable social relationships – with only 150 others [Dun93]. Several articles and studies have shown that Dunbar's number is also applicable in the context of OSN friends[12] [GPV11][13]. In 2011, Facebook stated that a user has, on average, 130 OSN friends. In Section 5.4, we show that today's Facebook users have an average number of more than 200 OSN friends and the most recent JIM study states that the respondents between twelve and 19 years claimed that they even have, on average, 272 friends on Facebook (cf. 2010: 159; 2011: 206 friends on average). Moreover, we found that the standard deviation of the number of friends is remarkably high, e.g., in the latest study on Facebook profiles, we found some user profiles with a friends list containing significantly more than 8,000 profiles. These large lists of friends indicate that it might be impossible for some (or even most) users to perform an adequate risk assessment as a basis for their individual identity management, i.e., sharing of PII only with a dedicated audience as a result of appropriate adjusted privacy settings. In this context, the authors of [KV10] define the term "self-disclosure" as the "amount of information shared on a user's profile as well as in the process of communication with others". In this dissertation, we investigate the self-disclosure of OSN users as a basis for the subsequently presented studies that quantify risks regarding privacy.

### 4.5.1 Related Work Regarding Publicly Available PII

In this part of the related work section, we introduce research that aims at quantifying the self-disclosure of OSN users, i.e., how much PII users share via their OSN profiles. In particular, at least since 2005, researchers investigate publicly available information accessible via Facebook. In the course of time, users' awareness has changed and, therefore, the amount of publicly accessible PII decreases from study to study. In the following, we introduce selected studies that investigated the availability of PII. Based on the findings of the presented related work, we provide an overview of the progress and change of the actual use of privacy settings in Table 4.2. These results can, additionally, be compared to the contributions presented later in this dissertation (cf. Section 5.2).

In 2005, Gross and Acquisti investigated Facebook profiles of 4,000 Carnegie Mellon University students in order to determine the corresponding privacy settings those users configured to hide sensitive information from third parties [GA05]. The authors found that, at least, 80 % of the analyzed profiles provided information that is sufficient to identify the corresponding user. 89 % of the users provided their full name on their Facebook profile and 90 % shared a photo of themselves. However, only about 1.2 %

---

[12]http://www.businessweek.com/printer/articles/90538-the-dunbar-number-from-the-guru-of-social-networks [Last downloaded 2013-05-28].

[13]http://www.forbes.com/sites/tjmccue/2013/01/15/social-media-maximum-150-friends/ [Last downloaded 2013-05-28].

| Attribute | [GA05] | [LES07] | [DHP07][1] (survey) | [BHI+08] | [SKT09][1] (survey) | [DJR12] NYC 2010 | [DJR12] NYC 2011 |
|---|---|---|---|---|---|---|---|
| real name | 89% | n.a. | 100% | n.a. | 55% | n.a. | n.a. |
| profile picture | 91% | n.a. | 99% | n.a. | 66% | n.a. | n.a. |
| friends lists | n.a. | n.a. | n.a. | 86% | 39% | 82.7% | 47.4% |
| Number of friends (avg.) | 133 | 179 | n.a. | n.a. | n.a. | n.a. | n.a. |
| date of birth/age | 88% | 84% | n.a. | 87% | 43% | 1.5% | 1.4% |
| gender | 99.6% | 94% | n.a. | 82% | n.a. | 58.9% | 52.8% |
| hometown | ca.72% | 83% | 93% | n.a. | n.a. | 10.4% | 24.0% |
| current residence | 51% | 45% | n.a. | n.a. | n.a. | 31.3% | 36.5% |
| address | 51% | 14% | n.a. | n.a. | 3% | n.a. | n.a. |
| e-mail | n.a. | 92% | 94% | n.a. | 13% | n.a. | n.a. |
| (mobile) phone number | 40% | n.a. | 38% | n.a. | 2% | n.a. | n.a. |
| instant messaging | ca.78% | 68% | 71% | n.a. | 18% | n.a. | n.a. |
| website | n.a. | 29% | n.a. | n.a. | 27% | n.a. | n.a. |
| university/(high) school | 87% | 87% | 84% | n.a. | n.a. | 13.4% | 9.1% |
| relationship status | 63% | 79% | 74% | n.a. | n.a. | 11.3% | 4.9% |
| sexual orientation | ca.54% | 51% | 78% | n.a. | n.a. | 7.7% | 6.4% |
| political direction | ca.53% | 61% | n.a. | n.a. | n.a. | n.a. | n.a. |
| interests/details | ca.65% | 78% | n.a. | n.a. | n.a. | n.a. | n.a. |
| favorite music | ca.66% | 78% | n.a. | n.a. | n.a. | n.a. | n.a. |
| favorite books | ca.60% | 67% | n.a. | n.a. | n.a. | n.a. | n.a. |
| favorite movies | ca.66% | 80% | n.a. | n.a. | n.a. | n.a. | n.a. |
| favorite TV shows | n.a. | 47% | n.a. | n.a. | n.a. | n.a. | n.a. |

[1] These findings are based on a questionnaire/survey. The authors of [LGKM11] found that in most cases users' expectations of adjusted privacy differs from their actual settings.

Table 4.2: Publicly available personally identifiable information in OSNs (unrestricted access, mainly Facebook) – findings of the presented related work.

of the users restricted the search-ability of their profile, i.e., the possibility to find a specific profile within the OSN based on, for instance, a user's name. Moreover, at this point in time only 0.06 % of users have hidden their profile so that it is not visible for other users than their OSN friends.

Lampe et al. investigated 38,407 Facebook profiles in 2007 (data gathered in April, 2006) [LES07]. At that time, Facebook was divided into sub-networks, e.g., universities had their own network and users interacted with other users within their own network. However, the authors' aim was to analyze which pieces of PII are actually provided by the analyzed users in order to find potential correlations to the number of their OSN friends. Actually, Lampe et al. could only analyze 30,773 of the profiles because 19 % restricted the audience of their shared information so that no data could be gathered from those users' profiles, i.e., already 19 % of users made use of privacy settings. However, the other share of analyzed Facebook members provided a lot of information via their profile pages, i.e., "On average, users complete 59 % of the fields available to them, and in some fields display a significant amount of information" [LES07]. In 2007, the authors of [DHP07] surveyed OSN users to figure out how trust in the OSN providers and other users, as well as privacy concerns affect the willingness to share information and to develop new relationships. Details on their results regarding publicly available information can be found in Table 4.2 (see column [DHP07]).

In 2008, the authors of [BHI+08] analyzed 7,919 Facebook profiles of Facebook's sub-network of the university of Michigan. This study aims at investigating whether or not users provide sufficient information to get context-aware spam, i.e., e-mails that are tailored to a user's characteristics and his/her PII. In their sampled data, the authors found that 68 % of profiles were visible to any other member of the network. 86 % of these profiles provided a public list of friends. In the same year, Krishnamurthy and Wills published their study on privacy in OSNs [KW08]. They analyzed several popular OSNs, such as Facebook, MySpace, and Twitter and found that, on average, 72.4 % of Facebook users (between 55 % and 90 % depending on the sub-network) let their profile viewable for any member of their sub-network and 79% of MySpace users retained the default configuration of provided privacy settings. Based on a previously carried out sampling [KGA08], Krishnamurthy et al. also analyzed how many Twitter users retained the default privacy settings of the OSN. At this point in time, only 1 % of users changed the default configuration and, thus, restricted the visibility of shared content. In 2009, Schrammel et al. published their investigation of the "Information Disclosure Behaviour [sic] in Different Types of Online Communities" [SKT09]. The study is based on a questionnaire and answers of 856 respondents (mainly "from German speaking countries" [SKT09]) carried out in 2008. See Table 4.2 for more details on their results.

Table 4.2 also contains the results presented by the authors of [DJR12] who repeatedly sampled the same large sample of Facebook users living in New York City. They found that privacy awareness of users has even been increased during the 15 month between the two last samplings. The attribute availability of the analyzed pieces of PII is shown in the table. These and the provided results of previous studies can be compared to the findings we present in the following chapter. In particular, Table 4.2 can be compared to Table 5.1 that shows the results of a sample we gathered in 2011, as well as to Table 5.2 that provides a comparison of profile analyses based on the 2011 sample and a sample gathered in 2012 (see Section 5.2 of the following chapter). By comparing the findings of previous studies and the results we provide, it becomes even more obvious that privacy awareness has been increased during recent years. However, for some pieces of PII, we can also observe a contrary "evolution" of privacy awareness, e.g., the attribute hometown was provided by 10.4 % of users in 2010 and by already 23.3 % of users in 2012, which might induce increased risks regarding privacy leakages. Inter alia, we address this particular threat by the findings presented in the following chapter.

The authors of [KW10a] analyzed the technical opportunities on top of which third parties can extract PII out of OSN profiles, in 2010. They analyzed twelve individual OSNs and show, inter alia, that in ten of these OSNs users' list of OSN friends are publicly accessible by default. In a follow-up study of these authors, they analyzed 13 OSNs that provide mobile access [KW10b]. The authors show that in six mobile OSNs the list of friends are always publicly accessible. In another six of the analyzed OSNs the friends lists are, at least, publicly available if users retain the default privacy settings pre-configured by the OSN provider. Just a single OSN restricted the access to friends lists by default. In this dissertation, we show that still most users of Facebook and other OSNs share a public friends list, which constitutes one of the key threats investigated in the following chapter.

## 4.5.2 Related Work Regarding Linkability Risks

Referring to the specific research questions stated in the context of the potentially existing linkability of several OSN profiles of a single user, we introduce selected related work in the following. Mislove et al. showed that not only the number of registered users in Facebook is growing, but also the number of users of other OSNs, such as Flickr[14] [MKG+08]. Therefore, it might be worth for attacking third parties to bring information together that is shared by a single user via different OSNs because the individually shared content might reveal different pieces of PII. On the contrary, Torkjazi et al. analyzed 360,000 MySpace profiles and report that the interest of users regarding the use of a specific OSN gets into a downturn after its (in this case, exponential) growth [TRW09]. They found that 41 % of the analyzed profile IDs (randomly chosen from the MySpace ID space) belong to profiles that have already been deleted. However, the authors also show that 75 % of users with public profiles have not been logged in to MySpace for more than 100 days. Thus, many users tend to do not delete OSN profiles that are no more in use and, hence, at one time publicly shared PII is often still accessible for any third party.

Even worse, if third parties can link users' OSN profiles, they might get access to sufficient information to link the gathered information to a particular person. In this context, as early as 2000, researchers found that 87 % of U.S. citizens can be uniquely identified by just three attributes: their gender, zip code, and date of birth [Swe00]. In 2006, these findings have been revisited and almost completely confirmed by Philippe Golle [Gol06]. Therefore, the linkability of users' OSN profiles poses a risk if different information is shared via different OSN profiles and, in particular, if users keep their "old" OSN profiles and publicly shared PII online.

The authors of [LM05] state that some users registered profiles in several OSNs. However, they estimate an overlap of only 15 % between two web-based OSNs. In 2007, a study carried out by the company *compete.com* demonstrates that 64 % of Facebook users also have registered a profile at MySpace, whereas only 20 % of MySpace users also registered a Facebook profile[15]. In the same year, the company *Rapleaf*[16] reported that 43 % of users of the OSN Hi5[17] are also registered at MySpace and that "Facebook users tend to use 2.9 major social networking sites on average"[18]. Motoyama and Varghese identified criteria in terms of attributes that are sufficient to re-identify a user of one OSN in another [MV09]. For their study, they sampled 68,277 user profiles out of the OSNs Facebook and MySpace. However, they observed that only 25.2 % of Facebook members overlapped in MySpace and 27.56 % vice versa. The authors explain the different values of overlap compared to the compete.com study due to the increase of the number of Facebook users that possibly did not register a MySpace

---

[14]http://www.flickr.com/ [Last downloaded 2013-05-28].

[15]http://blog.compete.com/2007/11/12/connecting-the-social-graph-member-overlap-at-opensocial-and-facebook [Last donwloaded 2013-04-02].

[16]http://www.rapleaf.com/ [Last downloaded 2013-05-28].

[17]http://www.hi5.com/ [Last downloaded 2013-05-28].

[18]http://readwrite.com/2007/11/12/opensocial_and_facebook_statistics [Last downloaded 2013-05-28].

account because of its decreased popularity. Furthermore, Motoyama and Varghese demonstrate that 44% of the users whose profiles have been analyzed and who are registered in both OSNs configured their privacy settings similarly. The other share adjusted their individual privacy settings differently depending on the OSN. This indicates that in some OSNs a user potentially shares information that is not publicly provided within another OSN, so that linking of his/her profiles might be worth for learning more about the user. In fact, at least, for 52 % of users attacking third parties can gain information by linking their OSN profiles. However, the authors also report that friends lists of Facebook and MySpace profiles of a single user just rarely overlap. We show in this dissertation that, in many cases, this little overlap constitutes a sufficient basis to link profiles without exploiting additional information.

Zafarani and Liu also introduced a methodology to link profiles [ZL09]. The investigated strategy aims at the revelation of users' registered names across several OSNs, i.e., they demonstrate that and how a user name registered in one OSN can be exploited to find user names of the same person used in other communities, such as OSNs. Another approach to link OSN profiles is introduced by the authors of [VHS09]. Their matching approach is based on representations of users' individual types of content shared via a profile page as vectors. A similarity score calculated between two vectors indicates matches. The authors applied the introduced algorithm to find overlaps of Facebook and StudiVZ and achieved a 83 % success rate. In [RCD10], the authors presented a framework to link profiles based on a weighting of attributes performed manually or even automatically. Furthermore, they implemented string and semantic metrics to calculate the similarity of attribute values and applied aggregation functions to decide whether or not a profile belongs to the same user. The authors tested their approach in an environment of automatically generated OSN user profiles.

In contrast to these studies, we exploit the network of friends (users' friends lists) to investigate the profile linkability. Whereas some types of attributes are provided in just very few profiles (cf. next chapter) and, in general, users share very diverse information via their profile pages, in popular OSNs more than a half of the users share their friends list. In contrast to the other pieces of information users share (or do not share), a friends list is a well-structured attribute that can easily be parsed even for attacking third parties that do not utilize sophisticated linking algorithms. Therefore, analyzing friends lists might be the first choice of a "casual attacker" in order to establish links between profiles of a single targeted user (see Section 5.1.2 for further details on the attacker model assumed for the studies presented in this dissertation). Another study that also exploits the friendship connections of users for linking profiles constitutes the work of Veldman [Vel09]. In particular, she introduce a two phase approach for linking profiles[19]. In the first phase, the shared content of potentially matching profiles out of two OSNs is compared, which results in a candidate list. Profiles contained in this list are compared with respect to their "network", i.e., a user's OSN friends. Whereas the second step is very similar to the linking approach we present in this thesis, her algorithm (only) refines the results by comparing OSN friends. In contrast, we just analyze the friends lists in order to establish links between

---

[19]http://doc.utwente.nl/68263/ [Last downloaded 2013-05-28].

OSN profiles of a particular user, which is a significantly less sophisticated approach in light of investigating "low cost" linkability.

Wondracek et al. demonstrate the linkability of a person to his/her OSN profile(s) based on so-called group memberships. In particular, they "show that information about the group memberships of a user (i.e., the groups of a social network to which a user belongs) is often sufficient to uniquely identify this user, or, at least, to significantly reduce the set of possible candidates" [WHKK10]. In contrast to linking several OSN profiles to each other, they try to identify one of a user's OSN profiles at this point in time he/she visits a (maliscious) website. Thereby, they exploit common methods to steal users' browser history and the fact that the set of group memberships of a user can function as kind of a fingerprint. A similar investigation has been carried out by Krishnamurthy et al. [KW10a]. The authors of this paper show how website providers can get knowledge of users' OSN profiles, or rather PII that is shared via these profiles. It has been shown that third parties can establish a link between a particular person and his/her shared PII, or even his/her OSN profiles. In contrast, we investigate the linkability of several profiles a single user registered in different OSNs, i.e., we aim at quantifying the risk that third parties can gather individually shared information due to compile a comprehensive digital image of a person. Thereby, we assume a more or less casual attacking third party that do not utilize large computing resources or sophisticated linking algorithms, such as, for instance, identifications by face recognition techniques (cf. [SZD08]).

The related papers introduced in the following have been published more or less contemporaneously or even subsequently compared to the submission and publication of the paper that contains the results we present in this dissertation, i.e., [LTH11]. However, this definitively does not imply an out-dated character of the findings we gained. The authors of [PCKM11] demonstrate an approach to link a user's profiles based on the user name used for the OSN profiles. In particular, it is shown that the entropy of a user name affects the probability of successful linking based on just this attribute. The approach either utilizes an estimation of the uniqueness of a user name used in several OSNs or links different identifiers. The fact that information about a user can also be gathered by just searching the Internet based on some (eventually insensitive) seed information is shown by the authors of [YLL+12]. In [BKP+12] and [MTW+12], the linkability of OSN user profiles is investigated as well. In contrast to the attacker we assume, these authors utilize a much more sophisticated approach for linking a user's profiles. For instance, the authors of [BKP+12] introduce a so-called "Joint Link-Attribute approach" to identify profiles of a single user across different OSNs, i.e., a graph-based algorithm. Thereby, they explicitly state that linkability constitutes (primarily) an advantage, at least, from the perspective of online marketers, but also for the users, for instance, in terms of improved automated merging of contacts on a mobile phone. However, from the perspective of a user, or rather from a privacy perspective, it might be not in the interest of users that, for instance, online marketers are provided with advantages to carry out their business and, therefore, such an "improvement" might also constitute a privacy threat for users. The authors of [JK12] published another investigation on the linkability of

OSN profiles that is, inter alia, based on the results we published in 2011 [LTH11]. In contrast to exploit only the friends list of users, such as we investigated the linkability, the authors exploit also the profile itself and content that is shared. They tested their system to find overlaps between Facebook and Twitter. Based on a sample of 543 Twitter profiles randomly selected out of a larger sample (about 500,000 profiles) the authors achieved an accuracy of 40.5 % by finding the corresponding Facebook profiles. Recently, the authors published another paper that explains their "identity search algorithm" in detail [JKJ13]. Certainly, such an integrated approach can result in a better accuracy than just exploiting the friends lists to link profiles, such as utilized for the investigations we present in this thesis. However, in every presented OSN study, we aim at assuming the "weakest" attacker that is imaginable and, thus, we provide lower bounds on, for instance, the accuracies of profile linking attacks. We are fully aware of the fact that the more side information an attacker can access the more precise he/she can link a user's OSN profiles. In turn, accessing and processing more content implies the need for more computing resources and the application of more sophisticated algorithms than a more casual attacker could apply. In 2013, the authors of [GLP+13] introduced a study that assumes an attacker "with moderate resources", i.e., an attacker who has access to just a few computers and the ability to rent some cloud resources. In contrast to this paper, we assume an any more casual attacker. In fact, the linking of user profiles based on provided friends lists can even be performed in a "manual" manner, i.e., with a simple algorithm executed by a single computer or even (without any computer-aided executed algorithm) by the attacker him-/herself. However, for linking OSN profiles, the authors of [GLP+13] exploit users' posts, or rather corresponding meta-information, such as the geo-locations and timestamps that are available for any post in some OSNs. Furthermore, they analyze how a post is written, i.e., "the user's writing style as captured by language models". In the context of low cost linkability, the authors of [CSS12] also present a "cheap and efficient" approach for mapping OSN profiles. The authors filter Twitter posts in order to identify posts induced by an action within another OSN, such as Youtube[20]. Afterwards, explicit links to the content shared via the other OSNs are extracted and, finally, uniquely identifiable profile information provides the link to the corresponding user at the other OSN in order to anrich the data shared via Twitter with further information provided in the other OSN. The authors of [CGNP12] present a model that "elucidates potential linkages between data" that is, for instance, shared via OSNs and show that it is sometimes remarkably easy how data can be gathered from different sources. The latter two papers referenced the linkability paper we published in 2011 [LTH11].

In this section, we presented related work regarding profile linking attacks or approaches to consciously link users' OSN profiles. In the following, we present related work regarding attacks that aim at inferring users' non-provided attribute values, or rather PII, for instance, based on information shared by others.

---

[20] https://www.youtube.com/ [Last downloaded 2013-05-28].

### 4.5.3   Related Work Regarding Attribute Prediction Risks

The authors of [MSLC01] demonstrate how the following old saying can be applied to social networks: "Birds of a feather flock together". The idea of this saying goes back to a quote by Democritus – an ancient Greek philosopher (c.460 B.C.E.) – who said: "*Creatures flock together with their kind, doves with doves, cranes with cranes and so on*"[21]. According to [MSLC01], already Aristotle and Plato took up this saying. In the year 360 B.C.E., Plato stated that "*similarity begets friendship*" [tbRB68] and, in 350 B.C.E., Aristotle wrote "*love those who are like themselves*" [tbHR34]. In 2001, in this context, Domingos et al. demonstrated that friends in a network potentially share similar interests and characteristics [DR01]. Moreover, the authors show that social network friends are so similar that they can even influence a user's decisions regarding whether or not to buy a product. The company *Anderson Analytics* underpinned the similarity hypothesis by carrying out a survey. This survey revealed that only 10 % of the respondents would accept any random OSN friendship request (i.e., potentially requests of dissimilar users). In contrast, 45 % of users only connect their profiles with those of family members and friends of their "real life" and another 18 % state that they would only connect with users they have met in "real life"[22]. Therefore, we can assume that the similarity of people induces not only friendships in general, but also and in particular in OSNs. However, the similarity of OSN friends can constitute the basis for inferring attributes that are actually not publicly shared by a user. To give an example, Brown et al. showed that 24.1 % of their sample of Facebook users are vulnerable for shared-hometown-attacks, i.e., a third party can send context-aware spam to this user by, for instance, utilizing his/her hometown. In this thesis, we show that a prediction of a user's non-provided hometown can be performed by third parties with an even significantly higher accuracy. Moreover, if sufficient information can be accurately inferred, third parties might be even more able to identify a particular person (cf. the study of [Swe00] that demonstrated that just three pieces of PII are sufficient to identify a particular person). In the following, we present related research in which the risk for inferring users' PII by third parties is investigated.

In 2006, He et al. utilized a Bayesian network approach "to model the causal relations among people in social networks" [HCL06]. Based on this model, the authors investigated the risk that third parties might be able to infer users' non-provided attributes due to PII shared by their OSN friends. The authors also state that only the selective hiding of OSN friendships has the potential to result in a non-threatening situation regarding privacy. The authors of [XZL08] studied the risk that third parties can infer users' non-provided pieces of PII also based on a Bayesian network approach. In this paper, the main focus is set on the prediction of the attribute *gender*. However, the authors also state that their algorithm can be used for predicting other pieces of PII. In 2009, Zheleva and Getoor demonstrated that attribute prediction poses still a risk for OSN users([ZG08], [ZG09]). Based on the list of OSN friends, as well as group memberships, the authors show eight

---

[21]http://ezinearticles.com/?id=1401521 [Last downloaded 2013-05-28].

[22]http://adage.com/article/digital/social-media-anderson-analytics-reveals-users-habits/137792/ [Last downloaded 2013-05-28].

attacks – utilizing different classifiers and features – that can potentially threaten users' privacy. They map the problem to a relational classification problem, i.e., classifying data out of a relational data set, and evaluate the proposed attacks on data sets sampled from four different OSNs. Whereas we investigate the attribute prediction primarily based on friends lists, the authors, additionally, exploit the group memberships to increase the accuracy of prediction. However, we show in this thesis that just the analysis of pieces of PII shared by a user's friends are in some cases sufficient to infer non-provided PII of the user him-/herself. In this context, Jernigan and Mistree state that "public information about one's coworkers, friends, family, and acquaintances, as well as one's associations with them, implicitly reveals private information" [JM09]. In particular the authors investigated whether or not the gender and sexual orientation of OSN users are inferable by third parties. They analyzed 6,077 Facebook profiles associated with an MIT-related sub-network sampled by the use of a software named *Arachne* to show that third parties can infer users' sexual orientation. 167,000 Facebook profiles are investigated by Lindamood et al. [LHKT09] in order to demonstrate the potential risk regarding attribute prediction. The authors exploit the social graph and present an inference attack that outperforms traditional Bayes and Links algorithms. A very similar approach to this and the study we present is utilized by the authors of [MVGD10]. In contrast to the findings presented in this thesis, they gathered profiles only from two selected sub-networks of Facebook (4,000 student profiles and 63,000 profiles from another network) and used a profile that is also member of a targeted sub-network, which induce more accessible information (e.g., an accessible friends list in any case) than available for an ordinary third party that is just a member of the OSN but potentially not of the same sub-network than the targeted user. Furthermore, the authors exploit specific sections of the social graph, i.e., they detect communities within a list of friends that have a higher degree of interconnection and, thus, shared information of members of these communities indicate non-provided information more adequately. Instead, we just concentrate on the information shared by a user's OSN friends as a whole regardless of the degree of interconnection of specific groups of a user's friends. This constitutes the basis to investigate whether or not also a casual attacker can infer PII, i.e., an attacker that do not have large computing resources at one's disposal or is able to exploit sophisticated prediction algorithms, such as an algorithm to perform community detection within a friends list. As a result of the assumption of such a casual attacker, "we demonstrate quantifications of risk based on the minimal knowledge a third party can get from OSN profiles and, thus, present a 'lower bound' on *how much* PII can be predicted in OSNs" [LWMH13].

In 2010, Facebook researchers published that users' non-provided location can be predicted by analyzing the location of corresponding OSN friends because the likelihood of friendships increases with shorter distances, i.e., users interconnect more often with other users who live in their proximity. The authors show that "the likelihood of friendships drops monotonically as a function of distance" [BSM10]. Furthermore, they predict the maximum-likelihood location of a user based on his/her Facebook friends. The authors found that in 67.5 % of the analyzed cases 16 or more friends live in a 25 miles or less distance to the user whose location is to be predicted. The aim of this study is very similar compared to the investigation of location prediction presented in the following chapter. However, instead of using data only accessible for Facebook itself, we study the risk regarding attribute prediction based on PII that is *publicly* available. Based on this attacker model, we observed that in about 56 % of the cases the city of the analyzed users exactly equals the most frequently provided city within a friends list. Thus, we demonstrate that even a third party is able to predict users' location, or rather current city based on PII *publicly* shared by their Facebook friends.

A completely different approach that enables to infer user's PII is investigated by Rao et al. [RYSG10]. Based on an algorithmic approach that targets semantic information, the authors analyzed users' posts on Twitter in order to "classify latent user attributes". On the contrary, we focus on investigating the *similarity* of users' shared pieces of PII. In [GA11], also an algorithmic approach is introduced to infer PII. The author states that "all liaisons are dangerous when all your friends are known to us" [GA11] and presents a study in which a novel graph labeling algorithm is applied to infer PII. He also used data shared on Twitter to test the algorithm. Instead of using Twitter data, we quantify the risks regarding attribute prediction based on an extensive sample of 1.3 million Facebook profiles. Furthermore, as mentioned before, we investigate privacy risks, such as the attribute prediction based on a model that assumes a third party that tries to attack at low cost.

The fact that some pieces of PII can be inferred is also shown by the authors of [LGK11] who indicate that provided favorites, such as favored books, movies, and music, can be inferred by third parties. Their results show that among the 100 most popular preferences, correlations of attribute values can be detected within a group of OSN friends regardless of the fact that 64 % of observed favorites are provided by just a single profile. In contrast, we focus not only on favorite attributes, but also on PII that might be more sensitive and, in general, cover a broader set of potentially inferable pieces of PII. The authors of [SKB12] present an attack to infer users' links, i.e., their friendship connections, and their location. However, also these authors utilized a sophisticated approach for predicting PII, i.e., an individually implemented algorithm.

In 2011, the authors of [AAF11] demonstrated that also third party providers of Facebook Apps can get access to sufficient information to infer non-provided pieces of PII. Additionally, they propose a scheme that can be used for risk assessment. In [GTM+12], the risk of attribute prediction was investigated based on algorithms that are adapted with a so-called social-attribute network model and data gathered from the OSN Google+. The risk of hometown predictions based on geotagged photos posted via Flickr profiles is investigated in [JKS12]. However, these studies differ from the investigations we present in terms of the approach and the source of information exploited to predict PII.

Recently, Chaabane et al. exploit interests stated on Facebook, or rather users' *Likes* to predict specific pieces of PII, i.e., users' gender, country, relationship status, and age [CAK12]. Based on the *Likes*, the authors selected specific communities of users – those who *liked* semantically identical content – and inferred users' non-provided pieces of PII based on information shared by the selected portion of users. Because of the possibility that such a selection of specific users might not be feasible for the casual attacker because he/she would have to crawl the largest data set possible, we concentrate on exploiting the information as it is shared by the users' friends, which can even be analyzed in a non-automated manner. In 2012, Blenn et al. published an investigation of the attribute prediction risk based on a large sample of users of an OSN mainly provided for users from the Netherlands, i.e., Hyves.nl[23] [BDSVM12]. Similar to the study on possible attribute predictions presented in this dissertation, the authors focus on whether or not and how accurate the age and location attributes can be inferred by third parties. Furthermore, they demonstrate the accuracies of inferring, at least, a nearby area of a user's actual location. However, the findings are based on a sample of a less popular OSN compared to Facebook that we analyze in the following chapter. Furthermore, the authors quantify the risk in a less detailed manner compared to the results we provide. The authors of [CAK12] also state that the age is inferable despite the fact that just a few users share this attribute. Similar to the results we present in this thesis, the authors demonstrate that it is possible to infer, at least, an *age range* that probably apply to a user. Based on their algorithm, they observed a success rate, or rather accuracy of predictions of up to 58 % for the youngest users. By utilizing a much simpler approach, we give evidence that this specific prediction accuracy can be reached, on average, for any user regardless his/her actual age. We also show that the most accurate predictions can be observed for predicting younger users' age. In fact, we calculated a prediction accuracy of up to 94 %. Another study that investigated the accuracies of attribute predictions is presented in [KSG13]. The authors analyzed *Likes* provided by 58,466 volunteers acquired via a Facebook App (on average, 170 *Likes* per user). The authors show that some potentially sensitive pieces of PII, such as users' sexual orientation, ethnicity, religious and political views, etc. can be inferred at a remarkable high accuracy. To give an example, on the basis of about 250 provided *Likes*, the authors could predict the user's age at an accuracy of 75 %. However, as already mentioned, we focus on attribute predictions based on publicly shared PII of users' friends in light of the assumed model of a more or less casual attacker.

In summary, we investigate which pieces of PII can be inferred by analyzing attributes shared by one's OSN friends if a friends list is publicly shared. In this context, the authors of [TWX+11] show that third parties can even obtain friends lists if users' do not share this information publicly, i.e., based on a reverse lookup via others' friends lists and the non-congruent privacy settings of OSN members the list of friends of a user can be reconstructed. However, if a friends list can be accessed or reconstructed, the attacker gets access to information publicly shared by a user's OSN friends. We quantify the risks that – just based on this knowledge – third parties can infer a user's non-provided information. Thereby, we utilize only simple string comparisons to "simulate" a casual attacker that cannot exploit sophisticated algorithms and large computing resources.

---

[23]http://hyves.nl/ [Last downloaded 2013-05-28].

## 4.5.4    Related Work Regarding Privacy Enhancing Applications

In this part of the related work section, we focus on research papers that introduce privacy applications and discuss their potential to support users in deciding whether or not to publicly share pieces of PII, as well as to monitor who can get access, or already accessed shared information. "As early as 2004, Acquisti wrote that only the combination of the aspects *technology* and *risk awareness* has the potential of successfully solving the privacy problem whereas any of these aspects alone will most probably fail [Acq04]. Recently, Krishnamurthy wrote, 'From an awareness point of view, the situation is pretty bad' [Kri10]" [LTH11]. In the following chapter, we show that the content shared via OSNs ranges from insignificant information to remarkably sensitive PII. Therefore, we assume that just providing privacy settings is not sufficient to encourage people to use such settings adequately.

In the following, we discuss related work regarding user support that aims at bringing users into the position to consider potentially existing (unintended) data flows induced by participating in OSNs. In the context of several research projects, such as the projects PRIME[24] and PrimeLife[25] that are funded by the European Union (EU), privacy tools have been introduced that can be deployed in order to support users in controlling who can access which type and piece of information, i.e., keeping track of any party that is able to access a user's PII. "As early as 2005, in the context of the PRIME project, the authors of [BRP05] assessed the idea of a system that supports users in preserving their privacy. Inter alia, in [BPL+11], the privacy-enhanced social network site *Clique* is introduced. This site provides users with the capability of segregating the audience of PII that is to be shared. It also provides options to define the accessibility of shared PII in a fine-grained manner. The authors of [FHHW11] investigated a user interface called Data Track to support people in maintaining an overview of their provided PII. In 2009, XML co-developer Eve Maler[26] presented a similar mock-up (called *CopMonkey*) at the European Identity Conference (EIC)[27]. CopMonkey represents a system that serves as a tool for assessing the given privacy status of a user" [Lab12]. In [LXH09], an approach is presented to conceal shared PII and only provide access to a selected group of other users. By providing fake information and encrypted data, the actual information is shielded from others that are not intended to get the information. The authors of [FL10] developed effective ways of managing friend lists by applying community detection on the social graph for predicting the intended adjustment of privacy settings in order to support users in managing their privacy. They provide a wizard-based approach to support users in adjusting their privacy settings more appropriately. To give another example, members of the EU-funded research project *digital.me* implement tools to provide users with an aggregated overview of pieces of PII shared with certain services, such as OSNs. The project aims at introducing a centralization of the management of PII shared in/with different services (cf. [SGH+11], [BRS+12], and [CSRH12]). To give particular

---

[24]https://www.prime-project.eu/ [Last downloaded 2013-05-28].
[25]http://www.primelife.eu/ [Last downloaded 2013-05-28].
[26]http://www.xmlgrrl.com [Last downloaded 2013-05-28].
[27]https://www.id-conf.com/ [Last downloaded 2013-05-28].

examples, the authors of [BRS⁺12] developed a prototype that gathers data from OSN profiles and a corresponding algorithm that matches multiple OSN profiles to one person. In [CSRH12], the authors further aim at integrating multiple OSN profiles into one single profile in order to increase usability. However, in contrast to the focus on usability (which could also enhance privacy), we concentrate on how to demonstrate potential privacy leaks (the users might not be aware of) to the users themselves.

Further approaches to enhance privacy in OSN-related communication is presented in the context of the EU-funded project *PICOS*[28], i.e., privacy enhancements for mobile communities, such as mobile OSNs. In this context, the authors of [KBT⁺10] "outline the approach of the PICOS project" and motivate the necessity of privacy enhancing technologies in terms of appropriate identity management capabilities for users of mobile communities. One of the architectures proposed in the context of the PICOS project is published in [KCTR11]. This particular work aims at preserving privacy in OSNs without loosing the ability for advertisers to carry out their business. A more detailed view on the architectural structure of the approach, as well as its implementation is provided in [TKH⁺11].

Proactive privacy support is also addressed in the field of research on user-centricity [BSCGS07]. In particular, "authentication and authorization frameworks of projects, such as the Kantara Initiative UMA[29], OAuth[30], and OpenID[31], to name just a few, often include a proactive information management component, which can be adjusted to deny or allow third parties access to the PII requested (...) However, the implications of granting permission to access personal data are often not clear to users" [Lab12]. Therefore, such privacy features can only provide an overview of the pieces of PII shared in a certain context.

Whereas the introduced related work mainly aim at providing information about who has potentially access to PII that is to be shared, a reactive monitoring of the actual flows of PII is often not primarily focused. In fact, most published work presents measures and tools to proactively support users in managing their PII, i.e., support in deciding whether or not to share PII in a certain context *before* the data is shared and support in maintaining an overview of shared PII. However, this is only one perspective of, at least, three perspectives that are important to effectively assist users in managing flows of PII. The other two perspectives are (1) the necessity to be able to monitor the proliferation of PII, i.e., (reactive) capabilities to determine who has access to shared PII at a certain point in time, and (2) the disclosure of privacy risks induced by the current situation of a particular user with respect to his/her shared information and regarding third parties that can potentially access this data.

Referring to (1), some work has already been published that addressed this issue. For instance, the tool *Data Track* introduced in the context of the project PrimeLife provides users with capabilities to monitor the actual pieces of PII stored by a certain provider of a service. Furthermore, in the context of *PICOS*, the need for "control

---

[28] http://www.picos-project.eu/ [Last downloaded 2013-05-28].
[29] http://kantarainitiative.org/ [Last downloaded 2013-05-28].
[30] http://oauth.net/ [Last downloaded 2013-05-28].
[31] http://openid.net/ [Last downloaded 2013-05-28].

over usage and proliferation of PII" was stated as a major issue accompanied with the implementation of OSNs that preserve users' privacy [Wei09]. The authors of [HPH11] also introduce an approach to enhance privacy by supporting users in a reactive manner. In particular, they introduce a tool to bring users into the position to access parts of service log files in order to figure out whether or not shared PII was forwarded by the respective provider to another third party. However, unintended data flows are not only induced by communication processes between users and services, but also due to the analysis of users' shared PII by third parties that might be able to, additionally, even link this PII to a particular person. Therefore, information flows are not limited to the disclosure of PII to a certain service provider.

In Chapter 6 of this dissertation, we mainly address the second aforementioned issue (2), i.e., we introduce concepts to design privacy tools that demonstrate users their current situation regarding privacy and potential privacy threats. This demonstration of potential risks provides an individual view on (possibly unintended) flows of PII as a basis to adjust privacy settings adequately according to a user's own privacy demands. We argue that privacy tools should aim at systematically adapt users' mental models of possible data flows towards adequate perceptions of potential receivers of shared information and corresponding privacy risks. Certainly, also the demonstration of privacy risks is not a new idea. To give examples, the tools *Take this Lollipop*[32] or *Wolfram Alpha Personal Analytics for Facebook*[33] aim at drawing the users' attention to certain privacy risks. However, referring to the related research work presented in this section, we argue that today's research has not sufficiently addressed the conceptual basis of privacy tools that can effectively sharpen users' mental models of flows of PII. In particular, the mentioned tools that demonstrate privacy risks do not strictly follow a well-reasoned strategy, or rather are not built upon a well-designed methodological basis. In Chapter 6, we contribute exactly this fundamental strategy as groundwork on top of which promisingly effective privacy tools can be implemented that demonstrate potential flows of PII and corresponding privacy risks.

---

[32]http://www.takethislollipop.com/ [Last downloaded 2013-05-28].
[33]http://www.wolframalpha.com/facebook/ [Last downloaded 2013-05-28].

# 5

# Large-Scale Empirical Investigations of Online Social Networks

This chapter presents the contributions that have been compiled by large-scale empirical studies on OSN user profiles. In particular, we address the previously stated research questions with respect to (1) the amount of publicly available pieces of personally identifiable information (PII), (2) the risk that several profiles of a single user can be linked and shared PII be aggregated by attacking third parties, and (3) the risk that non-provided PII can be inferred based on information provided by users' OSN friends. We argue that this empirical "risk quantification" lay an essential foundation for more effective privacy enhancing technologies with which OSN users can be provided in the near future. As already mentioned, in [ACF12], the authors identified that the concept and measure of risk is a central point of the model, on top of which privacy tools have to be designed. It has also been demonstrated that novel privacy applications are necessary to further establish risk awareness with respect to privacy and to demonstrate privacy implications of shared PII and PII that is to be shared. The forth field of OSN research introduced in the previous chapter targets exactly this discussion on novel concepts to support users in monitoring and control of the flows of their PII. However, this particular field of OSN research is elaborated within Chapter 6, whereas the current chapter focuses on the empirical risk quantification.

Before we present the results of these empirical studies, we introduce the methodology of the corresponding investigations. First, we provide a detailed discussion on how research on OSN profiles can be performed in a compliant manner with respect to, for instance, the German law. This is an essential contribution in light of the fact that even the investigation of potential risks could threaten users' privacy regardless of the actual "positive", or rather non-malicious intent of the work. Second, we introduce the already mentioned attacker model in detail. Afterwards, we present the technical methodology utilized to analyze OSN users' publicly shared PII and point out measures today's OSNs take to avoid automated processing of user profiles and shared information. In summary, we introduce the conceptual basis of compliant and privacy preserving analysis of users' publicly available PII in OSNs. Subsequently to the introduction of the methodology, we present results of three empirical studies carried out at different points in time. For each of these studies, we implemented an individual analysis software that was utilized to investigate publicly available PII shared by thousands of randomly chosen OSN user profiles. Parts of the contributions presented in this chapter have been previously published in [LDH11], [LTH11], and [LWMH13].

## 5.1 Automated Analysis of Online Social Network Profiles

For the studies presented in this chapter, we previously analyze the legal situation with respect to carrying out statistical sampling of users' OSN profiles and empirical investigations of their publicly shared PII. This preceding investigation is based on the German law and, particularly, the German Data Protection Act, because compliance regarding privacy regulations is a must in the context of large-scale empirical studies of OSNs. Based on discussions with members of the *Center for Applied Legal Studies (Zentrum für Angewandte Rechtswissenschaft, ZAR)* at the KIT, we developed a concept to implement fully automated analysis software that samples and analyzes user's profiles in a both privacy preserving and compliant manner. In this section, additionally, the attacker model, on top of which the software is implemented, is introduced. Finally, we present the conceptual basis of the analysis software developed for the studies and give insights into the implementations. Furthermore, we analyze which countermeasures today's OSN providers take to prevent crawling of information shared by their customers, i.e., the OSN members.

### 5.1.1 Compliance w.r.t. the German Law and Data Protection Act

The German constitution (in particular, Art.2 Section 1 in conjunction with Art.1 Section 1, GG) and the German National Data Protection Act (BDSG) together constitute the basis for German peoples' rights regarding data protection, i.e., privacy and self-determination regarding their own PII. Thereby, the term "purpose" is essential for processing PII. Without a purpose, which has to be *communicated* to and approved by the owner of the data, a third party has no right to process personal data unless the law explicitly permits the processing. The requirement of designated purposes is, for instance, regulated in §4.3 and §4a.1 BDSG. This also means that only the users themselves can give their consent for processing their personal data if the processing is not explicitly permitted by law.

The purpose of sharing information via OSN profiles is unambiguously to participate within the respective OSN. The users do not provide content for further processing of the data by third parties. Several OSNs explicitly prohibit the extraction of personal data automatically performed by, for instance, a crawler software. In this context, we stated the following in a previous paper: "According to our analysis of BDSG, it is not possible to legitimize any extraction, processing, and archiving of users' profiles and contained personal data without a previously stated agreement of any affected user (permission facts). Neither §40 (BDSG) is applicable, which regularizes the processing and use of personal data by research institutions, because it is required that the research institution gathers the data from users on its own, nor the investigation of extracted OSN data is included in the category of market and public opinion research purposes, which are separately regulated in §28 (BDSG)." [LDH11]

However, in contrast to the extraction of PII publicly provided by OSN users and to process this data, we were only interested in statistical data. In particular, we investigated whether or not certain attributes, i.e., pieces of PII, are publicly provided by a user, regardless of the actual value of this attribute. Furthermore, we investigated interdependencies of attribute values, for instance, between attributes provided by different profiles of a user or by a user and his/her OSN friends. Again, in this case, the main focus was to gather statistical data and not the raw attribute values themselves, despite the fact that we compared the actual values. Therefore, we did not need to *extract* attribute values from the analyzed OSN profiles and store them within a database. On the contrary, the raw data was only necessary at this point in time the statistical data was calculated. Therefore, the main requirement imposed by and derived from the German law is to implement an analysis software that keeps the time as short as possible in which the actual attribute values are analyzed. Furthermore, the software has to discard analyzed attribute values immediately after calculating the statistical data. Moreover, the software has to keep the raw data transiently in main memory for the shortest possible period of time in which the statistical data can be calculated, which constitutes the crucial point for acting in a compliant manner. Due to such short-time processing of data, the analysis of users' PII and the analysis of merely statistical data can be completely separately performed. Therefore, the time span in which the raw data is kept in main memory and analyzed by the software separates two domains of jurisdiction, i.e., the handling of PII by the OSN, which is/should be permitted by the users themselves, and the processing of statistical data. These very short time spans are referred to as *"logical seconds"* [Win00]. However, the time span in which the statistical data is calculated on the basis of the raw data can only be seen as a *"logical second"* if it is ensured that (1) the statistical data cannot be used to find out which profiles have been analyzed to calculate the respective statistical values and (2) it is not possible to access the raw analyzed information by any natural person.

Thus, for actually acting compliant with respect to the German law, the implementation of the analysis software has to fulfill the following requirements. First, raw data is only processed during a so-called *"logical second"*, i.e., the shortest possible time span in which data is only present in the main memory of the machine that runs the analysis software. Second, the raw data cannot be accessed by anyone during the analysis process, and, finally, the statistical data calculated on the raw information do not allow any reference back to a "real" OSN profile, i.e., "nobody is able to recover personal attributes or profile information with a distinct link to a natural person or an OSN profile at runtime of the analysis software as well as afterwards. Hence, all processing steps in the analysis software have to be executed automatically." [LDH11]

## 5.1.2  Attacker Model

Referring to the related work presented in Section 4.5, it becomes obvious that most studies in the field of research on privacy risks of OSNs do not assume an attacker model of low complexity. The authors of the presented related work have often chosen a very complex model that represents the attacking third party (see, for instance, [BSBK09]). Thereby, they can estimate *how much* information can be gained by third parties from a user's OSN profile or any other information extracted from OSNs, i.e., these studies provide findings on the *maximum of information* that can be gained from information shared by OSN members.

In the studies presented in this dissertation, we assume a contrary attacker model. In particular, we assume a more or less "casual attacker", i.e., an attacker that could be one's (potential) boss, ex-partner, insurance agent, or just the (wo-)man at the cinema counter who saw a customer's name on his/her credit card. These casual attackers do not have access to large computing resources and are not able to utilize sophisticated algorithms to threaten users' privacy. Furthermore, we assume an attacker who do not exploit side-information, i.e., data stored in his/her own databases or, at least, information that can be found by just googling a person. Hence, a casual attacker tries to gather and infer information about the targeted person by comparing his/her several OSN profiles and the profiles of his/her OSN friends.

Thereby, we assume an attacker who analyzes each of any attribute that can be publicly provided by OSN members (initially) semantically separated from other attributes. With that, we consciously do not include relations between several shared attributes. In particular, an attacker that behaves according to the model acts as follows: he/she tries to gather and infer users' PII primarily based on users' friends lists if this information is publicly provided (remember, more than a half of the users of the most popular OSNs publicly provide their friends list). Furthermore, the attacking third party can act like an ordinary OSN user, i.e., it has access to any information publicly shared. Thereby, the attacker is not connected to any other member of the OSN in terms of an OSN friendship. With that, (1) we do not have to involve other users into the studies in terms of annoying them with friendship requests and (2) the results are not influenced by possibly differing access rights of OSN friends, friends-of-friends, and other users. Furthermore, the attacker do not utilize sophisticated algorithms to gather and infer users' PII. Instead, only simple string comparisons are used to demonstrate the linkability and risk of attribute prediction.

Therefore, the "risk quantification is consciously based on minimal knowledge a third party can extract from OSN profiles. Thus, the findings present a 'lower bound' on how much information is predictable (at low cost), i.e., we present results of the analysis of a large set of statistical data and focus on those probabilities that can be extracted from the data with a minimum of semantic interpretation or combination of findings" [LWMH13]. Although the main focus of the studies presented in this thesis is on a semantically separated investigation of publicly shared attributes in order to quantify privacy risks, we also go a step further and discuss the potential of correlations of several types of attributes and demonstrate examples for this, e.g., how student users behave different from other users.

However, quantifying lower bounds constitutes an essential contribution to provide a basis to be able to compare the studies presented in this thesis among each other, as well as to compare future measurement studies with the findings presented in this dissertation. Therefore, on this basis, the findings constitute a reference for former and future empirical studies on publicly available information within OSNs and corresponding privacy risks. Moreover, the findings can serve as a reference for impact analyses of future privacy enhancing technologies. Thus, choosing such a less complex attacker model prevents from too artificial results in terms of detected risks or other findings that can potentially occur only if several conditions are fulfilled. In turn, assuming a more sophisticated attacker model does not completely ensure the repeatability of the experiments because OSN providers develop their services further and deploy unpredictable changes. However, repeatability is an essential requirement in light of the fact that the findings should be comparable to former and, in particular, future quantification of users' privacy awareness and users' handling of the IT system *OSN*.

Although many studies have been published that investigate similar risks regarding OSNs, to the best of our knowledge, this dissertation and the correspondingly published papers are the first research work that aims at assuming such a *low cost attacker* in order to calculate the *lower bounds* on what and how many pieces of PII can be gathered and inferred. As mentioned above, this is indispensable knowledge when, for instance, the impact of future privacy tools have to be determined.

## 5.1.3   Methods of Profile Sampling

Certainly, it is not possible to analyze a whole OSN by crawling all of its profiles in reasonable time and reasonable effort. Therefore, in order to analyze privacy risks induced by publicly available PII, it is necessary to sample a subset of OSN profiles in the most possible uniform manner. In general, several options exist to sample profiles out of OSNs. Because of the fact that OSN profiles with the corresponding friendship connections can be seen as, or rather transferred to a graph (i.e., the social graph) known algorithms that are applicable for graph traversals are also applicable to sample OSN profiles. In particular, many studies implement a *breadth-first search* (BFS), which goes back to the work of Moore [Moo59] and also Lee's research [Lee61] (cf. also [NW01] as an example of applying BFS to crawl websites). In the context of sampling OSN profiles, several authors made use of the BFS approach, e.g., the authors of [MMG+07], [JM09], [WBS+09], and [MVGD10]. The principle of sampling OSN profiles based on a BFS constitutes the selection of, at least, one profile that is used as a seed. Starting from this profile, the profiles listed in the corresponding friends lists are added to the profiles that are to be sampled. In the next steps, the profiles listed in the friends lists of the profiles of the seed's friends list are selected and so on and so forth. The authors of [KMT10] state that most probably BFS is a popular approach because it is a "textbook technique" that is easy to implement. However, they demonstrate that a BFS, as well as other related techniques applied to an OSN do not result in a uniform sample, or rather result in a biased sample. Related sampling techniques are the *depth-first search*, the *forest fire* approach, i.e., like BFS but with a randomization that decides whether or not to include a certain node/profile, the *snowball sampling* technique, i.e., an approach based on BFS, but only a certain number of neighbors are included in the sample, as well as *random walk*, which constitutes also a specialization of the BFS approach in terms of that only a single randomly chosen neighbor of the current node is included into the sample and it is not excluded that a profile is sampled several times. However, a sample of OSN profiles gathered by the utilization of a BFS or similar approaches is biased towards nodes with high degrees (see also [BCDF06], [YLW10] and [CDMF+11]), i.e., the algorithm just samples profiles within a certain sub-community and the probability to leave this sub-community is too low to get a uniform sample. In turn, the reason for this sub-communities constitutes the structure of OSNs in which sub-communities are highly interconnected and between sub-communities just a few links exist. In other words, it is more likely to sample nodes/profiles with a larger number of connections/friendships than sampling nodes with a small number of edges. The authors of [KMT10] showed in a previous study that a BFS induces a sample with an average node degree that is 3.5 times higher than data that is sampled based on a ground-truth method [GKBM10].

A sampling method that is considered as a "ground-truth" approach (cf. [KMT10]), which is, for instance, also utilized in [GKBM10], constitutes the *acceptance-rejection sampling* [LG08] (also known as UNIFORM sampling [CDMF+11]). Thereby, profiles are sampled uniformly in the OSN's ID space, i.e., the range of identifiers used by the OSN provider to refer to the individual profiles. An analysis software that implements an acceptance-rejection sampling randomly picks an identifier out of the ID space of the OSN and tries to open a profile that belongs to the chosen identifier. To give a more technical example, a user's Facebook profile can be accessed by the use of the Facebook URL [RFC1738] plus the corresponding identifier of a profile, i.e., https://www.facebook.com/<identifier>[1]. If an HTTP [RFC2616] request based on the randomly chosen identifier results in a responded user profile, the profile is included into the sample. Otherwise, in case no profile can be found with the chosen identifier, a new identifier is randomly picked out of the ID space of the OSN. We make use of this method of sampling for the study on the quantification of the risk regarding attribute predictions.

For carrying out the empirical investigation on the profile linkability, we implemented a different sampling that is based on searches of randomly chosen names. To recap the aim of this particular study, we compare profiles out of different OSNs that potentially belong to the same user to find potential measures that can be utilized by attacking third parties to link a particular user's profiles. Therefore, we have to sample profiles that have something in common, i.e., in the case of the investigations presented in this dissertation, the same or similar user name used to register the OSN profiles. This approach of sampling is based on a random selection of names that are used to

---

[1]Facebook identifies profiles not only by identifiers, but also by "Usernames", i.e., a freely selectable string value. However, by the use of, for instance, the HTTP-based Graph API (https://graph.facebook.com/<Username>?fields=id) or the provided explorer on top of this API (https://developers.facebook.com/tools/explorer) the actual identifier can be obtained.

perform search requests to the OSNs that are to be analyzed. However, depending on the data basis from which the analysis software randomly picks and chooses search strings, e.g., user names, the resulting sample is more or less (consciously) biased. In fact, it is not uniformly sampled within the ID space of an OSN. However, this does not constitute a problem for the investigation of similarities of specific users' profiles. See Section 5.3.1 for a more detailed introduction of the utilized technique of sampling.

## 5.1.4   Implementation of Analysis Software

The algorithm of each software implemented to carry out the studies presented in this thesis follows a common procedure of analyzing user profiles out of OSNs: the software opens the login page of the OSN and provides credentials of a previously registered OSN profile (cf. the approach, for instance, used in [XHLZ12]). Afterwards, the software receives Cookies from the OSN, is logged in and can act like any ordinary user who makes use of his/her browser. Hence, HTTP requests, such as those performed by a user's browser, have to be implemented to be able to parse users' OSN profiles. In general, developers can implement the requests by themselves or, alternatively, can make use of browser controls, such as provided by the C# integrated development environment (IDE), i.e., an adaptation of an actual browser that can be controlled by implementing, for instance, mouse clicks and gestures.

As already mentioned, this approach is very common in the community of empirical OSN research. To give more examples, the authors of [JM09] make use of a software called *Arachne* to analyze Facebook. This software performs also a login, receives the cookies necessary to stay logged in and to communicate with the OSN, and downloads the targeted pages. The authors of [MVGD10] make use of a profile registered by a student of a certain university to automatically log into Facebook in order to analyze other users' profiles. In the context of utilizing analysis software to automatically sample OSN profiles, we state the same as, for instance, written by the authors of [CAK12], i.e., in light of legal and ethical restrictions regarding the analysis of OSN profiles, we have considered not to send too many requests to the analyzed OSNs to prevent a "Denial of Service" behavior of the analysis software and, furthermore, we also anonymized the statistical data permanently stored after analyzing the OSN profiles. In fact, we did not extract users' publicly shared data. Hence, the users' raw data is not accessible by any person who has access to the statistical data and users' privacy was/is not threatened by any of the investigations.

For the investigation of the risks regarding attribute predictions, we analyzed a large sample of OSN profiles. Since such large-scale empirical investigation would take much time if performed from a single machine, we out-sourced the analysis software to a cloud. In particular, we rent virtual machines from Amazon EC2[2] and deployed the analysis software onto these machines (machines with the deployed analysis software are referred to as *agents*). Therefore, we were able to analyze OSN profiles in parallel, similar to approaches utilized by other authors (cf., for instance, [GKBM10] or the multi-threaded crawler approach introduced in [DJR12]). Compared to the

---

[2]http://aws.amazon.com/ec2/ [Last downloaded 2013-05-28].

approach for parallel crawling introduced in [CPWF07], i.e., a master agent triggers crawls of individual OSN profiles at a certain crawling agent out of the available agents, we make use of a slightly different approach. In particular, we divided the ID space into ten uniform portions and each of ten agents randomly picks and chooses IDs out of the assigned part of the whole ID space. With that, we save the overhead of implementing and running a master agent. After the last agent parsed all profiles to be sampled, we gathered the statistical data stored locally at the individual agents in a central data base to perform the analysis on top of the data. Due to the way the individual analysis software acts and due to the out-sourcing of virtual machines that run the software, for the studies presented in this dissertation, we analyzed more than 1.5 million OSN profiles in total in a compliant manner.

## 5.1.5 Measures to Avoid Automated Profile Analyses

Today's OSN providers implemented a series of countermeasures with respect to crawler/scraper software. However, the implementation of such countermeasures constitutes a difficult task, because third parties try to emulate users' behavior, or rather the technical behavior of the users' browser utilized to participate within an OSN. Therefore, distinguishing actual users and software that crawls the OSN is the challenge OSN providers have to tackle with.

"It is obvious, the better a crawler emulates the behavior of a human being and a browser, the more difficult it is to detect such intruding software. Hence, crawlers use previously registered accounts and determine parameters such as initialization vectors and valid session identifiers to login into OSNs. Additionally, to stay logged in crawlers have implemented a handling for cookies. The data will be extracted via parsing of HTML pages and identifying the information by means of tags or keywords inside the HTML code. Such keywords are commonly static and self-explanatory.

OSNs implemented several countermeasures to thwart and prevent crawling. If an alleged browser tries to get responses more and faster than ordinary users would try, CAPTCHAs are presented before the requested content is replied. CAPTCHAs are pictures with distorted letters that a user has to type in to be able to carry on surfing. CAPTCHAs are a common possibility to disturb crawling attacks, but an OSN has to weigh the safeness of its users and the potentially decreasing usability with respect to the amount of occurrences of CAPTCHAs. Into the bargain, today's CAPTCHA-challenges are breakable by software, too [ZYL+10]. Apart from that, a fix delay between sent HTTP-requests is often sufficient sophistication to prevent the occurrence of CAPTCHAs. Since only a valid e-mail address and some not further validated personal information is needed to create an OSN account, any time a profile is yet blocked by a CAPTCHA the software is able to register a new account and re-login into the OSN. This is also effective if OSNs are blocking further browsing for 24 hours after a fix amount of HTTP-gets within a fix amount of time. However, as long as these measures can be circumvented by re-login with another account, it is only a low extra effort for attackers to implement a bypass inside their crawlers.

Beyond these countermeasures, switches between standard websites (www...) and sites for mobile devices support crawlers to avoid JavaScript (and its variations like AJAX) that are more difficult to emulate. Usually, the mobile pages that any common OSN provide are solely based on native HTML code and if the software is logged in into one of these alternatives the access to the other one is also open. It is obvious that such and other countermeasures are not sufficient to completely avoid automated data extraction." [LDH11]

Recently, Facebook tried to invent a feature that might represent a big hurdle for many third parties that try to register accounts, or rather profiles based on faked data, i.e., a new user has to provide his/her mobile phone number during registration and the number is validated by a code sent via SMS. This is a promising opportunity to avoid fake profiles. However, it does not constitute an insurmountable hurdle for attacking third parties and automated gathering of users' PII and, actually, Facebook reversed the deployment shortly after its implementation. In general, the detection of malicious activity constitutes a trade-off between usability and efficiency since false negative detections of alleged crawlers could annoy the OSN users.

## 5.2   Attribute Availability

In the following, statistical data is presented that has been gathered by two different runs of OSN analysis. The runs were performed between January and March 2011, as well as between July and August 2012. First, we show the results of the run performed at the beginning of 2011. In this run, we did not only analyze Facebook profiles, but also profiles of the OSNs *StudiVZ*, *MySpace*, and *XING*. In particular, we present statistical data based on 110,088 analyzed Facebook profiles, 43,615 StudiVZ profiles, 25,035 MySpace profiles, and 10,088 XING profiles. First, we compare the results gathered from these four networks among each other. Second, we discuss the diversity of information publicly provided via the analyzed OSNs. With this investigation, we show that the number of profiles that share specific pieces of PII varies dependent on the OSN. Based on this finding, we assume that for attacking third parties a gain in information can be achieved by linking several OSN profiles registered in different OSNs by the same particular person. Subsequently to the comparison of publicly available PII in different OSNs, the availability of attributes in users' profiles is contrasted to the amount of PII shared by users' OSN friends that are findings based on the second run of analysis, which is performed on a sample of almost 1.3 million Facebook profiles. Finally, a comparison of the results of the empirical studies and a summary of the results regarding the availability of attributes in OSNs is provided.

Note that PII and other information published via chats or walls are not considered in the analyses performed for achieving the results presented in this dissertation, i.e., we always analyzed only publicly available information provided on Facebook's *information* and *favorites pages* or the respective pages of user profiles of other OSNs.

| Category | Attribute | StudiVZ | Facebook | MySpace | Xing |
|---|---|---|---|---|---|
| General | name | 100.00% | 100.00% | 100.00% | 100.00% |
| | *no further information available* | 7% | 22% | 20% | n.a. |
| | **friends lists** | **48.13%** | **59.45%** | **67.04%** | **40.98%** |
| Number of... | ...friends (avg.) | 67 | 141 | 21 | 44 |
| | ...friends (std. deviation) | 74.01 | 216.32 | 75.47 | 85.39 |
| | ...friends (max.) | 918 | 5499 | 2058 | 2878 |
| Personal | graduation/title | 5.51% | $-^1$ | $-^1$ | 69.03% |
| | date of birth (dob)/age | **64.00%** (dob) | 0.84% (dob) | 32.06% (age) | 0% |
| | zodiac sign | 10.51% | $-^1$ | 20.72% | $-^1$ |
| | gender | 71.06% | 49.92% | 32.06% | $-^1$ |
| Contact | hometown | 23.74% | 8.77% | 6.49% | $-^1$ |
| | current residence/region | 48.46% | 10.32% | 32.04% | $(100\%)^2$ |
| | homeland or current country | 18.69% | n.a. | 28.78% | $(100\%)^2$ |
| | address | 0% | 0.11% | $-^1$ | 0% |
| | e-mail | $-^1$ | 0.62% | $-^1$ | 0% |
| | mobile phone number | $-^1$ | 1.19% | $-^1$ | 0% |
| Job | company/occupation | 5.75% | 9.63% | 4.91% | $(100\%)^2$ |
| | type of job | 7.85% | n.a. | n.a. | $(100\%)^2$ |
| | income | $-^1$ | $-^1$ | 2.21% | $-^1$ |
| Higher education | university | 51.67% | 8.83% | n.a. | n.a. |
| | field of study or study path | 11.21% | n.a. | n.a. | n.a. |
| | languages | 10.04% | $-^1$ | $-^1$ | n.a. |
| | general education/cv | 23.71% | 2.81% | 6.35% | n.a. |
| | current school | $-^1$ | 16.00% | n.a. | $-^1$ |
| Oneself and relations | about myself | 16.33% | n.a. | 6.22% | $-^1$ |
| | relationship status | 26.51% | 13.12% | n.a. | $-^1$ |
| | status message | 49.85% | n.a. | 20.72% | $-^1$ |
| | physique | $-^1$ | $-^1$ | 6.93% | $-^1$ |
| | parentage | $-^1$ | n.a. | 6.02% | $-^1$ |
| | children | $-^1$ | $-^1$ | 7.61% | $-^1$ |
| Views and attitudes | sexual orientation | $-^1$ | 8.16% | 7.77% | $-^1$ |
| | interests/looking for... | 31.41% | 8.89% | 8.92% | $-^1$ |
| | political direction | 18.42% | 0.33% | $-^1$ | $-^1$ |
| | religious views | $-^1$ | 0.46% | 4.96% | $-^1$ |
| | smoking and imbibing | $-^1$ | $-^1$ | 5.52% | $-^1$ |
| Hobbies | interests/details | 25.44% | 8.50% | 20.72% | n.a. |
| | clubs/activities/groups | 16.57% | 14.29% | 0.77% | n.a. |
| Favorites | favorite citation | 21.00% | 4.78% | $-^1$ | $-^1$ |
| | favorite music | 26.02% | 16.75% | 6.84% | $-^1$ |
| | favorite books | 19.32% | 5.88% | 5.20% | $-^1$ |
| | favorite movies | 22.04% | 10.47% | 5.90% | $-^1$ |
| | favorite TV shows | $-^1$ | 12.73% | 5.51% | $-^1$ |

[1] This attribute does not appear in the respective OSN profile by default.
[2] It is mandatory that this attribute is publicly available.

Table 5.1: Publicly available PII – Data collected in 2011 [LTH11]

## 5.2.1   Attribute Availability Concerning Four Popular OSNs

Table 5.1 shows the percentage of the sampled profiles that publicly provided a specific piece of PII for each of the four analyzed OSNs. Additionally, numbers that characterizes the sample itself are presented, such as the average friends list size. Referring to the attacker model introduced in Section 5.1.2, the given numbers represent the percentage of sampled profiles that provided a specific attribute for any logged in user, i.e., without any additional access restrictions due to, for instance, adjustments of the default privacy settings. The analyzed attributes are divided into certain categories that indicate the type of information represented by the attribute. The categories are provided in the first column of the table.

The category *general* includes the availability of the users' names and their friends lists. Whereas the names were publicly available in every analyzed OSN, the friends lists were left open for public access by about a half of all members whose profiles were analyzed by the software. The availability of these two attributes constitutes the basis for the detailed analysis of privacy risks. Additionally, the first category indicates the ratio of analyzed profiles, in which the access to every piece of information was restricted or even the respective attributes were not provided at all, i.e., only information that cannot be concealed by the user were accessible in those analyzed profiles. In Facebook and MySpace, only about 20 % of users completely hided their shared PII from strangers or unknown third parties. Moreover, in StudiVZ only in about 7 % of the analyzed profiles no actually concealable attribute was accessible.

The second category is labeled with *number of...* and provides insights on the sizes of publicly available friends lists. In this category, it can be seen that StudiVZ, MySpace, and XING profiles had an average number of 21 to 67 friends listed as connected to the analyzed profile. However, Facebook showed an average number of already 141 friends per profile. Besides the average size of the friends lists, this category indicates the standard deviation and the maximum number of friends in the analyzed friends lists.

The category *personal* subsumes identity information that is almost never changing, such as the title, date/year of birth, and the gender. Whereas in XING[3] almost 70 % of profiles contained information about a user's graduation and/or title, in StudiVZ only 5.51 % of users reveal this piece of PII and the other OSNs did not show this attribute at all. In StudiVZ and MySpace about 10 and 20 % shared their zodiac sign. However, this attribute, as well as the attribute gender, which is provided in many of the analyzed profiles, could also be inferred by third parties just by analyzing the date of birth and, for instance, the name of a user, respectively. The date of birth is provided in 64 % of all analyzed StudiVZ profiles, which is surprising if considered that, on the contrary, only 0.84 % of profiles sampled from Facebook have disclosed this information in 2011. This detected diversity of the availability of some pieces of PII leads to the investigation of the risks regarding the linkability of a user's OSN

---

[3]Note that "Xing allows four levels of privacy. Users can choose whether their provided data can be seen by direct friends only or by friends and their friends. They can also adjust the settings to less restrictive levels with which friends of friends have access to shared information, up to a 4 level indirection. Since the crawler does neither have a direct nor indirect connection to any crawled profile, only the name, the title and in almost 60% of all profiles the friends lists could be analyzed. Other attributes remained hidden. However, the more friends an account owns, the higher is the probability of having access to further information, because many users still use the 'level four' setting mentioned above. It is straightforward that such connection chains are large enough to get access to many 'level four' restricted data in light of the well-known six-degree separation experiment [TMTM69]" [LTH11].

profiles. If profiles are easily linkable and, for instance, 64 % of StudiVZ members publicly share their date of birth, for those users it would make only minor sense to hide this attribute in Facebook. However, we further discuss this topic in Section 5.3.

The category *contact* includes the attributes hometown and homeland, the current city/residence and the current country, the address, e-mail address, and the mobile phone number. At the time the sample was gathered, about a half of the StudiVZ users publicly provided their current city, whereas only about 10 % of Facebook users shared this information with any logged in user. In the remainder of this section, we show that this availability has changed over time. However, the *hometown* and *homeland* were the most frequently publicly provided attributes in StudiVZ as well. About one-third of MySpace users also publicly shared the current city, but only about 6.5 % of them shared the attribute hometown. The analyzed Facebook users shared the hometown in about 9 % of all cases. In XING, the release of the attributes current city and current country is mandatory. Despite the fact that the other attributes of this category are very sensitive information and three of four analyzed OSNs does not reveal the corresponding attribute values by default, up to more than one percent of Facebook users publicly share their address, information about their e-mail contact, and their mobile phone number.

The categories *job* and *higher education* subsume information about users' occupation and educational background. Most of the attributes gathered in these categories were publicly provided by less than 11.5 % of the analyzed user profiles. However, publicly sharing of information about a user's employer and his/her type of job is mandatory in XING and, therefore, at 100 %. In StudiVZ more than 51 % of analyzed profiles provided the current or former university and about a quarter of users revealed further information on their educational background.

The category *oneself and relations* represents attributes related to a user's family and relationships, as well as information about the physical shape and current frame of mind. Remarkably, a half of all StudiVZ profiles permitted access to the users' status messages, which can contain very sensitive information if considered that users post status messages when they are, for instance, traveling so that their flat is temporarily unoccupied.

The three latter categories – *views and attitudes*, *hobbies*, and *favorites* – subsume attributes that characterizes the individual user concerning things he/she is often doing or thinking, e.g., a user's political, religious, and sexual orientations, as well as interests and favorites with respect to different objects. Whereas only a few MySpace users revealed attributes associated to these categories, the data shows that each of the analyzed attributes were provided by, at least, about a fifth of the StudiVZ profiles.

## 5.2.2 Attribute Diversity from OSN to OSN

On the one hand, the presented statistical data gives an impression on what kind of data was still publicly available (in 2011) regarding the four analyzed OSNs and that some pieces of information are publicly provided by many of the respective users. On the other hand, it is remarkable that the availability of information differs from

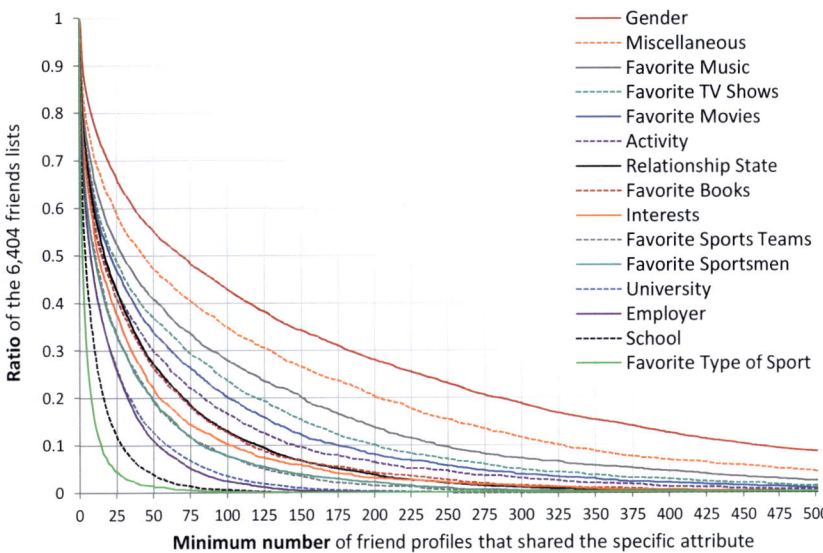

Figure 5.1: Ratio of the 6,404 analyzed friends lists that contained a minimum of x friend profiles that shared the specific attribute [LWMH13].

OSN to OSN, e.g., 64 % of the analyzed StudiVZ profiles revealed their date of birth, whereas less than one percent of Facebook members publicly shared this particular attribute. However, not only the analysis of the attribute *date of birth* resulted in diverse findings, but also the analysis with respect to the attributes current city, hometown, university, cv, relationship status, and some other attributes. In Section 5.3, we discuss that the diversity of available information induces significant privacy risks if users' several OSN profiles can be linked by third parties. The reason for this constitutes the fact that linked profiles, in which different information about a user is provided, result in the risk that third parties can gather a comprehensive digital image of a user, whereas the user actually decided for each of any OSN he/she participate which kind of information he/she discloses in the respective context. Therefore, users might be not aware that information shared in one OSN and data published in another context can be linked by third parties.

## 5.2.3   Attribute Availability Concerning Users' Friends Lists

In this section, we present parts of the findings with respect to the investigation of almost 1.3 million Facebook profiles that we analyzed in the mid of 2012. In particular, we show how much information is publicly available for third parties that analyze the friends lists of a targeted user. The corresponding findings induced the investigation on predictable attributes presented in Section 5.4.

The plot shown in Figure 5.1 indicates the ratio of analyzed friends lists (y-axis) that contained, at least, x user profiles that publicly provided a specific attribute, i.e., an analyzed attribute is publicly provided by, at least, x OSN friends of a user in $y * 100$ % of the analyzed friends lists. For instance, it is indicated "that in about 31 % of the analyzed friends lists a minimum of 175 friends provided the attribute *gender*, the attribute *miscellaneous* is in 20 % of the friends lists provided by 200 or more friend profiles. Each of 20 % of the analyzed friends lists contained a minimum of 150 profiles that provided the attribute *favorite music*" [LWMH13]. This plot demonstrates that for some attributes, on average, a lot of profiles can be found within a friends list of a user that share this attribute. In turn, this forms the basis for attacking third parties that try to predict an attribute that is not publicly shared by a user, but by many of his/her friends. Therefore, the risk regarding attribute prediction is estimated as high if many friend profiles provide access to an attribute that is not shared by the owner of the friends list. However, this is not true for attribute values that do not correlate among OSN friends and the owner of the friends list. In particular, the stronger the correlation the more accurate can a potential prediction be estimated and the less OSN friends are needed to be analyzed by an attacking third party to infer non-provided attribute values.

## 5.2.4   Comparison of the Statistical Data

In Table 5.2, we compare the statistical results gathered by the two empirical studies that form the basis of the research findings presented in this thesis. In the first two columns of the table, the attribute availability is shown as it is measured at the beginning of 2011. The next two columns present the same results but based on the study carried out in 2012. Since the results of the analysis of randomly sampled profiles remarkably differ from the results concerning profiles of users' friends, we present another two columns that represent the attribute availability within profiles of OSN friends of the randomly sampled user profiles that have also been analyzed in the 2012 study. These additional two columns are important in light of the investigation of the risk regarding potential attribute predictions because this attack is based on information a user's OSN friends publicly share.

The left column of each of the three parts of this table represent the overall results, i.e., students *and* other users, whereas the right columns (gray background) show the results concerning only those profiles that could be explicitly identified as profiles of students (indicated by a publicly provided university). However, since we cannot rule out that some of the analyzed profiles are profiles of students that we cannot identify as such (because no university is publicly provided), we cannot provide data on only non-student users. Therefore, it has to be considered that the results of the analyses of students' profiles are slightly biased in terms of that we consider only those profiles that have, at least, publicly provided their university, which is an actually concealable attribute, and, thus, the corresponding users might not the ones that are completely privacy aware.

However, first we compare the left columns among each other. The most interesting results can be found by comparing the first and the third column, i.e., the statistical data gathered by the analysis of randomly sampled profiles. In 2011, only 22 % of

| Attribute | 2011 randomly sampled profiles | 2011 students | 2012 randomly sampled profiles | 2012 students | 2012 friends of randomly sampled p. | 2012 student friends of randomly sampled p. |
|---|---|---|---|---|---|---|
| name | 100.00% | 100.00% | 100.00% | 100.00% | 100.00% | 100.00% |
| *no further information* | 22% | 0.27% | *37.84%[1]* | *1.53%[2]* | *14.20%[3]* | *0.39%[4]* |
| **friends lists** | **59.45%** | **88%** | **52.19%** | **80.71%** | **64.30%** | **82.00%** |
| # of friends (avg.) | 141 | 149 | 219.56 | 285.27 | 716.96 | 795.08 |
| # of friends (std. dev.) | 216.32 | 206.9 | 323.31 | 378.55 | 865.46 | 897.24 |
| # of friends (max.) | 5499 | 4,807 | 3,817 | 3,817 | 8,398 | 8,092 |
| date of birth | 0.84% | 0.14% | 2.29% | 4.83% | 5.32% | 7.78% |
| year of birth | n.a. | n.a. | 1.54% | 3.61% | 3.19% | 4.84% |
| gender | 49.92% | 78.72% | 85.78% | 91.81% | 82.00% | 85.38% |
| hometown | 8.77% | 23.55% | 23.20% | 44.92% | 38.33% | 54.64% |
| current city | 10.32% | 25.17% | 27.00% | 52.69% | 44.70% | 62.44% |
| address | 0.11% | 0.35% | 0.31% | 0.55% | 0.88% | 1.19% |
| e-mail | 0.62% | 1.30% | 0.10% | 0.04% | 0.34% | 0.49% |
| company/occupation | 9.63% | 46.76% | 18.37% | 55.17% | 28.13% | 58.01% |
| university | 8.83% | 100% | 19.40% | 100% | 28.72% | 100% |
| current school | 16.00% | 77.34% | 25.53% | 74.71% | 36.15% | 77.03% |
| about myself | n.a. | 8.84% | 10.31% | 23.24% | 16.47% | 27.35% |
| relationship status | 13.12% | 35.43% | 13.38% | 28.24% | 21.66% | 34.87% |
| sexual orientation | 8.16% | 20.88% | 14.79% | 31.26% | 18.96% | 31.75% |
| interests/details | 8.50% | 18.84% | 5.93%[1] | 13.28%[2] | 14.77%[3] | 22.92%[4] |
| clubs/activities/groups | 14.29% | 34.55% | 8.90%[1] | 20.01%[2] | 24.19%[3] | 35.03%[4] |
| favorite citation | 4.78% | 14.92% | 2.58% | 6.01% | 3.44% | 6.26% |
| favorite music | 16.75% | 37.80% | 18.58%[1] | 38.25%[2] | 42.29%[3] | 57.42%[4] |
| favorite books | 5.88% | 18.09% | 9.59%[1] | 22.96%[2] | 19.49%[3] | 30.58%[4] |
| favorite movies | 10.47% | 26.35% | 12.90%[1] | 29.63%[2] | 28.61%[3] | 41.73%[4] |
| favorite TV shows | 12.73% | 32.24% | 14.32%[1] | 31.29%[2] | 33.22%[3] | 46.59%[4] |
| **Number of analyzed Facebook profiles** | 110,088 | 9,203 | 12,270 ([1]9,628) | 2,380 ([2]1,694) | 1,280,827 ([3]741,926) | 367,814 ([4]208,627) |

Table 5.2: Publicly available PII in Facebook (unrestricted access) – comparison of the data samples gathered in 2011 and 2012.

profiles were completely closed, i.e., no further information than attributes that are not concealable was provided. In contrast, already about 38 % of users completely restricted the audience of their shared information in 2012. This finding underpins the increasing privacy awareness of OSN users mentioned in the previous chapters. Referring to the students' profiles, we can only observe about 0.3 % of profiles in 2011 and only 1.5 % in 2012 that do not provide any further information public except their university and the information that is not concealable at all by the use of privacy settings. Also more than 85 % of all analyzed friend profiles provide public access to, at least, one piece of actually concealable information.

For the availability of public friends lists, we can observe a decrease from almost 60 % to slightly more than 52 %. However, more than a half of users still publicly provide their friends list. Moreover, the analyzed profiles of students indicate that this group of users seems to be even less restrictive regarding the accessibility of their friends lists. In particular, more than 80 % of users who provided a university also shared their friends list in 2012 (88 % in 2011). Therefore, linking users' profiles based on friends lists might still pose a risk for users with several OSN profiles in which different pieces of PII are publicly shared.

Whereas in 2011 a friends list contained an average number of 141 friend profiles, until the sampling in 2012, the number increased to more than 200 friend profiles. Students tend to have even more friends on their friends list[4]. The maximum number of friends detected within the data has also been grown to more than 8,000 profiles. However, it has to be considered that Facebook still limited the maximum number of friends in 2011. In general, we can state that the detectable increase of the number of friends per user result in a higher risk that users' non-provided information can be inferred by analyzing users' OSN friends, or rather their publicly shared information because probably more friends can be found that publicly provide the attribute that an attacking third parties is about to infer.

By comparing the data gathered in 2011 with the 2012 sample, it becomes obvious that some attributes were less frequently provided publicly in 2012. However, the availability of a significant number of other attributes has been increased within the about 1.5 years between the two samplings. Pieces of PII, such as the gender, hometown, current city, further address information, information on users' jobs and even on the users' sexual orientation, etc., were more likely publicly accessible in the profiles sampled in 2012. In contrast, the availability of some other attributes, such as the users' relationship status and their favorite music, remained more or less unchanged. However, against the observable increase of privacy awareness, the comparison of the studies show that some attributes are even more likely accessible for any third party than in 2011, which further motivates the research on risks regarding publicly available PII.

Furthermore, it can be seen that those profiles that can be identified as students' profiles publicly provide some attributes more likely compared to the sample of all randomly chosen user profiles. To give an example, the hometown was publicly provided by almost 9 % (about 23 % in 2012) of ordinary users, whereas the students provide this attribute in about 24 % (about 45 % in 2012) of the cases. In turn, this situation indicates that probably a prediction of students' non-provided attributes based on attributes provided by their friends might be more accurate than for other users.

## 5.2.5  Summary and Conclusions

We showed that still many OSN users are unduly generous in sharing PII. We demonstrated that not only in Facebook users share, on average, a lot of information, but also via other OSNs. Furthermore, we discussed the diversity of the set of attributes that is

---

[4]The remarkable difference between the average number of friends of a randomly sampled user profile and the sample of friends' profiles is explainable due to the fact that a user with more friends is also more likely interconnected with an analyzed randomly sampled user. Thus, we can observe the effect of a non-uniform sampling, which is the case for analyzed friend profiles because these profiles are not randomly sampled itself.

publicly provided with respect to the OSN. Afterwards, we demonstrated that it is very likely that, at least, one OSN friend of a user publicly provides a specific piece of PII. This finding indicates that attribute prediction might still pose a risk if the attribute values additionally correlate. Finally, we compared the results of two samplings, i.e., a sample gathered in 2011 and data sampled in 2012. Thereby, we demonstrated that users' privacy awareness has been increased with respect to some pieces of attributes. However, some other attributes are still publicly provided in 2012 as in the sample of 2011. In particular, the users' friends lists are still provided by more than a half of all the randomly sampled users and students provide public access to their friends list in more than 80 % of the cases. In general, privacy awareness has been increased during the about 1.5 years between the studies in terms of that, for instance, the number of profiles increased that completely restricted the access to PII to a dedicated audience. However, compared to the situation in 2011, some attributes are publicly provided by more analyzed profiles in the second sample, e.g., the hometown and the current city, which are both investigated in the context of this thesis and, in particular, in light of the investigation of the risk of attribute prediction.

## 5.3   Linkability of OSN Profiles

In this section, we present the results of the investigation of the profile linkability. In particular, we analyze whether or not and how profiles of different OSNs registered by a single user can be linked by a third party at low cost, i.e., at low computational power, low implementation effort, and low sophistication of utilized algorithms. We already discussed in Chapter 4 and the previous sections of the current chapter that linking of profiles might be worthwhile for attacking third parties because of the gain in knowledge about a particular person that can be estimated. This gain is caused by the fact that users tend to not synchronize their privacy settings adjusted in different OSNs. Thus, different information might be publicly available in different OSN profiles of a single user.

In a broad sense, potentially many pieces of PII shared via a user's OSN profiles might be adequate to link the profiles. To give examples, a semantic analysis of the user's status messages could be exploited, or a face recognition software that can identify a user on a picture, e.g., this approach could be applied to the profile pictures used within the OSN profiles. Furthermore, other pieces of PII can be compared with each other to find correlations. However, since we are searching for the easiest and most often promising way to link a user's profiles, we hypothesize that comparisons of the lists of friends reveal profiles that correspond to a particular user and constitutes an attack that can be successfully performed at low cost.

Depending on the OSN, friends lists are publicly provided by 40 % up to 67 % of all analyzed profiles. Furthermore, comparisons of friends listed within a friends list only require simple string comparisons, which can even be done without computational support. In this context, we show that even known overlap metrics have not to be applied to compare the friends lists, i.e., we do not have to calculate, for instance, the *Jaccard index* that includes the number of friends into the calculation [Jac12].

On the contrary, we show that the number of friends can play only an insignificant role in sufficiently determining whether or not OSN profiles belong to the same user. In the following, we demonstrate that and how links between several OSN profiles of a single person can be established by third parties that have only access to publicly shared friends lists.

## 5.3.1   Sampling and Statistical Basis

The sample gathered for investigating the linkability of users' OSN profiles is carried out as described in the following. We implemented a JAVA™-based analysis software that fulfills the requirements stated in Section 5.1 and is implemented on top of the concepts also presented before. In particular, the software generates pairs of randomly chosen first and last names out of a large list of popular German names. Afterwards, the software performs search requests within the four analyzed OSNs by the use of a picked name pair. Therefore, the software samples profiles out of the four OSNs that potentially belong to a particular user. The potential belonging to a particular user is simply caused by the fact that the profiles are registered with equal names[5]. As a next step, the analysis software automatically compares each of the sampled profiles of each of the four OSNs with every profile found in the three other OSNs that are registered with the same user name. The statistical data calculated during these comparisons is stored in a local data base and the raw data of analyzed user profiles, i.e., the friends lists and attribute values itself, are discarded subsequently to the comparisons.

For the investigation of the linkability risks, we sampled OSN profiles and gathered statistical data by two different runs of the analysis software. First, we sampled about 50,000 Facebook profiles and about 15,000 StudiVZ profiles and compared the publicly provided friends lists in order to get a feeling of "what is possible" with respect to profile linking based on names listed in an OSN friends list[6]. In the second study, we sampled 110,088 Facebook, 43,615 StudiVZ, 25,035 MySpace, and 10,088 XING profiles and compared the profiles among each other, i.e., we compared the friends list of a profile out of an OSN with the friends lists of every potentially matching profile sampled from the other OSNs. This procedure was done for every profile and every OSN, so that we got data of comparisons of, for instance, Facebook and StudiVZ profiles and vice versa, MySpace and Xing profiles and vice versa, StudiVZ and Xing profiles and vice versa, etc. (in total, 12 combinations of comparisons). In summary, by this second run of the analysis software, we analyzed more than 180,000 OSN profiles and performed more than 7,000,000 comparisons of pairs of profiles. In the following, we present the results of both the preliminary and the comprehensive study in detail. Beforehand, the methodology of comparing friends lists is introduced.

---

[5]Note that we also sampled profiles with just similar names and observed the same findings compared to the investigation of profiles with equal names.

[6]Note that this data sample is not considered in the previous Section 5.2.

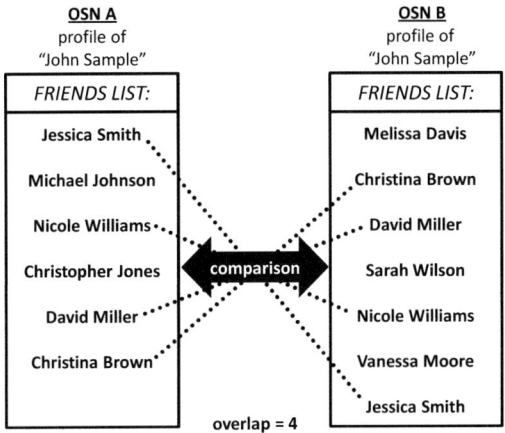

Figure 5.2: Exemplary comparison of two friends lists [LTH11].

## 5.3.2  Methodology of Profile Comparisons

The analysis software is implemented to compare friends lists in a fully automated manner based on the methodology presented in the following. The software divides each of the sampled friends lists in a list of entries. Each entry represents a user name that appears as an OSN friend within a sampled friends list. Subsequently, the software picks two of these lists that correspond to profiles that potentially belong to the same user (same/similar name) and calculates the number of those entries that appear in both friends lists. We refer to the number of friends' names that are present in both compared friends lists as the *overlap* of two friends lists. For instance, the overlap of friends lists $F_1$ and $F_2$ can be seen as $F_1 \cap F_2$. Figure 5.2 shows an exemplary overlap of two compared friends lists. In this case, the friends list of OSN A contained six entries and the one extracted from a profile found in OSN B contains seven entries. Four names appear in both of these two friends lists and, therefore, the overlap is equal to four.

Maximum Overlap Metric

Based on this comparison concept, the software calculates the overlap of each of the friends lists of one OSN and the friends lists of another OSN extracted out of profiles that potentially belong to the same user. Therefore, for each of the sampled OSN profiles $p$ of OSN A, we performed a number of $n_p$ comparisons, where $n_p$ is the number of friends lists sampled from another OSN B that are publicly provided within profiles that might belong to the same user as the user of profile $p$. We refer to the comparisons of one friends lists with a set of other friends lists as a *comparison set*. Figure 5.3 illustrates the comparison set concept. Figure 5.3a shows a single comparison set, i.e., the comparisons performed with respect to a single profile sampled from one OSN. A comparison set can also be seen as a 1:n comparison because one single friends list is compared with n friends lists of another OSN. Figure 5.3b

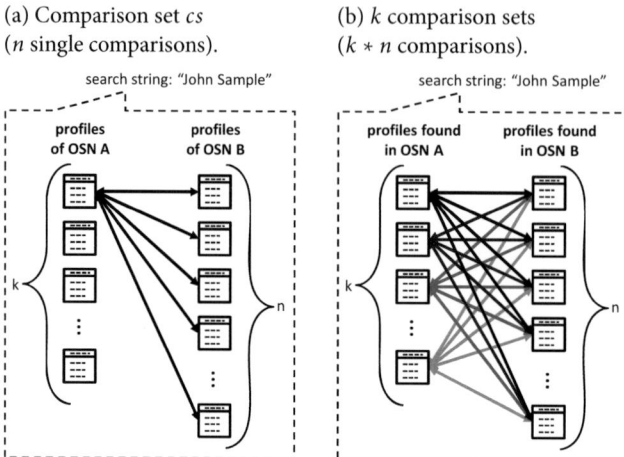

Figure 5.3: Illustration of the comparison set concept [LTH11].

shows $k$ comparison sets that cover all comparisons performed between profiles found in two OSNs based on the same search request (here, "John Sample"). Therefore, we show in this figure $k$ 1:n comparison sets. "For example, suppose we search for a person named 'John Sample' in two OSNs, OSN A and OSN B. Assume that the search returns 200 profiles in OSN A and 100 profiles in OSN B with the name 'John Sample'. To identify the same user of a specific profile $p$ of OSN A within the 100 profiles of OSN B, we firstly compare the friends list of the profile $p$ with all 100 friends lists of users named 'John Sample' from OSN B. These 100 comparisons form a comparison set ($cs$) consisting of 100 single comparisons (1:100, compare Figure 5.3a). To check each of the 200 profiles found in OSN A, the comparison procedure has to be executed for each of the 200 found profiles, resulting in 200 $cs$ of 100 comparisons each (compare Figure 5.3b)" [LTH11], i.e., 20,000 individual comparisons in total.

We define the overlap $o$ by the function $o(cs)$, where $cs$ represents a comparison set:

$$o(cs), cs \in \{comparison_i | 1 \le i \le n\}$$

With this function, we can express the maximum overlap that can be found within a single comparison set as $max(o(cs))$. In particular, $max(o(cs))$ is the maximum number of equal entries that can be found by comparisons of the friends lists of a single comparison set. We assume that a maximum overlap within a comparison set, i.e., the friends lists that corresponds to $max(o(cs))$, most likely indicates a *match* of two compared profiles, i.e., profiles that belong to the same particular user. If just a single comparison of a comparison set results in $max(o(cs))$, we refer to the respective comparison as the *target comparison* in the remainder of this part of the thesis. In other words, the function $f(max(o(cs)))$ represents the number of those comparisons of a single comparison set that resulted in the maximum overlap. There-

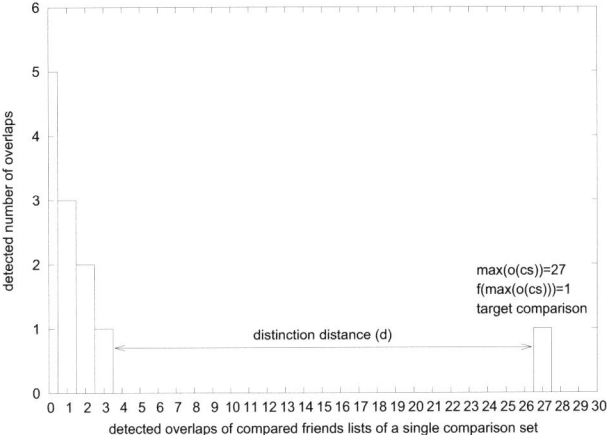

Figure 5.4: Histogram of detected comparison overlaps for an exemplary (1:12) comparison set *cs* [LTH11].

fore, if $f(max(o(cs)))$ equals one, we found a target comparison, which even more indicates that the corresponding two profiles might belong to the same particular user.

In the context of this methodology of comparisons, a *1:n* comparison set can also be visualized as a histogram. In Figure 5.4, we show an exemplary histogram of a comparison set with twelve single comparisons. In particular, such a histogram represents the comparisons of a single profile's friends list found with a search request *r* within OSN A and every friends list of the profiles found in OSN B by the use of *r*. In the illustrated example, we have detected a maximum overlap of 27. Furthermore, the comparison that resulted in this maximum overlap constitutes a target comparison because no other comparison could be found that resulted in the same overlap. Expressed as formulas, $max(o(cs)) = 27$ and $f(max(o(cs))) = 1$.

### Distinction Distance Metric

Besides the metric *maximum overlap* and the occurrence of a *target comparison*, Figure 5.4 illustrates another important metric for comparing entries of friends lists, i.e., the *distinction distance*. The distinction distance *d* measures the gap between the value of the maximum overlap and the value of the next lower overlap. In the exemplary visualized case, *d* equals $max(o(cs)) - 3$ because three is the maximum overlap of the remaining comparisons, i.e, all comparisons of a comparison set except the one that resulted in the maximum overlap. Hence, *d* quantifies how distinct the maximum overlap and, therefore, the target comparison stands apart from all other detected overlaps. In this context, the metric *distinction distance* describes the discriminative power of the maximum overlap.

The distinction distance is a crucial metric when to decide whether or not profiles potentially belong to the same user. With this metric, we can express the unambiguousness of the indication that is provided by the occurrence of a single comparison

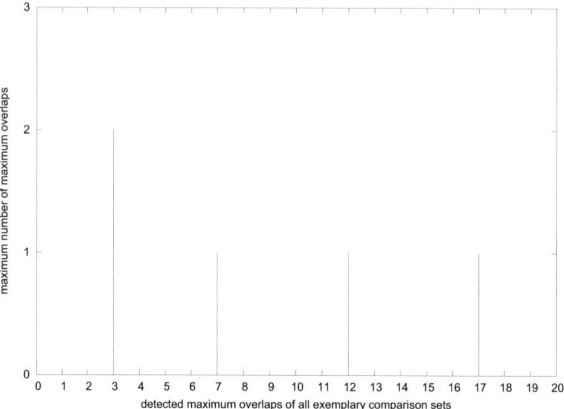

Figure 5.5: Exemplary aggregated max-overlaps graph (maximum number of maximum overlaps) [LTH11].

that resulted in a maximum overlap. Referring back to the example illustrated in Figure 5.4, $d$ remarkably distinguishes the maximum overlap from all other comparisons, which increases the probability that the two compared friends lists are owned by the same user.

Analysis of the Gathered Statistical Data

With a focus on comparisons that result in a maximum overlap, we are, particularly, interested in whether or not a detected maximum overlap constitutes also a target comparison and how distinct the overlap stands apart from other detected overlaps within the same comparison set. In the following, we introduce the concept of the further analysis that is based on both introduced metrics.

We start by an aggregation of the histograms that result from the different comparison sets. In particular, we take the peak that indicates the maximum overlap of each histogram that represents a single comparison set (for instance, in Figure 5.4 the peak at an x-value of 27) and aggregate those peaks in a single histogram. Thereby, we only aggregate comparison sets that resulted due to comparisons of single profiles of a specific OSN A and all potentially matching profiles of a specific OSN B. To give an example, one of the aggregated histograms only shows the comparison sets that are based on comparisons between several single Facebook profiles with potentially matching StudiVZ profiles. For this approach of analysis, it is further important that we aggregate peaks of maximum overlaps at the same x-value by plotting just the highest peak of all peaks. With that, we can observe what was the maximum occurrence of a maximum overlap within, at least, one of the respective comparison sets, i.e., a y-value of one indicates that maximum overlaps at a certain x-values only occurred at a maximum of one time per comparison set. In turn, a y-value larger than one indicates that in, at least, one of the respective comparison sets more than a single comparison resulted in the maximum overlap of this comparison set.

"An exemplary plot of such a graph is shown in Figure 5.5. For this diagram assume five comparison sets $cs_i$, $i = \{1,2,3,4,5\}$ for which the maximum overlaps are as follows: $max(o(cs_1)) = 3$, $max(o(cs_2)) = 7$, $max(o(cs_3)) = 12$, $max(o(cs_4)) = 12$ as well, and $max(o(cs_5)) = 17$. Assume that the maximum overlap of three is detected in two single comparisons in the first comparison set $cs_1$" (i.e., $f(max(o(cs_1))) = 2$). "The corresponding aggregated graph shows four peaks, as seen in Figure 5.5. Three of these peaks indicate a maximum overlap with a maximum number of one because in each of the corresponding four $cs$ these values are not detected or just detected in one single comparison. Note that the peaks indicate the *maximum* number of a maximum overlap and do not indicate the number of $cs$ with a specific determined maximum overlap. In this example, only one comparison within each of two corresponding comparison sets existed whose overlap matched the maximum overlap of 12. In contrast, the peak at three has a y-value of two because we assumed that this maximum overlap is found two times in $cs_1$ so that the maximum number of such specific maximum overlap three is two. We refer to such graphs as *aggregated max-overlaps graphs*, i.e., graphs in which the maximum overlap of every $cs$ is plotted against its maximum number within every $cs$" [LTH11].

In addition to the aggregated maximum overlaps, according the introduced concept of aggregation, we show in the aggregated plots also the average distinction distance of the maximum overlaps, as well as the corresponding standard deviations to get a feeling of how significant a maximum overlap indicates a comparison of two friends lists that probably belong to profiles of the same user. If the distinction distance at a certain x-value converges to this x-value, the corresponding maximum overlap stands considerably apart from all other overlaps detected in the respective comparison set(s). A maximum distinction distance that is equal to its x-value (i.e., the overlap) means that the detected maximum overlap was the only overlap that could be detected in the respective comparison set. In the following results section, we demonstrate that distinction distances are always next to the x-value so that maximum overlaps represent not only the largest overlap, but also an outlier with respect to the actual overlap of all other comparisons within a comparison set.

## 5.3.3   Results of the Empirical Study on the Linkability

Before the aggregated histograms are shown, we present Figure 5.6 that represents the results of the preliminary study we carried out to investigate the linkability of OSN profiles, i.e., the study based on 50,000 Facebook and about 15,000 StudiVZ profiles. In this plot, the overlap is shown in percentages on the x-axis. The y-axes represent the relative number of comparisons that resulted in a specific overlap. The gray curve (with its y-axis on the right) constitutes the cumulative distinction function (CDF) of the black curve (left y-axis). Referring to the black curve, it is obvious that a lot of comparisons resulted in a very small (or even no remarkable) overlap. However, the curve increases a little bit before and at an overlap of 15 % to 20 %. That means, we can observe many comparisons with small overlaps but some with a higher overlap.

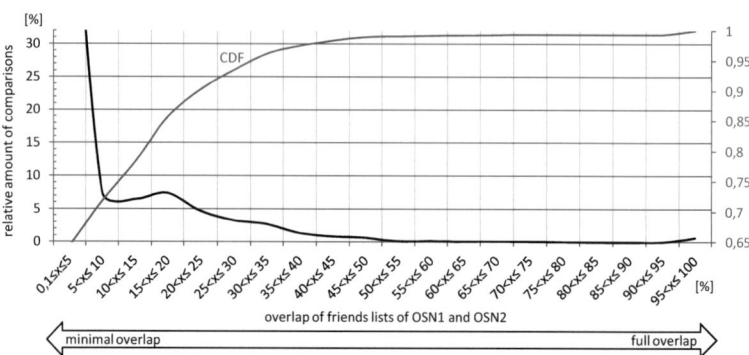

Figure 5.6: Histogram that shows the probability of the friends lists overlap of two profiles from different OSNs with respect to the extent of the overlap and a corresponding CDF [LDH11].

In the following, we show an aggregated plot, such as introduced in the previous section, to investigate these higher overlaps in more detail. Figure 5.7 shows one of the twelve aggregated histograms generated on the basis of the different comparison sets. In particular, the plot represents the results of choosing Facebook profiles and compare each of the corresponding friends lists with the friends lists of every potentially matching profile found in StudiVZ. Therefore, each of the included comparison sets includes comparisons of one single Facebook profile with all StudiVZ profiles found with the same search string. Because the other plots are very similar compared to the one shown in this section, we show the other plots in Appendix B.

The plot demonstrates that beginning from a certain x-value, i.e., the maximum overlaps detected in the respective comparison sets, the corresponding y-value is always just one (here, beginning from an x-value of four). According to the methodology of aggregation of the results presented in the previous section, this observation means that if maximum overlaps larger than three occurred, these overlaps could be identified just by a single comparison of the respective comparison sets. In other words, we cannot find a comparison set with a certain maximum overlap larger than three that is reached by two different comparisons of the same comparison set. Therefore, the comparisons of every single comparison set resulted in different overlaps, but the maximum overlap is only observable in one of these comparisons, i.e., every detected maximum overlap larger than three also indicates a *target comparison*.

Furthermore, the plot shows the average distinction distances and the corresponding standard deviations (y-axis on the right). Herein, we can make two different observations. First, each of the average distinction distances is close to the corresponding x-value. That means, on average, every maximum overlap stands considerably apart from all other overlaps detected in the same comparison set. The second observation is the fact that the standard deviations are always tiny, i.e., not only the average distinction distances are close to the corresponding x-values, but also we cannot detect a significant number of outliers with respect to the average distinction distance.

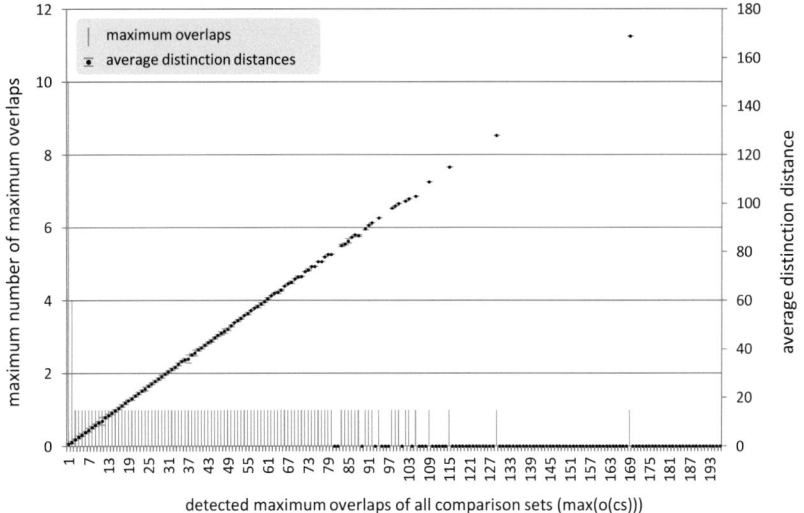

Figure 5.7: Maximum overlaps and distinction distances of all comparison sets of comparisons between Facebook and StudiVZ [LTH11].

In general, we found only two different types of comparison sets by comparing friends lists: first, comparison sets in which just minimal overlaps of friends lists could be detected (between zero and three overlaps per comparison) and, second, comparison sets in which all comparisons except one resulted in such minimal overlaps and the excepted one resulted in a significantly larger overlap (larger than three). For comparison sets that resulted in the first type of overlaps, we cannot give evidence that we found two profiles that potentially belong to the same user. However, in the second case, we found a strong indicator for profiles that belong to the same particular user because of the outlier characteristic of the overlap of the corresponding friends lists. This observation implies that every maximum overlap with a value of larger than three corresponds to a target comparison and, therefore, a comparison of two profiles that result in a larger overlap than every other comparison of the same comparison set could indicate profiles of the same particular user.

Therefore, profiles whose friends lists have an overlap of more than three names of OSN friends most likely identify profiles of the same user. All other comparisons of potentially matching profiles that result in an overlap lower than four cannot be identified as profiles that belong to the same user. In the next section, we discuss the error rate of the indication of matching profiles. However, the stated assumption with respect to matches indicated by overlaps larger than three cannot be proven because we would have to involve the owners of the analyzed profiles into the study in terms of asking them whether or not two potentially matching profiles are both owned by them. In light of the presented restrictions imposed by the German law and the aim to carry out the empirical studies as privacy preserving as possible, an involvement of the respective users would not be compliant.

Nevertheless, to provide a more detailed analysis on whether or not the mentioned interpretation of the results is correct, "we implemented a module that enabled the analysis software to compare additional available information of OSN profiles, such as the given hometown, region, university, date of birth, etc. With this module activated we did another short run with which the software found about 300 comparisons that resulted in an overlap larger than three. In almost all of these cases the software found a minimum of one other information that appeared in both compared profiles equally. In more than half of all cases the profile image was exactly the same in both profiles. Other attributes that were often available in both profiles were the user's hometown, region, university or the date of birth. In none of the analyzed comparisons the software found two mutually exclusive pieces of information. This fact confirms the hypothesis that two profiles with the same user name and an overlap of friends lists larger than three are owned by the same natural person" [LTH11].

## 5.3.4  Discussion

In the following, we discuss the results regarding the risk that third parties can link users' profiles by comparing the information publicly provided and point out limitations of the presented study. We demonstrated the risk that third parties can link a user's OSN profiles even at low cost. In particular, we showed that just simple string comparisons of the names of the user's friends can indicate whether or not two profiles belong to the same particular user. A requirement for a high accuracy of this approach of profile linking is constituted by the name that is used to register in the OSNs. If a user registered his/her profiles by the use of the same user name, the risk that third parties can accurately link the profiles can be estimated as significantly higher than for profiles that are registered by the use of different names. However, since some OSNs try to force users to provide their given and last name to be used as the user name, the assumption that users often register their OSN profiles by the use of the same user name seems valid. For instance, Google asks their customers whether or not they like to use their real name, which is also used in Googlemail[7], if the users make use of a, for instance, phantasy name for their Youtube channel[8]. Also other OSNs temporarily implemented measures to force users to use their given and last name as their user name of their profile.

However, even if users make use of different names to register their OSN profiles, unintended profile linking poses a risk. Actually, it is feasible to link profiles if third parties can extract a sample of profiles out of two OSNs that contain the profiles of the targeted user. In this context, the authors of [ZL09] show that user names registered in one OSN can be used to identify user names used by the same users in other OSNs. "Certainly, profiles of two differently named users who have the same city or the same hometown in common might have a higher overlap than two profiles that are just set up with the same name. The probability that a user with exactly the same name as another user exists who, additionally, has same friends is

---

[7]https://mail.google.com/ [Last downloaded 2013-05-28].
[8]https://www.youtube.com/ [Last downloaded 2013-05-28].

probably very low. However, the probability that in an evaluated population of users living in the same city two users with different names can be found who have a high number of overlapping OSN friends is obviously higher because of overlapping groups of friends in 'real life'. Nevertheless, we are convinced that the metrics *maximum overlap* and *distinction distance* could also be sufficient to link profiles registered with different names" [LTH11].

Finally, we discuss potentially existing error rates regarding the linking of profiles based on friends lists. A third party cannot entirely ensure that profiles linked by the presented approach do *not* belong to the same user, i.e., the occurrence of false positives. In fact, in light of the restrictions imposed by the German law, we cannot figure out the actual error rate, or rather accuracies of linking profiles. However, it is also debatable whether third parties even care about some wrongly linked profiles. Certainly, the answer to this question highly depends on the actual attacker. An attacker who just targets a single user and tries to link his/her profiles might care about false positives and false negatives. However, for another attacker who just try to gather as lot of information as possible about a large group of users, it might not significantly impair his/her objective if just a few of the profiles are wrongly linked. The reason for this might be the expected profit induced by the profiles that are successfully linkable. In this context, the presented results indicate that the error rate is remarkably low because of the unambiguousness of the outlier characteristic of the overlaps that correspond to a target comparison. Therefore, we assume that "potentially existing false positives are negligible compared to the number of profiles that third parties are able to link correctly. Furthermore, the expected gain of information (...) countervails less probably [sic] occurrences of false positives from the perspective of third parties" [LTH11]. In general, we can state that the more PII is shared by an OSN user via his/her different profiles the more profile linking poses a risk because the more accurate an attacking third party can link his/her profiles.

## 5.3.5   Summary and Conclusions

In Section 5.2, we have shown that OSN users still publicly share a remarkable amount of PII and other information. In particular, about a half of the users provide public access to their list of friends. In this section, we demonstrated that the linkability of a user's different OSN profiles poses a risk, particularly, if the profiles are registered with similar, or even equal user names. Furthermore, we showed that profiles that belong to the same user can even be linked at low cost, i.e., just based on string comparisons of the names of users' OSN friends. If we combine the findings presented so far in this chapter, it becomes obvious that the linkability of OSN profiles not only poses a risk in itself, but also brings third parties into the position of aggregating information shared in one OSN together with information shared in another OSN. Since users tend to publicly share different information in different OSNs the linking of OSN profiles might be worthwhile for attacking third parties.

In summary, we revealed that even an overlap of just more than three friends is probably sufficient to link profiles that are registered with equal names and belong to the same particular user. Furthermore, we discussed that profiles can be linked by comparing friends lists even if the user name is similar or completely differs in two profiles of a user. In those cases, comparisons might only result in distinction distances that do not converge as strong as the shown distances to the corresponding x-value and the number of false positives might also increase. However, the large amount of publicly available PII demonstrates that third parties can exploit further attributes to increase the accuracy of linking profiles of a user who has not registered his/her profiles with equal user names.

In 2009, Motoyama and Varghese suspected that more information can be gathered by finding additional OSN profiles of a user [MV09] and the study presented in this thesis confirms this assumption. Moreover, if users have not adjusted their privacy settings in some of their OSN profiles the data is publicly available, no matter whether or not the user frequently make use of the respective OSN. In other words, although Facebook gains remarkable market share in recent years, some other OSNs are growing as well (cf. [MKG+08]), users use different OSNs for different purposes (e.g., Xing and LinkedIn for managing professional contacts and other OSNs for personal purposes), users probably tend to not delete old and no more used OSN profiles, and users do not synchronize their privacy settings as discussed previously. Therefore, the linkability of OSN profiles poses still a risk for users and third parties can profit from aggregating information shared via different OSNs.

## 5.4  Attribute Prediction based on PII of OSN Friends

In this section, we present the results of the investigation of the risk regarding potential attribute prediction introduced in Section 4.4.3. The basis for the attribute prediction risk also constitutes the availability of users' friends list. Following the presentation of the results regarding the linkability risk, we demonstrate that some pieces of information that have not even been publicly provided by a user can be inferred by third parties based on the data publicly shared by the user's OSN friends.

In the following, we compare publicly provided PII of randomly sampled Facebook users with the PII publicly shared by their Facebook friends. The investigation is based on a large sample of randomly picked Facebook profiles and the analysis of the profiles of the corresponding OSN friends. In total, we have analyzed almost 1.3 million profiles for this study. In the following, we primarily focus on the quantification of the risk regarding the prediction of location attributes, i.e., a user's current city (i.e., the city where a user pretends to live) and his/her hometown, as well as the prediction of the users' age. Whereas location attributes are provided by many profiles of users' OSN friends, the age is a rarely provided attribute. However, even for the age, or rather year of birth, we show strong correlations that are sufficient to predict the age of users with a remarkable accuracy even if this attribute is not provided by the users themselves. Subsequently to the analysis of location attributes and the users' age, we discuss the risk that other pieces of PII are predictable by attacking third parties. Thereby, it is demonstrated that for some attributes the risk of potential attribute predictions can be estimated as significantly lower than for the previously analyzed

| Randomly picked α-profiles | 12,500 |
|---|---|
| > *Profiles with a public friends list (FL)* | *6,404* |
| **Total number of friends in 6,404 FLs** | **1,278,478** |
| > *Average number of friends in 6,404 FLs* | *199.64* |
| **Total number of profiles analyzed** | **1,290,978** |

Table 5.3: Sample of OSN profiles [LWMH13]

attributes, at least, if a casual attacker is assumed. The reason for that is constituted by the fact that these attributes are less often publicly provided and that the attribute values barely correlate. The study presented in this section also lays a foundation for future technologies to support users in managing their PII by performing an adequate risk assessment regarding their own privacy situation. See Chapter 6 for a discussion on privacy tools based on the studies presented in the current chapter.

The current section is structured as follows. First, we provide information on the methodology of sampling and the gathered statistical data. Second, we show the investigation of location attributes and, afterwards, the results regarding the privacy risk posed by the possibility to predict users' age. Next, we demonstrate whether or not and how accurate also other attributes can be inferred by attacking third parties. Finally, we discuss the findings and conclude the section.

## 5.4.1  Sampling and Statistical Basis

For carrying out the study on the quantification of attribute prediction risks, we uniformly sampled Facebook profiles and corresponding friend profiles from the – at the time of sampling – entire 950+ million Facebook profiles[9]. The sampling was performed in July and August 2012 by use of a C#-based crawler, which constitutes also a compliant analysis software with respect to the German law and aims at analyzing user profiles as privacy preserving as possible. The software is implemented to utilize an acceptance-rejection-sampling as introduced in section 5.1.3. In particular, the software analyzes every profile found by the sampling and, additionally, all corresponding friend profiles if a randomly sampled profile provides public access to its friends list[10].

When a profile with a public friends list is found, the analysis software compares every piece of PII provided via the information page and the favorite page of the sampled profile with the respective piece of publicly provided PII of the corresponding friend profiles. The software discards all profiles that do not provide public access to the friends list. Subsequently to the fully automated comparison process of one sampled profile and its corresponding friend profiles, the software discards also the raw data provided within the compared profiles and stores only the statistical data calculated on-the-fly during the comparison process. With that, no piece of PII was extracted by the software and permanently stored within the local data bases.

---

[9]Status at August 2012; http://newsroom.fb.com/.

[10]"Others report that a maximum of only 400 friends can be accessed within a friends list. We did not observe this restriction with the utilized analysis software" [LWMH13].

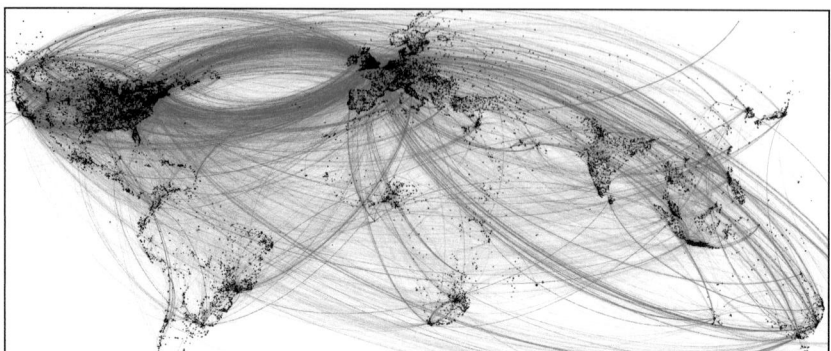

Figure 5.8: Graph with nodes geo-located with respect to the current cities of those randomly chosen users ($\alpha$-profiles) and their friends who provided this attribute (381,193 nodes). The edges represent the corresponding friendship relations. Illustration inspired by the visualization of Facebook friendships by Paul Butler (Facebook), Dec. 2010[11]. High resolution version can be downloaded at http://dsn.tm.kit.edu/img/content/fb-kit-2012.jpg [LWMH13].

Randomly sampled profiles that provide public access to the friends list are referred to as $\alpha$-*profiles* in the remainder of this chapter. Table 5.3 shows the number of randomly sampled profiles, the number of $\alpha$-profiles, as well as the number of friend profiles compared to its corresponding $\alpha$-profile. With the acceptance-rejection-sampling, we sampled 12,500 profiles. 6,404 of them publicly provided their friends list with an average number of about 200 friends. In total, we analyzed almost 1.3 million Facebook profiles for the investigation of the risk regarding predictable attributes.

"Figure 5.8 shows a graph with nodes geo-located with respect to the current cities of those users who provided this location information publicly. The graph shows current cities of $\alpha$-profiles (2,667 $\alpha$-profiles provided this attribute) and current cities provided by their friends. The distribution matches very well with the overall coverage and relationship visualization published by Facebook in December 2010[11]" [LWMH13]. Furthermore, compared to the "US population density of geolocated Facebook users" visualized by the authors of [BSM10], it can also be seen that the sample analyzed for this part of the dissertation constitutes a uniform sample of the whole Facebook "population".

### Statistical Basis for Comparing Profiles

In the following, we pick up the already discussed attribute availability observed in the sample (cf. Figure 5.1 introduced in Section 5.2.3). The statistical data is based on the analysis of the 6,404 out of 12,500 randomly sampled Facebook profiles that admitted public access to their friends list. For investigating potentially existing correlations of pieces of PII provided by a Facebook user and his/her OSN friends as a basis to infer

---

[11]https://www.facebook.com/notes/facebook-engineering/visualizing-friendships/469716398919 [last downloaded 2013-05-28].

| Attributes | A | B | C | D |
|---|---|---|---|---|
| Friends List | 6,404 | 100 % | – | – |
| *Personal Attributes* | | | | |
| Gender | 5,815 | 90.8 % | 6,345 | 99.1 % |
| Current City | 2,667 | 41.7 % | 5,900 | 92.1 % |
| Hometown | 2,316 | 36.2 % | 5,806 | 90.7 % |
| Relationship Status | 1,362 | 21.3 % | 5,669 | 88.5 % |
| University | 932 | 14.6 % | 5,201 | 81.2 % |
| Employer | 784 | 12.2 % | 5,134 | 80.2 % |
| School | 421 | 6.5 % | 4,715 | 73.6 % |
| Year of Birth | 117 | 1.8 % | 4,286 | 66.9 % |
| *Favorites* | | | | |
| Miscellaneous | 3,474 | 54.2 % | 6,092 | 95.1 % |
| Favorite Music | 2,400 | 37.5 % | 5,909 | 92.3 % |
| Favorite TV Shows | 1,884 | 29.4 % | 5,783 | 90.3 % |
| Favorite Movies | 1,688 | 26.4 % | 5,736 | 89.6 % |
| Interests | 1,370 | 21.4 % | 5,613 | 87.6 % |
| Favorite Books | 1,285 | 20.1 % | 5,572 | 87.0 % |
| Activity | 1,257 | 19.6 % | 5,632 | 87.9 % |
| Favorite Sports Teams | 778 | 12.1 % | 5,346 | 83.5 % |
| Favorite Sportsmen | 721 | 11.3 % | 5,320 | 83.1 % |
| Favorite Type of Sport | 180 | 2.8 % | 4,082 | 63.7 % |

A: absolute number of $\alpha$-profiles
B: percent of $\alpha$-profiles
C: absolute number of analyzed friends lists
D: percent of analyzed friends lists

Table 5.4: Column A and B: Absolute and relative number of the 6,404 $\alpha$-profiles that provided the attribute AND shared a friends list, in which a minimum of one friend also provided the attribute. Column C and D: Absolute and relative number of the 6,404 analyzed friends lists that contained a minimum of one profile that shared the attribute [LWMH13].

the user's attributes if he/she does not publicly share these attributes, we compare specific pieces of PII among each other. However, comparisons are, or rather could only be performed if the randomly sampled user profile and a minimum of one of the corresponding friend profiles provide the attribute. If the user and/or, at least, one of his/her friends does not publicly provide a specific piece of information, we cannot compare the $\alpha$-profile with the corresponding friends. Therefore, not every profile of the 6,404 $\alpha$-profiles can be included into the investigation of potential correlations of some of the investigated attribute values.

Therefore, Table 5.4 provides the number of comparable $\alpha$-profiles with respect to specific pieces of PII. In particular, the table shows, such as other tables of this chapter, several attributes OSN users (here: Facebook users) can reveal via the information and favorites pages of their profiles. In column A and B of the table, we show the number of profiles that publicly provide a certain attribute *and* a friends list in which a minimum of one friend also publicly provided the specific attribute (column A: absolute values, column B: relative values with respect to the 6,404 analyzed profiles with public friends lists). For example, we found 1,362 profiles (i.e., 21.3 % of the 6,404 $\alpha$-profiles) that publicly provided the attribute *relationship state* and a friends list in which a minimum of one friend also revealed this piece of information. Obviously, not every analyzed attribute is publicly provided very often, for instance, only 117 profiles contained the attribute *year of birth* and, additionally, a minimum of one friend, who also provided his/her year of birth.

Furthermore, Table 5.4 shows how many of the 6,404 friends lists contained, at least, one friend profile that provided a certain piece of PII (column C: absolute values, column D: relative values with respect to the 6,404 analyzed friends lists). The availability of the respective attribute within the $\alpha$-profile is consciously not considered in columns C and D. In general, we can observe that for some pieces of PII just a small portion of randomly sampled profiles publicly share a certain attribute *AND* a friends list in which one of the listed OSN friends also provide public access to this specific piece of PII. However, columns C and D show that even for those attributes that are rarely provided, we can find a lot of friends lists that contain a minimum of one profile that provided the attribute, which could be sufficient for inferring users' non-provided PII. To give an example, only 421 out of 6,404 users publicly share the *school* via their profile page and provide public access to their friends list in which a minimum of one friend also provide a value for the attribute *school*, whereas 4,715 of the 6,404 analyzed friends lists contain, at least, a profile that provided a value for this attribute. Inter alia, this statistical data indicates the actual risk regarding attribute predictions by attacking third parties if correlations of values of certain attributes can be shown.

In the following, we present the findings gained by comparing attribute values of specific pieces of PII provided by randomly sampled user profiles ($\alpha$-profiles) and by the corresponding friend profiles if a minimum of one friend also publicly provided the specific attribute.

### 5.4.2   Analysis of Location Attributes

Referring to the attribute *current city*, we found 2,667 $\alpha$-profiles that publicly provided this attribute *and* a friends list with, at least, one friend profile that also made the current city publicly available. In fact, about 44 % of a user's friends provided public access to their current city. We refer to a current city publicly provided by an $\alpha$-profile as an $\alpha$-*city* and friends that provide exactly the same current city as the $\alpha$-profile are referred to as *same-city-friends* in the remainder of this section.

Initially, by analyzing the statistical data, we figured out that, on average, more OSN friends of a certain $\alpha$-profile are same-city-friends than friends who publicly provided a different current city. In particular, in 56.3 % of the analyzed friends lists the most frequently provided current city equals the $\alpha$-city, i.e., those friends lists

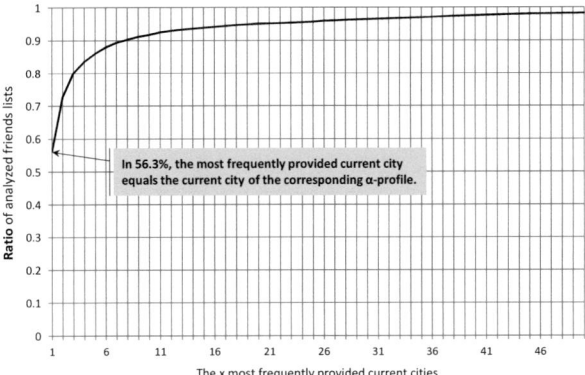

Figure 5.9: CDF of analyzed friends lists, in which the most, or rather the second, or the third,... (x-axis) most frequently provided current city is equal to the current city of the corresponding $\alpha$-profile [LWMH13].

contained more same-city-friends than friends in any other city. We show this result in Figure 5.9. Furthermore, the figure provides the probabilities on its y-axis that one of the two, three, four,... (see x-axis) most frequently provided current cities equals the $\alpha$-city. In fact, in 72.8 % of the cases the $\alpha$-city equals the most or second most frequently provided city. The probability that the $\alpha$-city is one of the three most frequently provided current cities within a friends list is at 80.2 %.

Therefore, it is most likely that the most frequently provided current city within a friends list equals the $\alpha$-city, i.e., the current city of the owner of the friends list. Hence, the most frequently provided city serves as a maximum likelihood estimator[13]. However, 56.3 % of accuracy is not remarkably high. Otherwise, we found, on average, 42 different cities provided in a single friends list and a maximum of 337 different locations in one of the analyzed friends lists. Therefore, we analyze the distribution of provided current cities in more detail in the following. In particular, we analyze how close friends are living around the $\alpha$-city, i.e., the average geographical spread of a friends list, in order to estimate the quality of the maximum likelihood estimator, or rather the actual inaccuracy of possible wrong predictions. For this investigation, we introduce another metric called the *discriminative distance*, i.e., the *air-line distance* between two publicly provided cities ("as the crow flies"). In order to plot a histogram of the distribution of friends with respect to the metric *air-line distance*, we calculated the number of friends in certain distances compared to the $\alpha$-city. Afterwards, these numbers are compared to the number of same-city-friends.

Figure 5.10 illustrates an exemplary histogram with the air-line distances on its x-axis and the percentage of friend profiles that provided a city in a certain air-line distance on the y-axis. Note that in this example the largest peak represents the same-city-friends, which is the case in only 56.3 % as mentioned above. Furthermore,

---

[13]Statistical model: Bernoulli distribution with $P(X = 1) = p$, i.e., the probability that the most frequently provided city equals the $\alpha$-city, and $P(X = 0) = 1 - p$ (in the opposite case).

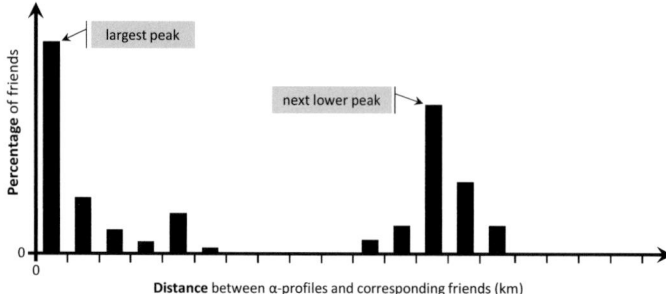

Figure 5.10: Illustration of an example histogram that shows the percentage of friends of an $\alpha$-profile who provided a city in a specific distance compared to the $\alpha$-city [LWMH13].

the next lower peak subsumes friends that provided a city in a certain air-line distance compared to the $\alpha$-city, or rather the current city of the same-city-friends.

Figure 5.11 shows an aggregated histogram of all histograms built upon the gathered statistical data of the individual friends lists in the aforementioned manner. The figure also shows the air-line distance on its x-axis and the *average* percentage of friends on the y-axis. Note that we only consider those friend profiles for calculating the relative numbers that publicly provided the attribute current city. Therefore, the whole number of friend profiles that share the current city represents 100 %. In turn, friend profiles that does not provide a current city are not considered for this and the following figures. As illustrated in the previous figure, the first bar of Figure 5.11 also shows the percentage of same-city-friends. We cut off the plot at a distance of 500 kilometers for the sake of legibility. The last bar shows an aggregation of provided

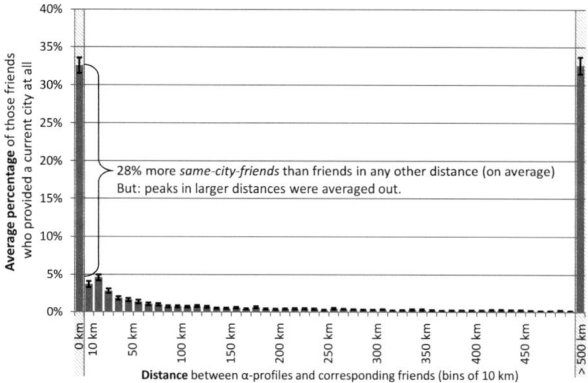

Figure 5.11: Average percentage of friends (y-axis) who provided a city in specific distances (x-axis) compared to the corresponding $\alpha$-profile. Additionally, the plot shows the corresponding 0.95 confidence intervals[12] [LWMH13].

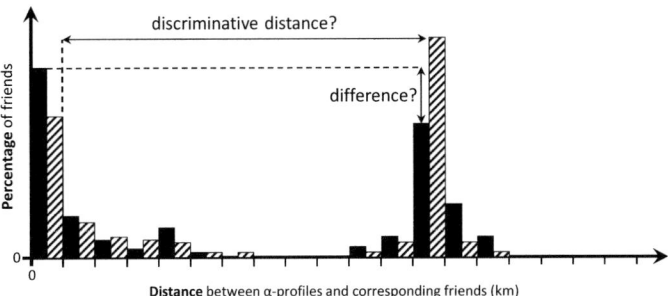

Figure 5.12: Illustration of how the difference (in percentage points) and the discriminative distance between two peaks is evaluated [LWMH13].

current cities within all air-line distances larger than 500 kilometers compared to the $\alpha$-city. Up to 500 kilometers each bar represents a bin of ten kilometers. Additionally, we show the 0.95 confidence intervals[13]. "It can be seen that on average 32.6 % (i.e., an absolute number of about 44 friends) of the friends who provided the current city are same-city-friends, which is 28 percentage points higher compared to other distance bins. However, the standard deviation of the 32.6 % of friends is at 26.9 and, additionally, occasional occurrences of (maybe large) groups of friends that do not live in the $\alpha$-city are averaged out" [LWMH13].

Therefore, we have to individually investigate each of the generated single histograms (cf. Figure 5.10) in order to study the actual geographical spread of friends lists. For this investigation, we divide the sample into two different cases: (1) those friends lists in which the most frequently provided city equals the $\alpha$-city (56.3 % of the cases) and (2) those friends lists in which the most frequently provided city is different from the $\alpha$-city. In Figure 5.12, once again, exemplary distributions of provided cities with respect to the air-line distances regarding the $\alpha$-city are shown. In particular, both case (1) (more same-city-friends; see black bars) and case (2) (less same-city friends; see striped bars) are illustrates in this figure. In the following, we investigate a dedicated metric for each of the two cases that provides further information on the distribution of friends around the current city provided by an $\alpha$-profile.

For friends lists of case (1), we investigate the *difference* between the two largest peaks within each histogram, i.e., a measure on how close a decision was if a third party successfully predicted an $\alpha$-city. Figure 5.13 shows these differences of the two largest peaks on the x-axis. In particular, we calculated the differences between the number of same-city-friends and the number of friends living in the second most frequently provided city in absolute terms and set this value in relation to the actual size of the respective friends list, i.e., the number of friends contained in the list. For example, we assume a friends list containing 100 OSN friends who provide a current city, of which 35 friends are same-city-friends, 25 friends are living in the second most

---

[13]Confidence intervals indicate the reliability of statistical values. 0.95 confidence intervals mean that the probability that the actual values of given statistical values are within the specified intervals is at 95 %.

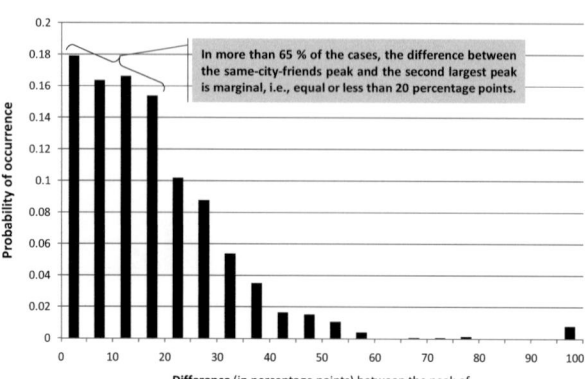

Figure 5.13: Probability distribution of the differences between the number of same-city-friends and the number of friends that correspond to the second most frequently provided city. The differences are expressed in relative terms w.r.t. the friends list sizes. Only the profiles are considered, in which the same-city-friends yield the highest peak [LWMH13].

frequently provided city, and 40 friends are distributed over the other provided cities. In this example, the *difference* between the two largest peaks (35 and 25) is equal to ten.

The y-axis of Figure 5.13 indicates the percentage of friends lists in which a certain *difference* can be detected, i.e., the probability of occurrence of a specific *difference*. The plot demonstrates, that in more than 65 % of the cases, the difference between the number of same-city-friends and the number of friends that provided the second most frequently provided city is marginal. In fact, it is equal or less than 20 percentage points and, therefore, a successful prediction based on the most provided city was very often a close decision.

In light of this finding, the question remains whether or not *wrongly* predicted $\alpha$-cities are close to the $\alpha$-city itself. To investigate this distance, we make use of the metric *discriminative distance*, i.e., the air-line distance between the most frequently provided current city and the $\alpha$-city for those cases in which these two cities are not equal. Therefore, we investigate the friends lists on top of which a prediction of the $\alpha$-profile's current city based on the most frequently provided city does not successfully result in the actual $\alpha$-city. In Figure 5.14, the aggregated results are shown. On the x-axis, we show the *discriminative distance* between the most frequently provided city and the $\alpha$-city pooled in bins of ten kilometers each. The probability of occurrence is shown on the y-axis, i.e., the percentage of friends lists in which we could detect a certain *discriminative distance*. The plot shows that in about 30 % of the respective friends lists the most frequently provided current city is located within a radius of 50 kilometers around the $\alpha$-city. However, whereas some most frequently provided current cities are very close to the $\alpha$-city, some others are remarkably far away.

Thus far, we demonstrated that an attempt to predict the $\alpha$-city based on the most frequently provided current city within a friends list induces a success rate of 56.3 %.

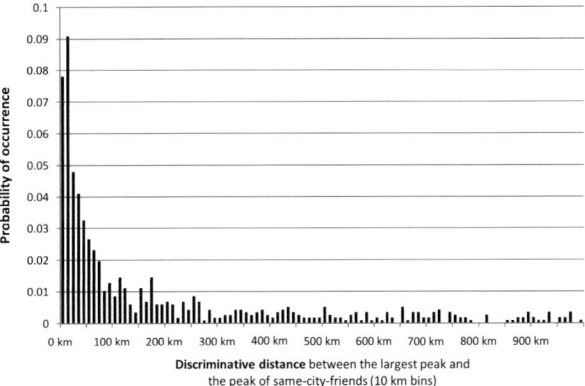

Figure 5.14: Probability distribution of the discriminative distances between the most frequently provided current city and the $\alpha$-city. Only the profiles are considered, in which the same-city-friends do not yield the highest peak [LWMH13].

We have also shown that successfully predicted cities are often close to other similarly frequently provided cities. In turn, some of the potentially wrongly predicted cities are very close to the actual $\alpha$-city. In the following, we soften the assumed attacker model a little bit in terms of assuming an attacker that is not interested in the exact current city of the user who corresponds to the $\alpha$-profile, but rather in whether or not the user is located in the nearby area of the actual $\alpha$-city. For instance, such an attacker is interested in whether or not a user lives within a 50 kilometer radius of Karlsruhe, Germany. Because of the fact that the investigation of friends lists with a most frequently provided city that differs from the $\alpha$-city has shown that a significant number of most frequently provided cities are located in the nearby area of the $\alpha$-city, we pursue the question how accurate, at least, a certain nearby area of the actual current city of a user can be predicted by exploiting a user's friends' provided locations.

Figure 5.15 provides the accuracies of predicting a certain nearby location of the $\alpha$-city. The plot answers the question in how many cases of the analyzed friends lists the number of same-city-friends plus the number of friends in a certain distance is larger than the number of friends who provided any other city plus the friends living in the specific distance of this city. The distance inaccuracy is shown on the x-axis as the "included radius around provided cities" (bins of one kilometer). On the y-axis, we show the percentage of friends lists that would induce successful predictions of a certain distance around the $\alpha$-city. At the very left of the plot the already mentioned 56.3 % success rate can be seen, which represents a distance inaccuracy of zero kilometers. However, at an x-value of, for instance, 50 kilometers the success rate is already at 68.2 %, i.e., if an attacking third party do not care about an inaccuracy of 50 kilometers the success rate of predictions based on friends' most frequently provided current city is at almost 70 %. Starting from about 70 kilometers inaccuracy the success rate increases to more than 70 %. The curve significantly flatten in its course. At a distance inaccuracy of 100 kilometers the success rate is at 71.7 % and at 250 kilometers at 75.3 %.

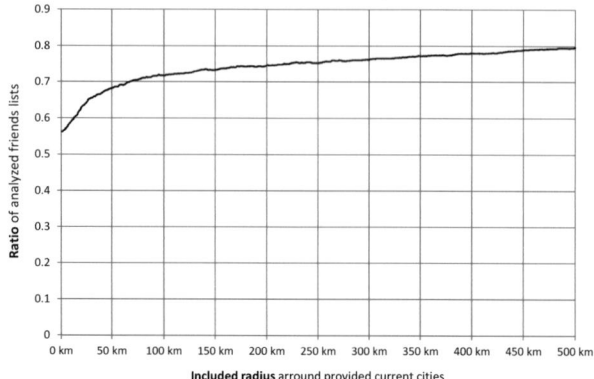

Figure 5.15: Ratio of analyzed friends lists, in which a city prediction would be successful if the number of friends in an x km radius around provided cities is included in the detection of the most frequently provided city or area, respectively [LWMH13].

"Therefore, on the one hand, it is worthwhile to exploit the number of friends in a small nearby area around provided cities if a third party is interested in predicting a user's city. On the other hand, the increase of the probability of a correct prediction diminishes if the radius is more and more increased, which is obvious if we take into account that most people live in the nearby area of their friends" [LWMH13].

Appendix C provides further results on the attribute prediction risk with respect to location attributes. In particular, we show the same analysis as presented before for the attribute *hometown*. Furthermore, we demonstrate how the accuracies of potential predictions of current cities and hometowns change if only those $\alpha$-profiles are considered that can be explicitly identified as profiles of current or former students.

## 5.4.3 Analysis of the Users' Age

In the following, we investigate the correlation of the attribute *year of birth*, or rather the *age*, within the users' friends lists. In contrast to the location attributes the year of birth is very rarely provided for the public. In fact, we found only 117 of the 6,404 randomly sampled $\alpha$-profiles that provided the attribute *and* provided a friends list in which, at least, one friend also provided this piece of PII (1.8 % of the randomly sampled profiles with a public friends list). Therefore, it is not possible to reach statistical significance by analyzing these 117 friends lists. However, we also found that 66.9 % of the friends lists contained a minimum of one friend who provided his/her year of birth (4,286 friends lists in total). Furthermore, about 9.5 friends of these friends lists shared the attribute, i.e., 40,672 friends in total. Hence, we analyzed the interdependences of the ages provided by the users' OSN friends.

"For this purpose, we took each profile $i$ and extracted the provided ages $a_{ij}$ of corresponding friends ($max(j)$ being the number of friends who provided the age). Next, we calculated the age difference $d_{ij}$ of each friend's age and the average age

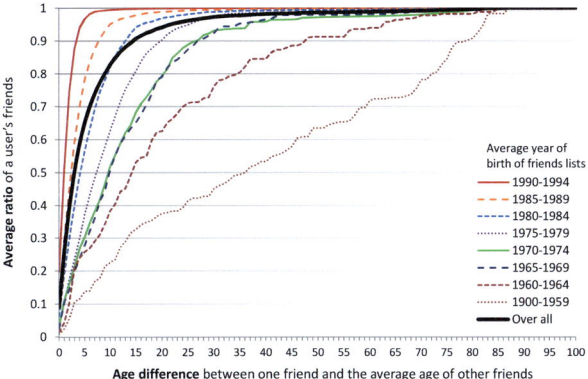

Figure 5.16: CDF: probability that a randomly chosen OSN friend has a maximum of a specific age difference to the average age of the friends list [LWMH13].

$\bar{a}_{ij}$ of all other friends of profile $i$. Afterwards, we calculated the CDF over all $d_{ij}$ of a profile $i$ (with $0 \le d \le 100$) and finally computed the average CDF over all profiles" [LWMH13]. This approach of investigation is similar to the "leave-one-out evaluation" utilized to investigate location predictions by the authors of [BSM10].

We show the resulting CDF in the bold curve of Figure 5.16. The x-axis of this plot represents the age difference between one friend and the average age of the other friends of the same friends list who provided this piece of PII. The y-axis shows the average ratio of a user's friends that are born a maximum of $x$ years (bins of one year) after or before the average year of birth of the other friends. In addition to the overall results, the plot shows separated results with respect to the average year of birth of the analyzed friends lists. These results are represented by the thinner curves. The average years of birth are pooled in ranges of five years. On average, we detected 431 friends lists per bin. Furthermore, we show another curve in this plot that represents the average years of birth ranging from 1900 to 1959 because we found only 58 friends lists within this range of years. Note that the year of birth of underaged users (younger than 18 years) is concealed from public by Facebook itself and, therefore, we analyzed only friends lists whose average year of birth is 1994 or earlier.

In general, the figure shows the probabilities that one friend out of a friends list who provided his/her year of birth is not older or younger than $x$ years with respect to the average year of birth of the other friends who provided this piece of PII. Hence, Figure 5.16 provides the accuracies with which an attacking third party can infer the age of a user's friends based on the analysis of years of birth provided by other friends of the same friends list. "As an example, if a third party determines the average year of birth of all friends that provided the attribute (except one), the probability that this excepted friend is not older or younger than four years concerning the average age is at 59 %. Moreover, if the average year of birth of the friends list lies between 1990 and 1994, this probability increases to 94 %. Thus, Figure 5.16 indicates, inter alia, that prediction of the age is more accurate the younger the friends in a friends list are" [LWMH13]. In general, the risk for users depends strongly on the attacker itself. If it is an attacker that is interested in predicting the exact age of the user, the accuracies might not be sufficient. However, if we assume an attacker that is, for instance, interested in whether or not a user is younger or older than 50 years, the average age of the user's friends list serves as a good indicator. Therefore, age prediction poses a risk despite the limited number of users who publicly share this piece of PII.

Since these are only valid findings for friends who provided the year of birth, we discuss the transferability of these results with respect to the prediction accuracy of the age of those friends who do not provide public access to the year of birth and, in particular, with respect to the actual age of the owner of a friends list, i.e., the $\alpha$-profile. The strong correlation of the age a few friend profiles publicly share indicates that also the year of birth of the owner of a friends list can be inferred by attacking third parties. However, we cannot proof this assumption because of the fact that we could not gather statistical data on the attributes that are not publicly shared. As stated at the beginning of this section, we cannot reach statistical significance by comparing the 117 years of birth provided by $\alpha$-profiles and the ages of the corresponding friends. However, a comparison of these profiles provide another indicator that the results of investigating the interdependence of friends' years of birth can be transferred to the respective $\alpha$-profile that does not publicly share this piece of information. The average difference between the average age of a friends list and the year of birth provided by the respective $\alpha$-profile is 3.9 years. Furthermore, for the group of friends lists that have an average age between 1990 and 1994 the average difference is at only 2.4 years. These results underpin the assumption that the results introduced above are transferable and, thus, age prediction poses a risk for owners of a publicly shared list of friends despite the low number of friends who reveal this piece of PII.

### 5.4.4  Analysis of Other Attributes

In the following, we discuss whether or not the current privacy situation regarding Facebook and adjusted privacy settings still provides the basis for attacking third parties to infer other non-provided attributes. A summary of the attributes analyzed besides the location attributes and the users' year of birth is shown in Figure 5.17. The x-axis designates the particular attribute, whereas the y-axis indicates the average percentage of a user's OSN friends. For each attribute, we show two bars. The right bars (gray) show the average relative number of friend profiles that provide public access to a certain attribute. The other bars (blue) show the average percentage of friends who provided exactly the same attribute value, e.g., if an $\alpha$-profile publicly provides the attribute value "in a relationship", the corresponding left (blue) bar indicates how many friend profiles of this $\alpha$-profile also publicly shared that they are in a relationship (in the case of the attribute *relationship state*, 10.9 % of a user's OSN friends share exactly the same attribute value as the user). To indicate the statistical significance of the results and, therefore, the accuracy of the provided percentages, we further show the 0.95-confidence interval in this plot. Note that some of the analyzed attributes are multi-value attributes, i.e., attributes that can take several

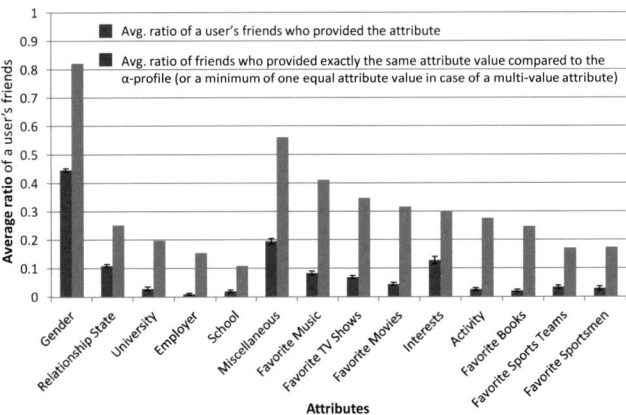

Figure 5.17: Correlations of other types of attributes provided by compared pro-files [LWMH13].

values in parallel. To give an example, a user can *like* Jazz Music, Classical Music, and Hip Hop Music so that all these three kinds of music appear as individual values of the attribute *favorite music*. Referring to the figure, the attributes *Miscellaneous, Favorite Music, Favorite TV Shows, Favorite Music, Interests, Activity, Favorite Books,* and *Favorite Sportsmen* are potentially multi-value attributes. We include a friend profile into the category of overlapping (multi-value) attribute values if just a single attribute value provided by the $\alpha$-profile equals just a single attribute value provided by a corresponding friend profile. Note that a Facebook user can also share his/her former universities, employers, and schools. However, for this plot, we only consider the current university, employer, and school if publicly provided at all.

For most of the attributes shown in Figure 5.17, we detected just a small overlap between a user's attribute values and those of his/her friends, i.e., about or less than 10 % except for some of the multi-value attributes and the attribute *gender*. However, the gender can only take two values, i.e., *male* and *female*. Therefore, it is no wonder that about a half of the provided attribute values of a user's friends equal the one provided by the user him-/herself. Referring to the multi-value attributes, we detected some users that share hundreds of individual values for some of these attributes. To give an example, users publicly share, on average, 16 individual values for the attribute miscellaneous and we found a profile that even provided 5,787 different items in this category. Based on this finding, it is also no wonder that we detected such an overlap for these attributes, just because of the fact that the probability that one of the shared items in one profile matches one that is publicly provided in another profile is significantly higher than for single-value attributes.

Other attributes are rarely publicly provided in general, e.g., on average, only 19.7 % of a user's friends reveal the name of their *university*, 15.5 % their current employer, and 10.9 % their current school. Additionally, the overlap is very small for these attributes, i.e., only 2.8 % of all friends of a user share the same university, about 1 % the same employer and 1.9 % the same current school. Even the analysis of the overlaps of the *favorite...* attributes resulted in very small values despite the fact that these attributes are multi-value attributes. An interesting finding is also constituted by the fact that some of the *favorite...* attributes are provided by many OSN friends of a user, e.g., we found a user profile that contained 554 publicly shared items of the attribute *favorite music*. However, the correlation of these types of attributes might be not that strong compared to, for instance, the strong correlation of friends' year of birth, because of the fact that the values such attributes can take are more independent from each other. "To give a concrete example for this, the prediction of a user's age might be easier than the prediction of his/her favorite music if, on the one hand, friends provide the years of birth 1991, 1992, and 1994 and, on the other hand, the music types *Classical Music*, *Hip Hop*, and *Jazz*. The reasons for this are the diversity and independence of the values the attribute *favorite music* can take" [LWMH13].

In general, the methods for investigating correlations of attributes provided by $\alpha$-profiles and corresponding friend profiles introduced in Sections 5.4.2 and 5.4.3 could also be applied for investigating the attributes shown in Figure 5.17. However, the small overlaps indicate that these values correlate not as strongly as the year of birth or the location attributes. In turn, since some of the attributes are rarely provided in general, the small overlaps could be a sufficient pattern to predict these attributes, for instance, by use of a more sophisticated prediction algorithm. Nevertheless, in light of the assumed "casual attacker", we estimate the risk regarding potential predictions of these attributes as significantly lower than for the age and location.

## 5.4.5 Discussion

In the previous sections, we provided results of the investigation of accuracies that can be estimated for inferring non-provided attributes by a third party based on information provided by a user's friends. The presented findings are based on two assumptions that are further discussed in the following. For the investigations we assume that the analyzed attribute values are not faked by the users. The second assumption is that the identified correlations of attributes publicly shared by $\alpha$-profiles and their friends are transferable to the correlations of attributes that are not publicly provided by the $\alpha$-profiles. Referring to the first assumption, we turn the tables and assume that users fake some of the publicly shared attributes, which seems realistic in general. However, unless friends do not make arrangements in terms of providing similar faked information, the occurring faked values mainly deteriorated the presented results. In light of the aim to calculate "lower bounds", a deterioration by faked attribute values implies only that predictions based on actually not faked information would result in even higher accuracies. The strong correlations detected by analyzing OSN friends' publicly provided PII weaken also the second assumption, i.e., non-provided attributes correlate as strongly as provided ones. Although this seems to be an unverifiable assumption, we have to ask the question whether or not any attacker care about some incorrectly predicted attribute values. Again, this depends on the attacker. In general, the estimated gain in information due to the prediction of non-provided attributes and the calculated accuracies seem to be sufficiently worthwhile from the perspective of an attacking third party.

Previously, we stated that the investigation of possible attribute prediction quantifies privacy risks. Certainly, for an appropriate risk quantification not only the accuracies of these predictions have to be taken into account, but also the probability of occurrence of successful prediction attempts of attacking third parties, as well as the expected "damage" for the users have to be considered. In this context, we already argued that the media published several articles stating that meanwhile companies, such as insurance agencies and others, perform analyses of OSN profiles to gain knowledge about the users who are, for instance, their customers. Therefore, there is no question whether or not the threat is existing. However, we have to ask what kind of damages can be expected due to such attacking third parties. Daniel J. Solove wrote an article in which he impressively discusses the weakness of the argument "I've nothing to hide" that users often state [Sol07]. Hence, there is no doubt about potential occurrences of attacks and about the damage. However, the quantification of these influential factors regarding privacy risk quantification are an issue in itself.

## 5.4.6  Summary and Conclusions

In this part of the thesis, we analyzed whether or not and how accurate third parties can predict users' non-provided attributes on the basis of attributes provided by the users' OSN friends. First, we demonstrated that location attributes can be easily inferred. In particular, we showed that in 56.3 % of the cases the most frequently provided current city of a friends list equals the current city of the owner of this friends list (54.1 % for the attribute hometown, see Appendix C). With an accepted inaccuracy of predicted locations, we demonstrated that these accuracies can even be increased. For instance, with an inaccuracy of 50 kilometers, we calculated a success rate of predictions of almost 70 %. Whereas location attributes are frequently provided by OSN friends, other attributes are very rarely provided to be accessed by any member of the OSN. An attribute that is often not publicly provided by OSN friends is the year of birth. However, also for this attribute we revealed that the few provided years of birth can bring third parties into the position to predict the age of a user with a remarkable accuracy. In particular, we demonstrated that the year of birth can be inferred at an accuracy of 59 % if an "acceptable" inaccuracy of +/− four years is assumed. For friends lists that have an average year of birth between 1990 and 1994, this accuracy increases to 94 %. Therefore, a publicly provided list of friends still threatens the corresponding user's privacy.

However, we also "discussed the interdependence of other attributes and showed that some are provided rarely and correlate little. Therefore, these results demonstrate that the situation concerning some predictable attributes is not that threatening. Except for the attributes investigated in detail, we consider the accuracy of attribute prediction to be low if attackers just analyze provided values of the targeted attribute in the friends list. On the other hand, we showed that OSN friends still threaten parts of users' privacy and, therefore, no all-clear signal can be given. Attribute prediction still poses a risk, at least, concerning some pieces of PII. The reason for this is not necessarily the availability of an attribute, but also the interdependence of PII shared by the OSN friends. At large, the more information can be publicly accessed the more PII can be predicted. Furthermore, if a third party applies, for instance, pattern learning mechanisms or other intelligent algorithms, OSN friends might reveal a lot more information about a user. Therefore, a strong reasoning for hiding friends lists in publicly accessible OSN areas is still given" [LWMH13].

## 5.5   General Conclusions

In the previous sections, we analyzed the availability of publicly provided pieces of PII and quantified the risk regarding profile linking and attribute predictions of certain non-provided pieces of PII based on the analysis of users' friends lists. The results presented in this chapter constitute an important basis to understand OSNs that are extensively used by millions of people today. The results contribute essential findings and data to the field of computer science to understand the interaction between humans and those kinds of IT systems. Furthermore, such understanding constitutes the basis for designing innovative privacy preserving technologies in the future. We show in Chapter 6 that the results presented in this part of the thesis already induced a foundation for a novel concept on top of which future privacy enhancing technologies can be implemented. The findings presented in this part of the thesis can also be utilized to evaluate the impact of future privacy tools if those tools are widely used by the participants of OSNs. Moreover, the contributions support users themselves in acting in a privacy aware manner, i.e., the contributions constitute a part of the *IT security and risk management* users actually have to perform on their own when participating in OSNs. In comparison to enterprise environments, in which developers and administrators have the ability to take care of security and risk management, these important management perspectives have to be recognized and addressed by the users themselves and, therefore, still constitute remarkable issues today.

# 6

# Avoiding Unintended Data Flows in OSNs: a Reflection

In this chapter, we reflect the findings presented in the previous chapters and discuss a concept that brings users into the position to understand which kind of flows of PII can potentially occur due to sharing content via OSNs. Such an understanding serves as an essential basis to make use of privacy settings in a more adequate manner than today's OSN users do. With this reflection, we address the research questions stated in Section 4.4.4. In particular, we introduce a design approach and an implementation of a technical measure that provides insights on who can (potentially) access, or even infer particular pieces of PII. This concept, on top of which novel privacy applications can be designed, provides support to synchronize users' own privacy demands with their adjustment of privacy settings. Thereby, the presented concepts aim at establishing an understanding of a certain user's current situation regarding privacy and, therefore, provide a clear and explicit demonstration of shared or predictable PII in combination with potential privacy risks.

Initially, we discuss users' general reasons for sharing PII to build up a basis for further discussion. Furthermore, from a psychological point of view (here: behavioral psychology), we elaborate which kind of measures would be most promising to force users to adjust privacy settings in an adequate manner. However, we also show that the probably most effective measures would not be realizable and not be accepted by users as well. We discuss that such approaches would result in negative effects for users and, moreover, would infiltrate users' urge for freedom of choice regarding the actual adjustment of privacy settings.

To get closer towards a concept of effective privacy applications, it is necessary to identify the essential aim of an *effective* privacy enhancing technology. In particular, we discuss that the combination of increasing privacy awareness and the possibility to adjust privacy settings are not sufficient for acting in a privacy aware manner. In point of fact, we hypothesize that the mental models of flows of PII users have got in their mind probably often do not match with the actual flows of PII. However, such mental models constitute the basis to adjust privacy settings according to a user's own privacy demands and, thus, are essential to act in a privacy aware manner. Therefore, we argue the need to provide a chance to match the often inadequate mental models to actually or potentially existing flows of PII. Moreover, we state that only the combination of privacy awareness, privacy settings that are easy-to-understand and easy-to-use, and, in particular, adequate mental models of data flows can result in a more appropriate use of privacy settings. In order to tackle this issue, we introduce an approach to provide decision support – in this context, support to appropriately adjust privacy settings – that is inspired by Thaler and Sunstein. These authors coined the term "nudge" as a measure that helps people to decide things appropriately (from a certain point of view) without taking off the possibility to behave inappropriately [TS08]. We apply the concept of "nudges" onto the design of applications that support OSN users in managing their shared PII adequately, i.e., according to their own privacy demands.

However, before the idea of providing "nudges" in the form of a special concept to design privacy applications as well as a respective implementation is introduced, we contrast such an approach with what we have learned from research on data flows within enterprise environments. We take the experience regarding IT services that are provided in enterprise environments (cf. Chapters 2 and 3) and contrast this to the privacy issues concerning OSNs. Parts of this chapter have already been published in [TLH12], [Lab12], [LDH11] and [LH11].

## 6.1 Psychological Discussion on Effective Privacy Tools

The media attention on privacy risks regarding the participation in OSNs urged a significant number of users to adjust privacy settings in a more restrictive manner and to behave in an increasing privacy aware manner. However, we showed in this dissertation that still a remarkable portion of analyzed OSN profiles provide public access to more or less sensitive PII and other information. In [Kri10], Krishnamurthy points out the significance of preserving privacy in OSNs. He "assumes that a possible reason for the complexity of preserving privacy is the ignorance of users regarding the protection of PII. Users share information through OSNs without thinking about possible consequences. Even if they have the possibility to secure their shared information by adjusting privacy settings, they are reluctant, maybe because of the urge for 'satisfaction of the needs for belongingness and the esteem needs through self-presentation' [KHG+08]" [LTH11]. Hence, we investigate what kind of measures could further educate users in terms of increasing privacy awareness (if they are not aware of privacy risks yet) and which type of privacy applications could help to adjust privacy settings in an even more appropriate manner than adjusted today.

One of the major reasons why people join OSNs is obvious. In the past, people tried to keep in touch with friends and others by communicating in an one-to-one or one-to-few fashion with respect to the number of communication partners. OSNs provide the possibility to reach a larger audience (one-to-many communication) with just a simple, single action, i.e., a post, a comment, an uploaded photo or video, etc. that can be accessed by a large group of users. That means, with just a single shared content element, a user can give the feeling of being present and, therefore, being part of the life of his/her OSN friends. Responses in terms of comments and *Likes* motivate even more to share information. Another motivation might be the possibility to meet and communicate with distant acquaintances (or rather strangers) in a familiar environment.

However, besides all the advantages OSNs provide for meeting and keeping in touch with people, sharing PII poses risks regarding privacy. In [LDH11], we have asked: "why do many users not think about these risks while providing personal data?" In the following, we pick up on the argumentation that answers can be found in behavioral psychology. This area of psychology explains the learning of human activities on the basis of rewards and punishments. If we transfer this psychological knowledge to the context of user behavior in OSNs, it is obvious that responses in terms of comments and *Likes* reward people for sharing their PII or other pieces of information. Furthermore, users' actions are rewarded directly, i.e., in a short period of time. The more content a user shares the more interest will his/her profile arise and the more responses he/she will get from sharing content. Additionally, by sharing information an individually distinctive urge for self-representation can be satisfied, which can serve as another reward for being active in an OSN. In summary, users expect benefits from publishing content and they are motivated to share information to get rewarded by their friends and other members of the OSN. Psychologists refer to the motivation to act in a specific manner because of anticipated rewards as "positive reinforcement" [Zim04]. In this context, the authors of [Joi08] state that the following categories are those features that are most frequently seen as gratifying characteristics of an OSN: "social connection, shared identities, content, social investigation, social network surfing and status updating. User demographics, site visit patterns and the use of privacy settings were associated with different uses and gratifications" [Joi08].

In contrast, a "negative reinforcement" effect is the motivation to stop doing something in the sense of conditioning of human behavior by punishments as a consequence of an action. In general, rewards and negative effects compete in influencing humans future behavior and motivation to do (or not to do) something. Thereby, not only the number of rewards and punishments matters, but also the intensity of the corresponding effects and the time gap between an action and the effect. The impact of effects that do not promptly occur subsequently to an action is known as the "deferred gratification" [Mis74][MM83], i.e., a gratification (in a positive *or* negative sense) that applies with a certain time gap between an action and the occurrence of a "gratifying" effect.

In the context of OSNs, a negative reinforcement would be a motivation for users to not share content. However, in today's OSNs – as argued above – rewards occur on a very short time scale, i.e., an action is almost promptly followed by responses of other OSN members, mostly in terms of comments and/or *Likes*. These responses constitute in most cases a reward for sharing content, e.g., Facebook does not provide a "Dislike button". For sure, social media can also be and is being abused, for instance, for bullying people. In 2012, according to the earlier mentioned German survey, 23 % of the respondents between twelve and 19 years stated that they know, at least, one other person who has been bullied via the Internet [JIM2012]. 15 % stated that they were confronted with undesirable content (photos, comments, etc.) about their own person, at least, once since they are active on the Internet. However, the number of positive responses on published content is probably much higher than the content that annoys users. Otherwise, users would not participate in OSNs in such an extensive dimension and would not share such amount of information via their OSN profiles.

In turn, if punishments occur at all, this effect is obviously realized on a significantly longer time scale. Consequently, potential punishments that occur some time after sharing a certain piece of information are less effective on users' future behavior, or rather on the motivation to (not) share information, than the rewards a user probably gets promptly. Therefore, a sustainable recognition of the potential privacy risks by negative effects of users' behavior regarding information sharing cannot be expected at present. To give an example, a published photo of the new pretty house a user has bought induces most probably (positively) gratifying comments and *Likes*. However, if a car dealer would have access to the picture, he/she probably tries to not give a discount to the user who posted the newly bought house because he/she knows that the customer has enough money to buy such a house, regardless whether the photo has been posted just a short time before his/her offering or long ago (in this context, cf. [Sol07]).

According to this theory, for developing users' awareness regarding privacy risks of information sharing, it would be necessary to intensify the punishments and/or to shorten the time gap between an action and the realization of negative effects. The principle objective would be a conditioning of the users. Psychologists refer to conditioning via regulated rewards and punishments as "operant conditioning". However, the question arises which punishments should be provoked to achieve an effect in terms of an increased privacy awareness. Moreover, negative responses in terms of punishments would cause detriments to users and OSNs would not endorse measures that punish people for participating within the OSN. Not least, the business model of OSN providers would stand in contrast to those measures.

Besides approaches on the basis of operant conditioning – that would not be deployable –, only approaches on the basis of educational work remain. Press reports and public discussions resulted in a significant increase of users' privacy awareness. Showing people the risks regarding the participation within OSNs quite plainly leads to the perception of these risks and is thought-provoking. The media attention is urging more and more users to adjust privacy settings adequately to hide parts of a profile from strangers and to be restrictive regarding information sharing with unrestricted access conditions. In the following, we discuss what types of measures could also be effective to educate users in terms of demonstrating them their current risks regarding privacy, which constitutes the basis to understand potentially existing unintended flows of PII and to adjust privacy settings according to the users' privacy demands.

## 6.2   Today's Privacy Settings and Users' Mental Models

Today's provided privacy settings are often comfortable to use. However, the offer of such settings might be not sufficient to enforce privacy aware acting in OSNs. Certainly, by providing such often well-designed and easy-to-use privacy controls OSN providers have, in principle, done their duties. However, just offering capabilities to adjust who can access which piece of PII does not induce privacy aware acting as discussed before. In particular, adjusting privacy is often very simple, but the induced effects are not clear to the users, or OSNs are even suggestive of comprehensive privacy (cf. the statement of Marc Zuckerberg quoted at the beginning of Chapter 1). In this context, Deuker et al. published a series of papers in which they investigate the motivation of users to make use of privacy settings ([Deu12] and [DRA12]) and study "the trade-off between privacy concerns and benefits associated to the usage" of OSNs and, in particular, third party Apps [SDAN13]. The studies are based on qualitative interviews of Facebook users. In general, these studies aim at providing a foundation to identify requirements for designing improved and more effective privacy setting. In particular, in [SDAN13], the authors identify an urgent need for providing "more transparency" of flows of PII. In this section, we discuss whether or not an improved design of privacy settings or another approach might be feasible and could induce more privacy aware sharing of PII via OSNs. In particular, we identify an essential building block that should, additionally, be considered for designing novel privacy tools.

### 6.2.1   The Need for Accurate Mental Models

Considered precisely, sharing PII in a privacy aware manner and the individual adjustments of privacy settings are not the same thing. In particular, a user who has adjusted his/her privacy settings provided by the OSN does not necessarily behave privacy aware, i.e., it is not sufficient for privacy aware acting to adjust privacy settings in some way, particularly, if potential flows of PII are not clear to the users. Ordinary OSN users seem to be overwhelmed with the task to adjust privacy settings according their own privacy demands. The reason for this might be simple: today's users demonstrably do not understand, or rather perceive each of any potentially occurring flow of information. In other words, the actual number of possible data flows exceeds the imagination of many users. Thereby, users do not necessarily recognize that they are overwhelmed, or rather that they are not acting privacy aware. In fact, as already discussed, not only other users of the respective OSN can possibly access shared PII, but also the OSN provider and, probably, even worse, third parties that aim at processing users' shared information as a basis of their own business. Hence, the transparency of possible unintended flows of PII is essential to adjust privacy settings appropriately and constitutes a key feature to bring privacy demands and privacy settings together. Therefore, providers of OSNs or others ought to offer services that aim at bridging the gap between the user interface provided to adjust privacy settings and users' *mental models*, i.e., their perception of flows of PII.

Whereas, so far, most related work regarding privacy in OSNs do not include aspects regarding mental models of potential flows of PII, the involvement of such mental models into the design of other services is already very common. In particular, the concept of mental models is considered in the area of designing user interfaces, i.e., a user's mental model represents his/her expectations of the functionality of the interface [SN93]. Even earlier, from a psychological perspective, users' mental models have been discussed in the context of physical systems and devices, as well as users' understanding of the corresponding functionality [Hil83] (see [Rap05] for a more detailed review on "cognitive and educational psychological research on mental models"). However, the field of *user interface design* adopted the term "mental models" and includes it in the development of interfaces from a practical point of view, i.e., the assumption that devices, physical systems, as well as other user interfaces along with their functionality are abstractly represented in users' minds as mental models (cf. [CRCC07]) in terms of small-scale simulations of the actual systems. The adaptation of mental models can induce different user behavior because mental models are applied to predict the real-world behavior of a system that is to be used. To give an example, even technically inexperienced users build their own mental model of the computer they use, although the model might be completely wrong, or rather different from the so-called *system model*[1], e.g., the time to boot is considered as a warm-up phase to reach operational temperature. In general, the users' mental models are often less complex than the actual model of the system.

In between a mental model and a system model stands the *represented model*[2]. This model includes the representation of the system model due to the design of the user interface and it can match the system model very closely or can be (even consciously) designed as representing something different, for instance, to give the users the feeling of comprehensible system behavior. Because of the fact that users can understand an interface better that is based on a represented model that is close to their mental models, interface designers should follow the mental models [CRCC07], i.e., for the design of ordinary interfaces a developer should adopt users' expectations instead of aiming to force users to change their current mental models.

## 6.2.2  Distinctive Characteristics of Privacy Settings

However, this approach works as long as the design of interfaces do not induce an incomplete, or even wrong understanding of the system behavior. In turn, if represented models support inappropriate mental models, users have no chance to really understand the implications of using the system. Referring to OSNs, today's privacy interfaces, i.e., privacy settings, are (eventually even consciously) designed to support users feeling of a privacy preserving environment if privacy settings are (somehow) adjusted. In this context, the authors of [SL08] conducted a study in a usability lab and found that the reason for not adjusting privacy settings according to the actual privacy awareness and privacy demands of users is caused by the design of the user interface. Additionally, not least, the use case introduced later in this chapter shows that current mental models do not match actual flows of PII. This

---

[1]The system model is also referred to as implementation model or programmer's model.
[2]The represented model is also referred to as design model, manifest model, or designer's model.

situation indicates the need for privacy tools that adapt users' mental models towards a comprehensive understanding of each of any potential flow of shared and even non-provided PII. In particular, adaptions of current mental models regarding data flows are necessary, at least, in light of the fact that PII once released to a third party cannot be claimed back, i.e., a shared piece of PII that unintentionally has been accessed by a third party constitutes an irreversible situation.

In general, we can identify three major differences between privacy settings and ordinary user interfaces that underpin the argumentation of the necessity to support the adaptation of users' mental models towards a privacy aware view on potential flows of PII: first, privacy settings are provided to manage PII that might constitute sensitive data and a disclosure of this data cannot be rescinded. In contrast to other user interfaces, a privacy management interface that lacks conformity with users' expectations does not only cause inconvenience, but can also cause harm. Second, as discussed in Section 6.1, users get rewards for sharing content, i.e., *Likes*, comments, etc.. However, potential negative effects that could harm users occur, if at all, on an often longer timescale. Theory of behavioral psychology says that deferred effects induce less impact on future behavior than effects that can be immediately recognized [LDH11]. Therefore, users are not necessarily motivated to adjust privacy settings appropriately. Third, OSNs, such as Facebook, provide a service that is free to use. In turn, the user shares personal data that can be exploited by the OSN vendor or its business partners for targeted advertising, which constitutes the underlying business model of OSNs. Users trade personal data for services. Thus, the OSN vendor is interested in gaining and spreading as much personal data as possible. Due to user demands and legal aspects, OSNs are forced to provide privacy management tools but at the same time the use of it is not necessarily in their interest. Therefore, today's provided privacy settings have the potential to induce unintended flows of PII due to users' inappropriate mental models of potential flows of possibly sensitive PII.

## 6.2.3   Divergent Mental Models Using an Example

Previously, we discussed that mental models of users are divergent compared to potentially occurring flows of PII. In the following, we manifest this hypothesis by use of an example, which shows that unintended flows of PII exist and that the unintended character of such flows is demonstrably not clear to the users.

Today, each of the 15 most popular Facebook Apps (cf. Section 4.1) are used by more than 18 million OSN members per month[3]. The authors of [GSMY08] investigate and characterize the "popularity and user reach of Facebook" Apps by a measurement-based study. For this, they gathered usage data of popular applications available via a third party service. Furthermore, the authors analyzed OSN profiles in order to determine how many Apps a user installs on average. Inter alia, the authors found that the total number of installed applications increases. In particular, they show that five randomly selected applications out of the 100 most popular Apps achieve a coverage of 30 % to over 50 % of all users.

---

[3]http://www.socialbakers.com/ [Last downloaded on 2013-05-28].

OSN Apps are often provided by third parties that can – due to the use of their provided Apps – potentially get access to personal data of the users and their OSN friends. At least, they get forwarded basic information about the user, including the friends list, which reinforces the mentioned risks regarding inferable data [LWMH13].

However, on the one hand, the privacy control interface of Facebook seems to be intuitive and well-designed in terms of providing the desired functionality to privacy aware users. All settings can be changed with a few clicks, including settings regarding friends' Apps. On the other hand, restricting the access to posts, photos, etc. to OSN friends, does not exclude certain App providers from accessing the data, even if the user him-/herself never installed an App. In particular, if other default settings of Facebook are not adjusted, even Apps installed by users' OSN friends can potentially access the users' PII. It only requires the friends to forward the permissions in an obligatory approval process, which is a prerequisite for installing most Apps and done via a standard interface during the installation process. In turn, Facebook users could easily exclude friends' Apps from accessing their own data by changing a specific setting provided on a different page compared to the other privacy settings. However, the small survey introduced in the following indicate that most users are even not aware of these potential flows of PII and, not to mention, often do not adjust the respective settings even if they would demand to prevent such flows. In this context, the authors of [BLSC09] investigate the access control model regarding shared PII in combination with the use of Facebook Apps. Thereby, they also show that "current applications put users at risk by permitting the disclosure of large amounts of personal information to these applications and their developers" [BLSC09] and demonstrate that not only the data shared by the user of a particular App can be accessed by this App, but also the data of his/her OSN friends. They further point out that OSN friends will not be asked for their consent before their data is forwarded via the actual user of the respective App. Even worse, App providers do not only request data that is necessary to provide a certain service, such as online games and other services, but also request data that could be interesting for further business, e.g., advertising, although such a behavior is not compliant to the terms of use of some OSNs, e.g., Facebook. In 2008, it is shown that more than 90 % of analyzed Facebook Apps unnecessarily request private data [FE08].

However, although privacy issues related to Facebook Apps have been discussed (e.g., in [WXG11], [KLS11], [HLL11]), the specific privacy problem discussed in this dissertation is often overlooked. Wang et al. report that participants of their study have mentioned the problem regarding the mass of data forwarded to App providers, while it is not considered in the design of their study [WXG11]. Interestingly, from the perspective of Hull et al. the problem is an obvious and "egregious violation" of the norms of distribution [HLL11]. Therefore, at the end of this chapter, we present an implementation of the introduced concepts in the form of a privacy application that provides transparency of flows regarding this specific use case. In particular, this privacy tool is implemented as a Facebook App and demonstrates users which pieces of their and their OSN friends' PII they potentially forward to a third party App provider. Moreover, the App tries to infer users' non-provided attributes (cf.

Figure 6.1: Extract of the Facebook questionnaire: participants of the study were asked who can see a post with the privacy options "Only Me", "Friends", "Friends of Friends" and "Public".

the contributions presented in Chapter 5) in order to make possible risks even more explicitly comprehensible. We refer to the introduced use case several times in the remainder of this chapter to apply the discussions and introduced concepts for novel privacy tools onto a specific demonstrable deficiency concerning flows of PII that are often not perceived by OSN users.

## 6.2.4   Survey on Users' Actual Mental Models

On the basis of a small survey, we demonstrate an indication of the unintended character of potential flows of a user's PII to third party providers of Apps a user's OSN friends have installed. We developed a questionnaire that is shown (in part) in Figure 6.1 with which we asked the respondents who can actually access shared PII if certain privacy settings are adjusted, i.e., "Only Me", "Friends", "Friends of Friends" and "Public". The aim of this survey was to find out whether or not users are aware of the fact that third party providers of Apps used by their OSN friends can access their shared PII even if the accessibility is set to "Friends".

Two groups participated in the survey. The first group consisted of 39 computer science students participating a lecture on Web development. The other group was formed by 41 members of several sports teams. The participants were between 15 and 35 years old. The results are shown in Figure 6.2. The very left bar represents the overall result, which shows that more than 80 % of the 80 participants were not aware of the fact that shared information can be accessed by Apps used by others. In addition, the figure shows the results divided into three types of users, i.e., those who are using Facebook on a regular basis, those who stated a seldom usage and those

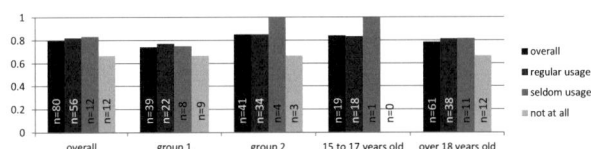

Figure 6.2: Results of the survey: part of the participants that were *NOT* aware of the fact that Apps installed by their OSN friends can get access to their data if the default privacy settings are not changed.

who are using Facebook not at all. Furthermore, we split the results into the two test groups (group 1: students, group 2: sports team members). Moreover, we divided all participants into those who are 18 years or older and those between 15 and 17 years.[4] However, we could not detect significant variances in the divided results. We are also fully aware of the fact that the results cannot be unconditionally generalized because we asked only 80 respondents. However, already in this small survey it becomes apparent that it is likely that Facebook users, regardless of their age or education, are not aware of the fact that third party providers of Apps used by a user's friend can get access to his/her data without asking the user him-/herself. Based on the survey, we conclude that unknown and also unintended data flows still exist and users are often not able to understand these flows as a basis to adjust privacy settings in an adequate manner. Therefore, this example serves as the exemplary case used to implement the concepts introduced in the remainder of this chapter.

## 6.3  Bridging the Gap Between Users' Privacy Awareness and Actual Adjustments of Privacy Settings

As already pointed out, it would not be feasible to intensify negative effects of information sharing or to shorten the period of time before such effects occur to enforce privacy aware acting. We further argued that solely providing privacy settings is not sufficient to induce privacy. In turn, although the aim to educate users in terms of increasing their privacy awareness – as induced by the media attention regarding privacy in recent years – is essential, awareness does not solely induce privacy aware acting in each of any situation with respect to OSNs. Moreover, even the combination of both the offer of privacy settings and appropriate privacy awareness is not enough. Therefore, we can identify a gap between these essential building blocks of preserving privacy, i.e., a missing understanding, or rather inappropriate mental models of the actual flows of PII that can potentially occur in the context of OSNs and third party providers. Figure 6.3 illustrates the chain of necessary building blocks for privacy aware acting in OSNs and, furthermore, shows corresponding influential factors. The figure points out that privacy awareness and privacy settings are already addressed by related research work in terms of improvements and tools that support to increase awareness and/or that simplify the adjustments of privacy settings (cf. Section 4.5.4). However, the figure also indicates that establishing adequate mental models is less addressed compared to the other building blocks of privacy aware acting.

Certainly, OSN providers could also change their privacy interfaces to support users to understand potential flows of PII. However, as discussed before, OSN providers have a distinctive (and also comprehensible) urge to keep their users sharing information, not least, in light of their business models. Hence, it would be pointless to try to encourage OSN providers to change their implementations of privacy settings. The

---

[4] Additionally, we interviewed 25 children between 12 and 14 years. However, although most of these respondents already registered a Facebook profile and also already made use of third party Apps, they did not even know that third parties are involved by using Facebook and its Apps.

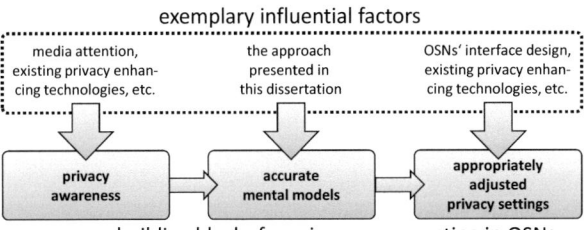

Figure 6.3: Influential factors on the chain of necessary building blocks of privacy aware sharing of PII via OSNs.

other option constitutes the offer of more transparency of potentially occurring data flows in terms of a clear and understandable demonstration of individual privacy risks with respect to a user's current situation concerning shared PII. In other words, the gap between privacy awareness and the adjustment of privacy settings could be bridged by providing support to sharpen users' mental models of intended and unintended flows of PII that occurred or can occur in the future. In short, whereas OSNs provide privacy settings and the media attention regarding privacy in OSNs raised privacy awareness, an essential building block is still missing: interactive tools that provide transparency in order to sharpen users' mental models of potential data flows. In the following, we discuss the approach of providing transparency in light of the concept of "nudges", i.e., supporting people to take appropriate decisions.

## 6.3.1   Basic Concept of "Nudges" to Induce Appropriate Decisions

The following introduction of the concept of providing "nudges", which is a more or less psychological support to enforce smart decisions (smart from a certain per- spective), is based on the findings presented in a book of Thaler and Sunstein [TS08]. The authors introduce an example of *a canteen within a school* to explain the concept of nudging people towards smart decisions: placing healthy food, e.g., produce, at eye-level of children and junk food not at that same level constitutes a nudge in light of the aim to enforce eating healthier food. In contrast, providing junk food not at all is not a nudge because it is a non-libertarian approach to enforce smart decisions, i.e., the freedom of choice would be limited by not offering such unhealthy food. The fundamental basis of the concept of nudges is the assumption that the cognitive costs to decide in one or another direction are different. Referring to the canteen example, the cognitive costs to grab an apple is lower than necessary to search and take the junk food. Consequently, most of the children get a healthier diet. Therefore, providing nudges is a conscious change of the incentives of taking one or another option (here: pieces of food) in terms of a change of the cognitive costs required to opt for something (here: a certain type of food). In this context, those who support others in taking decisions are referred to as *choice architects*. The decision support that aims at not eliminating the opportunity to decide inappropriately is referred to as *libertarian paternalism*. [TS08]

Thaler and Sunstein further refer to thumb rules, or rather judgmental heuristics used by humans that systematically induce biases, which goes back to Tversky and Kahneman [TK73] [TK74], i.e., (1) the adjustment from an anchor, (2) the availability heuristic, and (3) the representativeness heuristic. Referring to (1), decisions made on top of this heuristic are influenced by a certain more or less comparable example in users' minds, i.e., an anchor. Thaler and Sunstein state that people living in a larger city estimate the number of inhabitants of another smaller city larger than those people living in an even smaller city. In the context of OSNs, users potentially estimate the number of guests joining a party announced via Facebook significantly lower than it actually can happen[5]. The reason is probably the comparison to "real-life" party announcements and the resulting number of guests following such an invitation. Another example constitutes the sharing of photos: a photo pinned at the wall of a user's flat can only be seen by a few people, i.e., only those who are/will be physically at the user's flat. However, photos uploaded to the Facebook wall can be accessed by a much broader audience, which might be underestimated by the users because of the feeling of pinning a photo to an actual wall. The second heuristic (2) subsumes decisions based on the presence of examples, e.g., some people feel like it is more likely to become a victim of terrorism compared to the probability to have a car accident, which is a wrong assumption often made just because terrorism is more "available" in peoples' minds due to, for instance, its media attention. In the context of OSNs, this effect can also be observed: some users might feel that the risks posed by publicly shared or inferable PII is not existent because they do not know anyone who suffered detriment from sharing PII. The third category of decision rules constitutes the representativeness heuristic, which subsumes decisions made on top of a comparison of the current situation to another well-known thing/situation/etc., e.g., Thaler and Sunstein provide the example of a very tall American guy (e.g., 2.10 meters); most people might believe it is more likely that the guy is a professional basketball player than another guy who is only 1.70 meters tall. The authors say, that sometimes stereotypes are right, however, in general, such comparisons lead to biases. Transferred to OSNs, we can identify an example for biases based on the representativeness heuristic in the context of OSN friends. Whereas the definition of a friend in "real-life" is most likely clear to the users, an OSN friend is something completely different. However, users might forget about the differences from time to time just because they think about friends when they refer to OSN friends. According to [TS08], nudges can help to avoid these biases and, therefore, we argue that the examples provide sufficient reasons to include the concept of nudges into future privacy tools.

## 6.3.2   "Nudges" for Adequate Adjustments of Privacy Settings

Thaler and Sunstein further state that if people feel like they are rid of risks than they are more likely neglecting useful precautions. Therefore, people who run risks

---

[5]Cf., for instance, http://worldnews.nbcnews.com/_news/2012/09/22/14028638-thousands-descend-on-tiny-dutch-town-after-facebook-invitation-goes-viral and http://www.bbc.co.uk/news/uk-england-beds-bucks-herts-11376350 [Last downloaded 2013-05-28].

because of unrealistic optimism could benefit from the offer of nudges as well. [TS08] In the context of designing privacy applications, the concept of nudges could also be applied to prevent users from unrealistic optimism regarding the probability of occurrence of certain privacy leaks. Hence, the concepts presented in this chapter follow the principle of providing nudges in terms of a demonstration of privacy risks.

Wang et al. also identified the concept of "nudges" as a basis for effective privacy support. Implementations of such privacy tools, as well as an exploratory study on the impact of "privacy nudges" are presented in [WLS+13], which has been published subsequently to the main writing phase of this dissertation. Thereby, the authors mainly focus on the privacy tools themselves, as well as the corresponding impact assessment. In contrast, we show a more detailed transfer of the concepts and theories presented in [TS08] with respect to the context of OSNs. Furthermore, the design and implementation of privacy tools presented later in this chapter provides *reactive* features to identify potentially unintended flows of PII based on already shared or even non-published information, whereas the "privacy nudges" presented in [WLS+13] focus on a *proactive* support to determine, for instance, the audience of PII that is to be shared. However, both reactive and proactive features that support users in managing their privacy are necessary to induce privacy aware acting. Furthermore, the discussion, design concept and implementation presented in this dissertation, as well as the findings of Wang et al. both underline the assumption that "nudging" users to act in a privacy aware manner might be an effective approach. According to Wang et al. "nudges could potentially be a powerful mechanism to discourage unintended disclosures in social media that may lead to regret" [WLS+13]. Therefore, the contributions of both this dissertation and [WLS+13] complement each other perfectly and build the basis for more effective privacy support for OSN users.

## 6.4   Contrasting Privacy Apps and Enterprise IAM

In the following, we contrast privacy tools that improve users' mental models based on the concept of "nudges" with another field of research. In particular, we review the experiences gained by investigating IAM systems in order to identify existing capabilities of administrators and developers to avoid unintended flows of PII that are not provided for today's OSN users. With that, we try to transfer requirements from the context of enterprise environments to the design of privacy applications.

In enterprise environments, developers and administrators are capable to control and monitor flows of PII. To give an example, in up-front provisioning systems (as introduced in Section 2.2.1) developers design each of any flow of information in terms of the implementation of rules and policies. Additionally, these flows are "typically monitored and governed by various overview boards" [Lab12], at least, in the form of imposing the rules and policies to be implemented by the technical staff. Certainly, it is not excluded that something can go wrong and unintended flows of PII are missed (cf. Section 2.5.1). However, most likely, unintended data flows occur less frequently than in OSN environments. In contrast, the management of PII is on the discretion of OSN users themselves, i.e., no other instance is responsible for the control and monitoring of flows of a particular user's PII. As shown by presented results of the empirical studies on publicly available PII in OSNs, it seems to be already an issue for users to determine who can potentially get access to shared information. It is even more difficult to monitor flows of PII after sharing information.

Hence, the question arise whether or not we can learn from capabilities administrators and developers of enterprise IAM systems are provided with in order to provide support for OSN users to be able to manage their PII more adequately.

In an enterprise environment processes are defined by the companies involved in the processes, i.e., the processes, or rather flows of PII are per se provider-engineered, whereas the data flows in the context of OSNs are not only provider-engineered, but also and in particular built by the users themselves. To give an example, a user shares a certain piece of PII and makes use of a third party OSN App. In this scenario, the user has "engineered" a flow of information to a third party, regardless of whether or not the user intended this data flow. Whereas the flows of PII in enterprise environments are based on implemented policies and rules, flows that occur in OSN environments are induced by the combination of certain "circumstances" that are joined by the users themselves. Even worse, not only a user him-/herself contributes to these data flows, but also his/her OSN friends (cf. the use case introduced in Section 6.2.3). Another example for information flows induced by several users constitutes the combination of contact lists on smartphones and the use of mobile Apps provided by the OSNs. In particular, if a user connects his/her smartphone with his/her OSN account, the contact lists of the smartphones are often uploaded to the OSN provider so that the user induces a flow of information (here, for instance, mobile phone numbers of people on his/her contact list that are sent to the OSN provider).

However, the main difference between managing PII in enterprise and in OSN environments constitutes the fact that the rules and policies that induce flows of information are not in the hands of the users. On the contrary, the impetus for information flows, i.e., sharing information and using certain OSN features, is incumbent upon the user. On the one hand, in [Lab12], we stated that "if users are responsible for the configuration of data flows outside of organizational borders, to some extent, they are also responsible for ensuring privacy." On the other hand, if users induce flows of information they have to be provided with capabilities developers and administrators of IAM systems are provided with. Therefore, since OSN users do not implement their own rules and policies with respect to potential flows of information, it is necessary to show users the consequences of a certain action in terms of a comprehensible demonstration of potential data flows and corresponding risks.

In summary, we can state that, in principle, the requirements for understanding potential flows of PII are very similar in enterprise and OSN environments. However, we stress the point that users do not impose the rules and policies regarding the data flows they induce by participating in OSNs. Certainly, administrators and developers also only implement the rules and policies. However, they have to have a clear and comprehensive understanding of the implications of these rules and policies. In light of this "condition" regarding enterprise environments, we can derive the following requirement for privacy tools, which we already stated in the previous sections: users have to be supported in understanding potential flows of PII in a comprehensive manner as a basis to control and monitor the proliferation of their PII.

## 6.5 Design and Implementation of an Effective Privacy Application

In the following, we introduce the concept of privacy tools that provide "nudges" to adjust privacy settings in a more adequate manner concerning the users' privacy demands. Afterwards, we present an implementation of the concepts. This particular *Facebook Privacy App* (FBPA) demonstrates a user his/her current situation regarding privacy and privacy risks according the actual data he/she and his/her OSN friends shared. The FBPA is based on the use case introduced in Section 6.2.3. Finally, we discuss the issues of bringing such an App up-and-running. In particular, we argue that legal restrictions impose hurdles that might inhibit a productive application and operation of such approaches in general and the deployment of the FBPA in particular.

### 6.5.1 Concept for Effective Privacy Applications

In principle, we already presented the concept of such novel privacy tools in the previous sections. Referring back to Figure 6.3, we identified the need to adapt users' mental models of flows of PII as an essential building block for privacy aware acting. Therefore, privacy tools should include the demonstration of potentially occurring data flows and corresponding privacy risks. In particular, privacy tools should be provided that demonstrate the following facts:

- Users and third parties who can potentially access a certain piece of information.

- The pieces of shared (and non-provided) PII accessible (or even inferable) by these users and third parties.

- The pieces of others' PII accessible by these users and third parties due to the use of certain OSN features, i.e., others' information that is (unintentionally) forwarded by the user him-/herself.

- A clear and comprehensible demonstration of corresponding privacy risks.

In fact, an App that provides the aforementioned aspects can also not solely induce privacy aware acting in OSNs. However, besides the offer of privacy settings and the establishing of privacy awareness in general, it serves as the third essential building block necessary to adjust privacy settings according to the own privacy demands. In particular, the adaptation of users' mental models of flows of PII bridges the gap between the two other mentioned building blocks in terms of a *mapping* of users' privacy awareness to adequate adjustments of privacy settings.

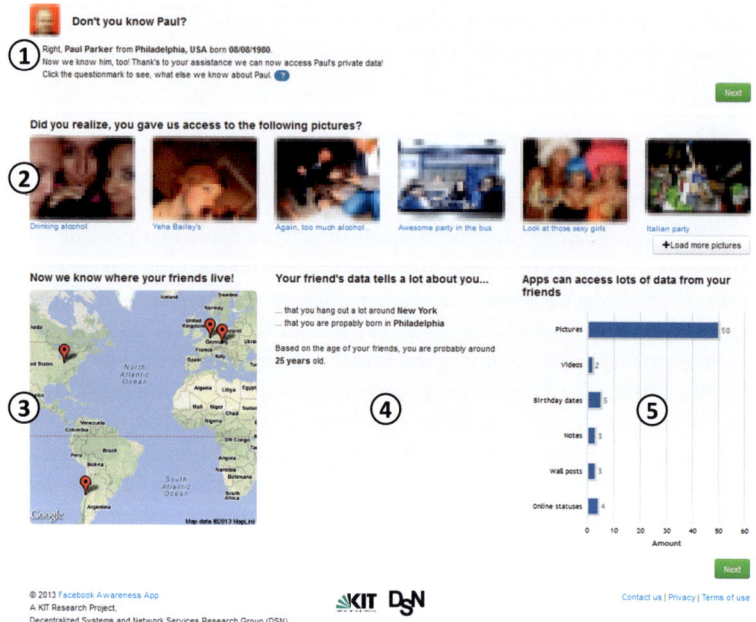

Figure 6.4: Demo-Screenshot of the main page of the FBPA implementation[6].

## 6.5.2   Facebook Privacy App (FBPA)

In Section 6.2.3, we introduced the use case in which a user potentially forwards PII shared by his/her friends to providers of Apps he/she makes use of if a specific part of the default privacy settings are not changed by the users' OSN friends. Therefore, a user can forward personal data of his/her OSN friends to third party providers without an explicitly stated consent of his/her OSN friends. In the following, we present a Facebook App, i.e., the Facebook Privacy Application (FBPA), that implements the concepts stated before to establish adequate mental models of data flows in users' minds with respect to the mentioned use case. The FBPA is implemented as a web application that can be integrated into the Facebook site as an App[6]. We developed prototypes in order to evaluate which features could be most promising for demonstrating privacy risks with regard to the forwarding of friends' data to App providers. The main page of the final solution, inter alia, includes the features shown in Figure 6.4 that we present in detail in the following (note that the numbers in the figure match the numbering of the detailed explanation of the individual parts of the App).

---

[6]Note that prototypes of the App have been implemented by a group of students participating within a practical course on the topic *Web Engineering* at the KIT (summer term 2012) and the prototypes have been developed further by the research assistants Alexander Wolf and Florian Werling. The author would like to thank these students and, in particular, his colleague Matthias Keller for the invaluable contributions.

(1) Attention getter: randomly picked OSN friend whose PII is presented

The first section of the App shows an OSN friend of the current user of the App in order to get this user's attention on the fact that he/she has (potentially) already forwarded PII of his/her friends. In particular, this part of the FBPA picks one of the user's friends (preferable one with a certain amount of shared PII) and displays a "thank you"-information to the user that says he/she (potentially) brought the App provider into the position to get data of a particular friend.

(2) Uploaded photos containing potentially precarious content

Next, the App shows photos picked out of the albums of the user's OSN friends that are tagged with one or more certain keywords that could indicate precarious content, e.g., alcohol, party, etc.. This particular section aims at further establishing mental models that include the potential flows of PII and other shared content to an App provider.

(3) Location Information

The third section displays the current cities of a user's friends on a map and claims another "thanks" to the user in the form of: "Now, we know where your friends live".

(4) Attribute Prediction

Based on the findings presented in Section 5.4, in the forth section of the App, we try to infer a user's current city, hometown, and age if the App provider is not provided with this information by the user. With that, we demonstrate that even non-shared PII is at risk regarding privacy and could be inferred by third parties. Furthermore, this part of the App aims at sharpen the users' mental models in the direction of perceiving potential privacy leaks due to data shared by their OSN friends.

(5) Statistical Data

In the last section of the FBPA, we provide statistical information on the whole set of data that could be accessed by the App. Hence, we show how many photos, videos, and other information a user would (potentially) forward by using an App.

Besides this main page, the FBPA provides also information on how users can adjust privacy settings so that their own PII cannot be forwarded to third party providers of Apps their OSN friends make use of. Furthermore, we explain the potentially unintended flows of PII induced by the installation of an App in a more abstract manner, i.e., the FBPA suggests users with content that demonstrates the principles on top of which the respective data flows can occur.

## 6.5.3   Issues with Respect to Providing Privacy Applications

In this last section on potentially effective privacy applications, we emphasize issues regarding the deployment, or rather productive operation of such technical support to establish adequate mental models. Certainly, a clear and comprehensive understanding of each of any potentially occurring flow of PII is essential to adjust privacy settings according to a user's privacy awareness and consequential privacy demands.

The tool presented previously contributes an essential building block towards such an understanding. However, in light of data protection in general and the German data protection acts in particular, it can be difficult to deploy such application to be used by today's OSN users:

Strictly speaking, the processing of data shared by a user's OSN friends by a third party App provider is illegal because of the non-existent consent of the OSN friends, at least, in light of the German data protection act (cf. Section 5.1.1). Since the FBPA is also implemented as a Facebook App, this App is also not allowed to process the data of users' OSN friends. This applies as a matter of fact regardless of the aim of supporting users to act more privacy aware. Consequently, such an App has to be implemented completely as executed at the client, i.e., the computing device of the user him-/herself. Furthermore, the App must not send any information gathered by analyzing the data of the user's OSN friends to a server of the App provider. Moreover, even with an implementation that ensures a complete execution at the client-side, we have to ask whether or not such a privacy App can be compliant, at least, in light of the German law. The reason constitutes the fact that with a client-side execution actually the user would analyze the data shared by his/her OSN friends, which could be an unintended behavior from the perspective of the OSN friends. However, if the implementation of the App ensures not any flow of PII to the provider of the App, the analysis of OSN friend's personal data is only be used to help the user him-/herself and the analysis is only be triggered by the user him-/herself. Therefore, we can argue that §1, Section 2, Number 3 BDSG and §27, Section 1, Sentence 2 could allow the deployment of such an App. In particular, these paragraphs allow the processing of PII for personal or familial use. If the mentioned requirements are fulfilled, with the help of FBPA a user would only process PII of his/her OSN friends for his/her own personal use, i.e., adapting his/her own mental models of potentially occurring flows of PII. Therefore, a deployment of a FBPA could be seen as compliant with respect to the German data protection act if completely executed at client-side and if the results of the analysis "stay" at the client-side.

Besides the legal restrictions, another issue of the productive operation of these kind of privacy tools is worth mentioning. In fact, it is not very difficult to copy the design of a privacy App that aims at helping the users adjusting privacy settings appropriately. Therefore, malicious third parties could implement such an App as a basis to carry out illegal business, i.e., these third parties could provide a "Trojan Privacy App" that pretends to be compliant, but actually gathers the data of a user and his/her OSN friends. Thus, the FBPA and similar privacy applications could only be deployed in a trustworthy environment. However, a privacy App is deployed within an OSN environment, which is far more open to the public than, for instance, enterprise IAM services. Thus, a provider has even more to consider security requirements. With that, a privacy tool that establishes adequate mental models of potential flows of PII could effectively support users in keeping track of their shared information without inducing additional threats to the users. Moreover, such an App would provide an understanding of possible unintended flows of PII as a basis to adjust privacy settings adequately [Lab12].

In general, in this part of the dissertation, we introduced a concept on top of which technical measures can be implemented that bridge the gap between privacy awareness and the actual adjustments of privacy settings. However, for a productive application of such a technical approach, we discussed that also issues have to be considered that are, for instance, induced by the individual data protection acts. Nevertheless, we indicated ways to advocate the application of such an approach, even in light of the very restrictive German data protection act (compared to other data protection acts). Therefore, in principle, the possibilities are existent to bring such user support up-and-running. In the future, just the three main influencing factors need to be brought even more in line, i.e., the technical design, the law, and the users themselves.

## 6.6   Summary and Conclusions

In this chapter, we discussed the estimated effectiveness of several approaches to support users in understanding and avoiding unintended flows of PII. In particular, we argued that the intensification of punishments and/or the reduction of the time gap between sharing PII and the actual realization of negative effects would be promising to enforce more restrictive privacy settings. However, we also discussed that such an operant conditioning would not be realizable because of the need to harm users. Therefore, we proposed to make use of another approach that could provide "nudges" in the direction of adequate adjustments of privacy settings, i.e., the demonstration of a user's current situation regarding privacy to the user him-/herself. Combined with a demonstration of the resulting risks, such an approach has the potential to clarify who can actually access shared PII and what are the consequences, or rather privacy implications. In turn, this understanding of possible data flows constitutes the basis to adequately adjust privacy settings according to users' privacy demands. In the process of this chapter, we contrasted technical measures that make use of this privacy "nudging" approach with IAM systems provided in enterprise environments. Afterwards, we presented the principle design of effective privacy tools and showed a prototypical implementation in terms of a Facebook App. Furthermore, we discussed legal and other issues that have to be considered to provide OSN users with those privacy applications. Finally, we pointed out that privacy tools that are based on the introduced concepts of "nudging" towards privacy aware acting in OSNs and the findings gained in this dissertation are promising and should be deployed in the near future.

# 7
# Conclusions and Outlook

Due to the fact that users like to, or rather have to consume IT services, they are confronted with the often obligatory transmission of pieces of their personally identifiable information (PII) to the service that is to be used. Additionally, the service consumption frequently implies not only the transmission of data to the service provider, but also the disclosure of PII beyond flows between users and consumed services (or rather the intended audience) that have to be considered. For instance, if users are unduly generous by sharing data in Online Social Networks (OSNs) and have not yet set their privacy settings adequately, probably a broad audience can get access to the shared information, i.e., even attacking third parties.

This dissertation presented research results on unintended flows of PII that may occur by using IT services. Thereby, two different areas of application, in which IT services are provided, were investigated. On the one hand, the thesis covered Identity and Access Management (IAM) systems deployed in enterprise environments, which are in charge of providing PII to services a user is going to consume. In particular, we introduced improvements of particular IAM services, i.e., SAML identity providers, in order to avoid unintended flows of PII. On the other hand, we investigated users' publicly available PII in OSNs with respect to possibly unintended data flows, or rather unintentionally publicly available information. Additionally, we identified and investigated risks that come along with publicly available PII in terms of measures a malicious third party can take to increase value of accessible information. Furthermore, we presented a concept to support users in managing flows of their own personal data. In general, the thesis demonstrated strategies, methods, and technology to avoid unintended flows of PII.

Within enterprise environments, IT services are often provided in an integrated manner and, therefore, based on locally operated IAM systems and services. These IAM infrastructures provide IT services with authentication services. Furthermore, attributes can be delivered to the services at this point in time a user is authenticated in order to provide a basis for authorization and for providing the service itself. IAM systems that are based on the *Security Assertion Markup Language* (SAML) are very popular, particularly in the academia. SAML-based IAM systems are not only deployed to be solely used within an organization, but also to collaborate with other organizations in terms of federated services, i.e., providing access to services provided by several organizations by the use of the credentials a user got from his/her own organization, i.e., the home organization. However, these federations impose restrictions with respect to the implementation of data flows within the local IAM systems. Furthermore, federations expand the range of recipients that are suggested with a user's PII when he/she is consuming an IT service.

In this dissertation, we presented solutions to ensure that only authorized entities can get access to PII, for instance, users' credentials, despite the restrictions and characteristics that emerge with the federation of SAML-based IAM infrastructures. In this context, we implemented a plug-in for Shibboleth-based infrastructures based on the concept of *JAVA™ Authentication and Authorization Services* (JAAS) that are already used by Shibboleth identity providers. This plug-in ensures that an identity provider sends a user's name and password only to the intended identity source to check whether the credentials are valid. Thereby, it also decreases the delay of authentication via a Shibboleth identity provider. We also implemented login modules that can be utilized by a Shibboleth instance of an identity provider to integrate proprietary identity sources. Additionally, we introduced a concept and an implementation of the integration of alternative authentication mechanisms into the frontend of SAML-based IAM systems, e.g., QR code-based authentication mechanisms and logins via accounts of third parties, such as OSNs. This integration can be useful, or rather essential, if users have to be authenticated while being located in an environment where others can spy on the person that is to be authenticated during, for instance, typing in his/her password. Furthermore, such alternative authentication mechanisms provide advantages if users have to authenticate at an open terminal where, for instance, key loggers can be installed.

The main contributions in the field of enterprise IAM systems are not only the innovative modules implemented. The main challenge in this area of application constitutes the development of modules that are deployable, operable, and easy to maintain during operation. Both, the solutions implemented for the backend and the integration of alternative authentication mechanisms into the frontend of SAML-based IAM systems were evaluated against these requirements. We demonstrated with proofs-of-concepts and productive implementations that the concepts are viable. In general, we have shown that the widely deployed SAML-based IAM systems can induce unintended data flows, in particular, if deployed in large organizations or if provided for users who cannot shield their input data from others. We introduced concepts and implemented modules to improve the flows of data and demonstrated that the solutions can be easily deployed in existing infrastructures. Furthermore, we showed that the modules do not break the established maintenance processes of the already deployed IAM systems. In summary, we showed that improvements can be integrated in such infrastructures in a "minimal invasive" manner and that customizations are operable despite the fact that they are not invented by the developer of the IAM system itself.

For the investigations in the area of OSNs, we analyzed the legal situation and identified a law compliant concept (w.r.t. the German law) to carry out empirical studies on publicly available information users share via OSNs[1]. This concept preserves users' privacy in terms of the fact that we are not able to determine the OSN profiles originally analyzed. Furthermore, during the runtime of the analysis of users' raw data shared via OSNs only anonymized statistical data is stored in the data bases. The statistical data, as well as visualizations and console outputs did not disclose the profile IDs or any other hint that provides a relation to analyzed user profiles. Subsequently, we introduced the concepts utilized for the automated and compliant analysis of publicly available PII provided within OSN profiles. We presented related work on which these concepts are based and gave insights into the implementation of the software. Furthermore, we showed how we parallelized the analysis with the help of cloud computing resources to enlarge the number of analyzed profiles and to reach statistical significance while preserving users' privacy at the same time.

With the analysis software, we performed three types of experiments, i.e., empirical studies on the *attribute availability*, the *linkability* of OSN profiles owned by a single particular user, and a study on the risks regarding possible *attribute predictions*. In particular, based on differently sampled data sets, we demonstrated the *attribute availability* of publicly shared PII within four different OSNs. Thereby, the diversity of information made public constitutes one of the most obvious findings. Due to the diverse information third parties can access via different OSNs, the question arose whether third parties are able to link different pieces of publicly available PII extracted from several OSN profiles that belong to the same particular person. A study on this question showed that linking profiles is not only possible, but can even be performed at low cost, i.e., attacking third parties do not need extensive computing resources and do not have to exploit sophisticated algorithms to link OSN profiles. We showed that friends lists, which are publicly available in about 50% of all OSN profiles (depending on the particular OSN), and simple comparisons of strings suffice for linking a user's profiles registered in different OSNs. In particular, if users registered their several OSN profiles by use of the same user name, just more than three overlapping friends of two compared friend lists indicate that the friends lists most likely belong to profiles of the same particular user. Moreover, those accessible friends lists constitute the basis to predict attributes that are not even publicly shared by an OSN user. If an attacking third party can access the profiles of a user's OSN friends, some attributes are predictable at high accuracy and without additional knowledge, i.e., side information from Google or other sources. In particular, we investigated the correlation of location attributes and users' age provided by users and their OSN friends. With that, we found that these attributes – if not provided by a user – can be inferred by attacking third

---

[1]The author would like to thank the members of the Center for Applied Legal Studies (ZAR) at KIT (in particular, Oliver Raabe) for the discussions on approaches to carry out empirical studies on OSN profiles in a compliant manner with respect to the German law.

parties just on the basis of PII shared by his/her OSN friends. However, we also showed that not every piece of PII can easily be predicted by third parties. We showed that privacy awareness has been increased such significant and privacy settings are more adequately adjusted (compared to findings presented in the related work) that the accuracy of the prediction of some pieces of PII can be estimated as significantly lower than for location attributes and the age, at least, if no additional knowledge is exploited, i.e., under the assumption of a low cost attacker model, i.e., an attack performed by, for instance, a "casual attacker".

With these empirical studies, we demonstrated still existing privacy risks, although privacy awareness has been demonstrably increased during recent years. In particular, we found that some pieces of attributes are even more frequently made public than observed in previous studies. Moreover, OSN friends threaten users' privacy because the disclosure of the list of OSN friends is often sufficient to, for instance, predict PII of a user. Therefore, no "all clear signal" can be given with respect to privacy in OSNs. However, we also showed that some privacy risks have even been demonstrably decreased, at least, if a casual attacker tries to attack a user's privacy who cannot make use of large computing resources or sophisticated algorithms. However, to further enforce adequate use of privacy settings it is not sufficient to only provide support for its adjustment and/or to apply measures to increase privacy awareness.

In the last part of the dissertation, we argued that between two already existing and also essential building blocks of acting in a privacy aware manner another third measure is not sufficiently addressed by today's privacy research, i.e., establishing adequate mental models of (potential) flows of PII in terms of measures that demonstrate users their current situation regarding privacy and emphasize corresponding privacy risks. We stressed the point that it is an issue for today's OSN users to take every receiver of PII into account that can potentially get access to information that is (to be) shared. We stated that some parts of measures to establish adequate mental models are already discussed and some are even implemented, even though the methodological basis was not sufficiently analyzed. In this dissertation, we provided a (in part psychological) discussion on the effectiveness of certain approaches to adapt users' current mental models of data flows and privacy risks. Subsequently, we contrasted the findings gained by investigating enterprise IAM systems with the issue of providing effective privacy applications. Based on this discussions and analysis, we demonstrated a fundamental basis on top of which novel privacy tools can be designed that provide the often still missing building block towards privacy aware acting in OSNs. Finally, we presented a Facebook application that demonstrates users their publicly available PII and those of their friends that can potentially be forwarded to third party App providers. Hence, we implemented the concepts introduced before concerning a particular use case of unintended flows of PII. Moreover, we discussed the legal issues of deploying such an application into a productive OSN environment. In summary, we demonstrated that acting more privacy aware can be achieved, or rather enforced by adding a third building block of privacy applications, besides measures to support adjusting privacy settings and the aim to increase privacy awareness, i.e., support to adapt users' mental models towards adequate considering of each of any potential flow of PII and corresponding privacy risks. Although some implementations of such tools are already productively deployed, this dissertation provides the fundamental basis on top of which those privacy tools can be designed.

In summary, we analyzed current flows of PII, identified possibly unintended forwarding of personal data, and investigated corresponding privacy risks. Furthermore, we introduced measures to avoid unintended flows of PII. In the context of enterprise IAM systems, we observed that improvements can be achieved very easily. However, developers and administrators of such systems are confronted with the issue to even determine unintended flows of PII. For identification of these flows it is necessary to understand the complex structure of flows of PII, involved systems, and implemented processes, which is provided by a detailed analysis in this dissertation. Furthermore, this thesis tackled another issue that is constituted by the fact that IAM systems are often already deployed, i.e., improvements have to be designed and implemented to be deployable and as operable and maintainable as the already productive IAM infrastructure. In the context of OSNs, avoiding unintended flows of PII is even more difficult, which is constituted by the fact that users induce the flows of PII on their own, which has to be considered when designing improvements of data flows. Today's OSN users have to be supported with effective privacy tools to influence their acting within OSNs as a basis of preserving more users' privacy. In the research area of OSNs, this dissertation contributed towards increased privacy aware acting in terms of quantifications of certain privacy risks and by discussing a novel concept on top of which potentially effective privacy support can be implemented.

In general, the contributions of this thesis can be used for further research in several ways. Certainly, some of the results constitute an interdisciplinary contribution. In particular, the results of the empirical studies are also relevant in the field of social science and, in particular, investigations of users' behavior in OSNs. However, the findings contributed mainly in the field of computer science. On top of the results gained by analyzing and improving enterprise IAM systems future IAM services can be built in order to ensure deployability, operability, and maintainability. Furthermore, the detailed and deep analysis of such IAM systems contribute an essential understanding of induced data flows as a basis for further research on and improvements of today's IAM systems and services. The empirical studies on publicly available PII in OSNs and corresponding privacy risks contribute a comprehensive understanding of the IT system OSN. The findings reveal the result of providing OSNs as IT services whose flows of PII are induced by the users themselves in contrast to other IT services that only consists of provider-engineered and, therefore, pre-configured processes and data flows. Computer scientists can build future OSNs by considering the findings of this research work regarding privacy risks induced by users actual interaction with the IT system OSN. Additionally, future privacy tools can be built upon the concepts introduced in the last part of this thesis in order to even more avoid unintended flows of PII in the future. Furthermore, the methodology used to analyze more than 1.5 million OSN profiles and corresponding "big data" can be reused for future studies on publicly shared PII. In this context, the findings provide a reference for future measurement studies and, in particular, impact assessments of privacy enhancing technologies deployed in the future. In particular, the specific attacker model, i.e., a model of a "casual attacker", assumed for investigating publicly available PII in OSNs leads to a fundamental basis for future research. Another research community of the field of computer science that can benefit from the presented findings constitutes the simulation community that we provide with more detailed data to model the actual user behavior within OSNs than existent before. Finally, the contributions provide a basis for adequate risk assessments by the users of OSNs themselves as part of their own IT security management, which also constitutes a field of computer science.

# A

# Integration of the JAAS Dispatcher

In this part of the appendix, we present the integration of the *JAAS Dispatcher* into productive IAM systems. First, we show the integration of the module into Shibboleth identity providers, which constitutes an implementation of SAML identity providers. Second, we discuss the interoperability of the *JAAS Dispatcher* with respect to other identity-related services that are already based on the JAAS concepts. The following sections are originated from the documentation of the *JAAS Dispatcher*. This guideline can be downloaded at `https://dsn.tm.kit.edu/3050.php`.

## A.1    Integration for Shibboleth Identity Providers

For the installation of the *JAAS Dispatcher* one has to copy the file *JaaSDispatcher.jar*[1] into the "lib"-folder (usually WEB-INF/lib) of the war-file (usually /opt/shibboleth-idp-x.y.z/war/idp.war) of the Shibboleth identity provider that is to be adapted. To configure the *JAAS Dispatcher* the file login.config has to be modified as follows.

The following lines have to be added to the top of the configuration file *login.config* (the <...>-parts have to be replaced with appropriate content):

```
ShibUserPassAuth {
        edu.kit.scc.dei.jaas.dispatcher.Dispatcher sufficient
                regExp.0="<RegEx1>" jaasContext.0="<JAASContext1>"
                regExp.1="<RegEx2>" jaasContext.1="<JAASContext2>"
                ...<Maybe more lines like the previous ones>...
        ;
};
```

---

[1]see folder JaaSDispatcher/JAR/ of the zip file that can be found by use of the following links: https://dsn.tm.kit.edu/3050.php [Last downloaded 2013-05-28] or https://www.aai.dfn.de/dokumentation/identity-provider/tools/ [Last downloaded 2013-05-28].

Note that each configured login module has to be encapsulated into a separated JAAS Context like the following example:

```
<JAASContext1>  {
        edu.vt.middleware.ldap.jaas.LdapLoginModule required
                host="<Host>"
                ...<more configuration>...
        ;
};
```

Subsequently, the file has to be stored and the identity provider restarted by restarting the application server.

## A.2  Generic Integration

The installation for other identity-related applications that make use of the JAAS concepts to authenticate users is as easy as the above presented installation description for Shibboleth identity providers. The only difference is that the name of the first JAAS Context (ShibUserPassAuth) has to be replaced with the appropriate name for the application that is to be adapted. Furthermore, the jar-file has to be placed into the correct library path. Note that the JAAS Dispatcher makes use of the framework slf4j for logging purposes.

# B

# Further Results on the Linkability Risks

This part of the appendix provides further results of the comparisons of two friends lists at a time that are extracted out of two different OSNs. The following plots are structured as Figure 5.7 shown in Section 5.3.3, i.e., aggregated plots are provided that show only the detected maximum overlaps of compared friends lists taken from two particular OSNs and the maximum number of occurrence within single comparison sets (*cs*). Furthermore, as in Figure 5.7 the plots visualize the average distinction distance between the detected maximum overlaps and the next lower overlaps of the same comparison set. Figure B.1 shows comparisons of Facebook friends lists with friends lists of possibly matching profiles found in XING. Figure B.2 shows these results for Facebook friends lists compared with MySpace friends lists. Figure B.3 and Figure B.4 present the results of comparisons of StudiVZ friends lists with Facebook and XING friends lists, respectively. Figure B.5 and Figure B.6 show these results from the perspective of XING profiles, i.e., we took profiles out of XING and compared each of the corresponding friends lists with any potentially matching profile out of Facebook and StudiVZ, respectively. Figure B.7 presents the results of comparisons between MySpace and Facebook. Since the analysis of comparisons between friends lists of StudiVZ and MySpace (and vice versa), as well as between friends lists of XING and MySpace (and vice versa) resulted in just minimal overlaps, we do not show the respective aggregated histograms in this thesis. Furthermore, because we could not detect significant overlaps, we estimate the linkability risk between these particular OSNs as significantly lower than for the other compared OSNs addressed in the plots shown in this thesis if the attacking third party only exploits the publicly provided friends lists.

Similar as interpreted in Section 5.3.3, the plots indicate that a maximum overlap occurs just a single time within a single comparison set (except some very low maximum overlaps, i.e., less than four overlapping friends). Furthermore, the average distinction distance of the maximum overlaps indicate that these overlaps stand almost always considerably apart from all other detected overlaps detected within a comparison set if this maximum overlap is larger than three. Hence, we conclude that linking profiles is feasible at low cost by just comparing names listed in friends lists of possibly matching profiles. However, the risks regarding linking profiles registered in MySpace with corresponding XING or StudiVZ profiles is estimated as significantly lower than for linking profiles between Facebook, XING, and StudiVZ.

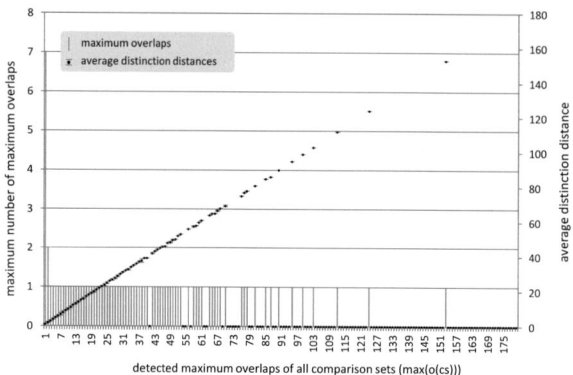

Figure B.1: Maximum overlaps and distinction distances of all comparison sets of comparisons between Facebook and XING [LTH11].

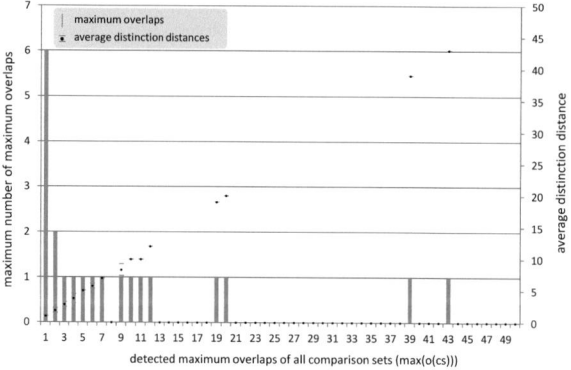

Figure B.2: Maximum overlaps and distinction distances of all comparison sets of comparisons between Facebook and MySpace [LTH11].

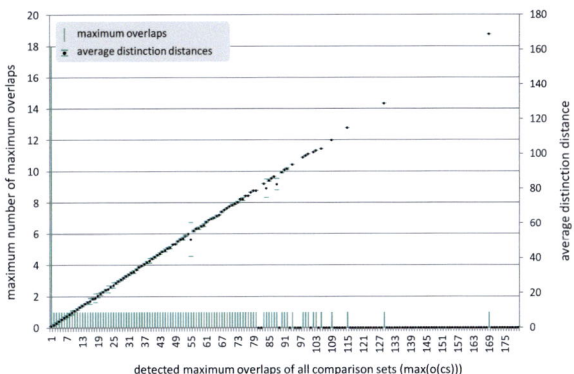

Figure B.3: Maximum overlaps and distinction distances of all comparison sets of comparisons between StudiVZ and Facebook.

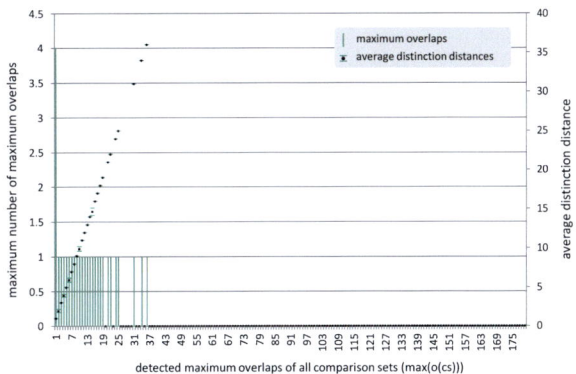

Figure B.4: Maximum overlaps and distinction distances of all comparison sets of comparisons between StudiVZ and XING [LTH11].

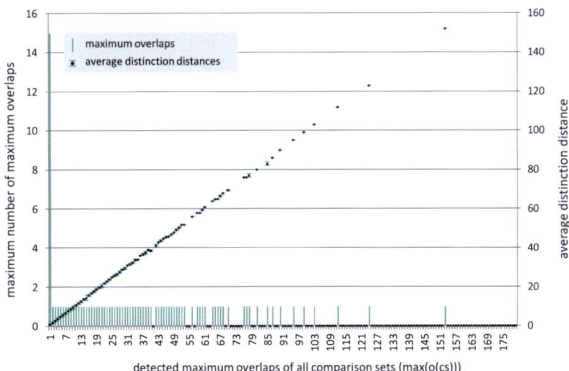

Figure B.5: Maximum overlaps and distinction distances of all comparison sets of comparisons between XING and Facebook.

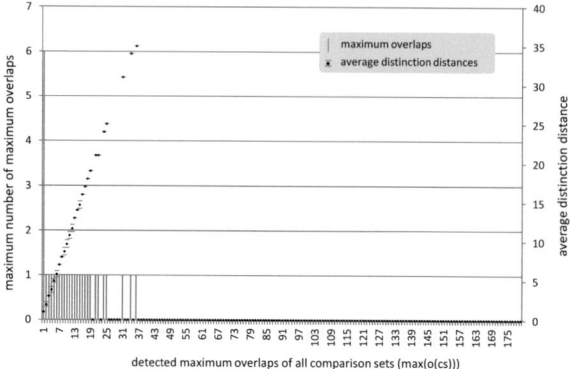

Figure B.6: Maximum overlaps and distinction distances of all comparison sets of comparisons between XING and StudiVZ.

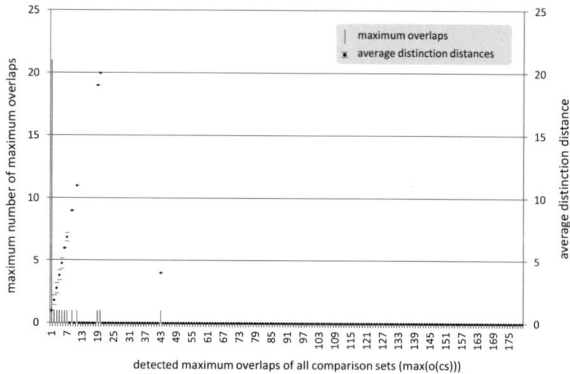

Figure B.7: Maximum overlaps and distinction distances of all comparison sets of comparisons between MySpace and Facebook.

# C
# Further Results on the Risks Regarding Location Predictions

In each section of this part of the appendix, we present four plots that show further results of the analysis of location attributes and the investigation of the risk that these attributes can be inferred by an attacking third party if the attribute is not provided by the user. The results are gained by comparing shared locations of users and those shared by their OSN friends. Whereas we analyzed provided current cities in Section 5.4.2, in the following Section C.1, we present the results with respect to users' and their friends' *hometowns*, or rather the interdependence of this attribute. In Section C.2 and Section C.3, we limit the analysis to comparisons of location attributes of those users ($\alpha$-profiles) who indicated that they are students and compare provided locations with those shared by their OSN friends. Section C.2 provides these results with respect to the attribute *current city*, whereas Section C.3 demonstrates the findings of the investigation of students' and their OSN friends' *hometowns*. The plots are similarly structured than those shown in Section 5.4.2, in particular, Figures 5.9, 5.13, 5.14, and 5.15. We show that the *results* presented in this appendix are also very similar to the findings gained by investigating the interdependencies of publicly shared current cities.

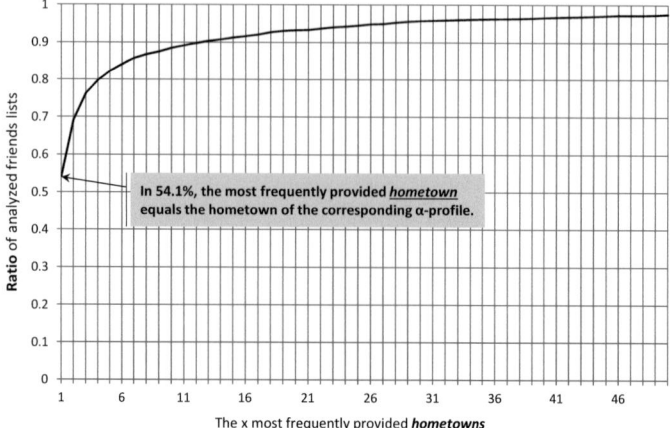

Figure C.1: CDF of analyzed friends lists, in which the most, or rather the second, or the third,... (x-axis) most frequently provided **hometown** is equal to the hometown of the corresponding α-profile [LWMH13].

## C.1  Prediction of Users' Hometown

In the following, we show comparisons of the attribute *hometown*. 2,316 α-profiles publicly shared this attribute, as well as a friends list that contained, at least, one OSN friend who also publicly provided the attribute *hometown*. "Figure C.1 shows that in 54.1 % of the analyzed friends lists the most frequently provided hometown equals the hometown of the corresponding α-profile. In more than 75 % of the cases, one of the three most frequently provided hometowns equals the one provided by the α-profile. Figure C.2 indicates that the difference of the two largest groups of friends who provided a specific hometown is often marginal. For the case of same-hometown-friends, in 77 % of the friends lists the second most frequently provided hometown is provided by a maximum of 20 friends less than the most provided hometown. However, for those friends lists in which the most provided hometown does not equal the hometown provided by the corresponding α-profile, Figure C.3 shows that the most frequently provided hometown is often located in the nearby area of the hometown provided by the α-profile. In Figure C.4, we show that 66 % of predictions resulted in a correct hometown with a distance inaccuracy of 50 kilometers and more than 70 % for distance inaccuracy of 100 kilometers. For a more detailed explanation of the plots in this appendix, we refer to Section 5.4.2, in which the corresponding plots are introduced" [LWMH13].

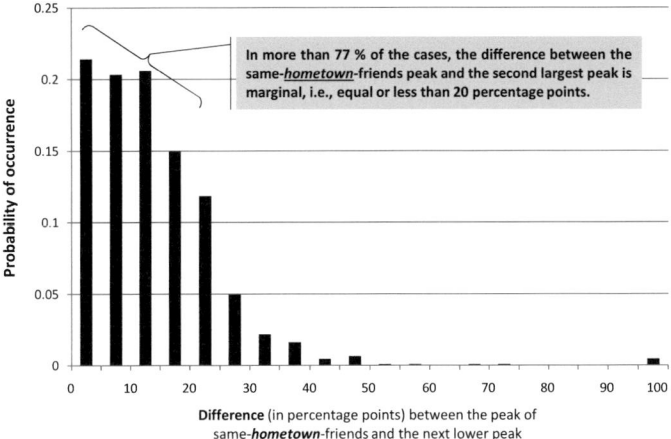

Figure C.2: Probability distribution of the differences between the number of same-hometown-friends and number of friends that correspond to the second most frequently provided city. The differences are expressed in relative terms w.r.t. the friends list sizes. Only the profiles are considered, in which the same-***hometown***-friends yield the highest peak [LWMH13].

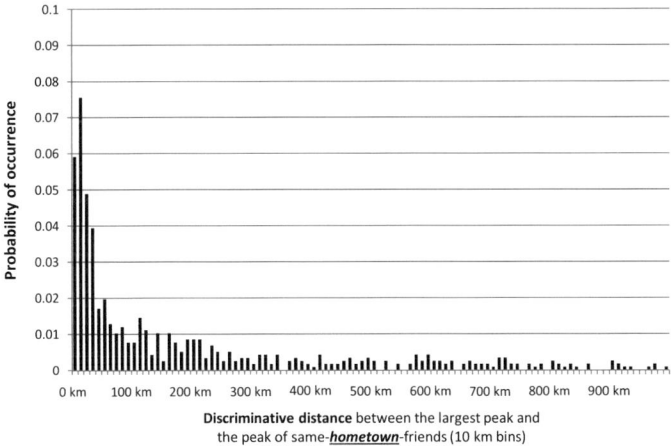

Figure C.3: Probability distribution of the discriminative distances between the most frequently provided ***hometown*** and the hometown of the $\alpha$-profile. Only the profiles are considered, in which the same-hometown-friends do not yield the highest peak [LWMH13].

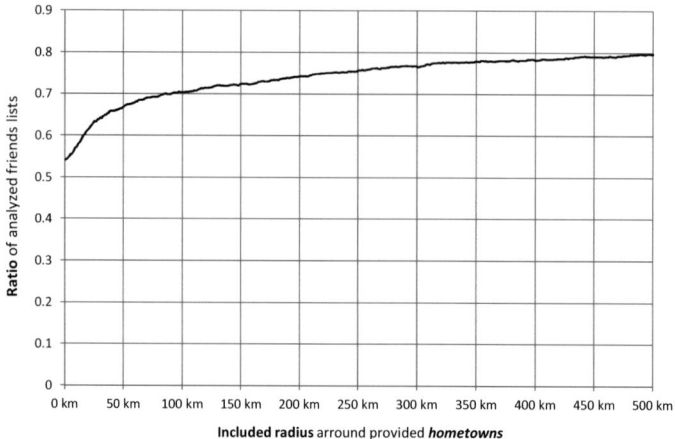

Figure C.4: Ratio of analyzed friends lists, in which a **hometown** prediction would be successful if the number of friends in an x km radius around provided hometowns is included in the detection of the most frequently provided hometown or area, respectively [LWMH13].

## C.2   Prediction of Students' Current City

In this Section, we present the results of interdependencies of publicly shared *current cities* of $\alpha$-profiles and their OSN friends. Thereby, the results only consist of those $\alpha$-profiles that could be clearly identified as profiles of current or former students. In particular, the comparisons consist of those students' profiles that shared their current city, as well as a friends list with a minimum of one friend who also provided this attribute (1,073 $\alpha$-profiles in total). With this investigation, we address the question whether or not location prediction poses a more remarkable risk for students. The first plot (Figure C.5) shows that in 56.4 % of the analyzed cases the most frequently provided city of a friends list equals the current city shared by the corresponding $\alpha$-profile (cf. Figure 5.9: 56.3 %). Even in the course of the curve, we cannot identify significant differences compared to the plots shown in Section 5.4.2. Figure C.6 also indicates no remarkable differences, i.e., in more than 64 % of the cases, the difference between the number of same-city-friends and the number of friends who shared the second most frequently provided current city is equal or less than 20 percentage points (cf. Figure 5.13: >65 %). However, it can be seen that the number of same-city-friends and friends who shared the second most frequently provided current city differs, on average, a little more compared to the results that consist of all $\alpha$-profiles. Figure C.7 confirms this little difference. Compared to Figure 5.14 the discriminative distances of the cases in which the number of same-city-friends is smaller than those living in, at least, one other city is a little bit larger, which could be explainable due to users who are moving to study in a certain city, e.g., they might still have a large number of friends living at their hometown. This observation also effects the accuracy of location predictions if a larger radius around the actual current city is "accepted". Figure C.8 shows these results for the $\alpha$-profiles of students. Herein, it can be seen that including a larger radius around the most frequently provided current city is promising from the perspective of an attacking third party. However, the effect is a little bit smaller than detected by considering all analyzed profiles, which is also explainable by the fact that many users are (physically) moving to another city for their studies.

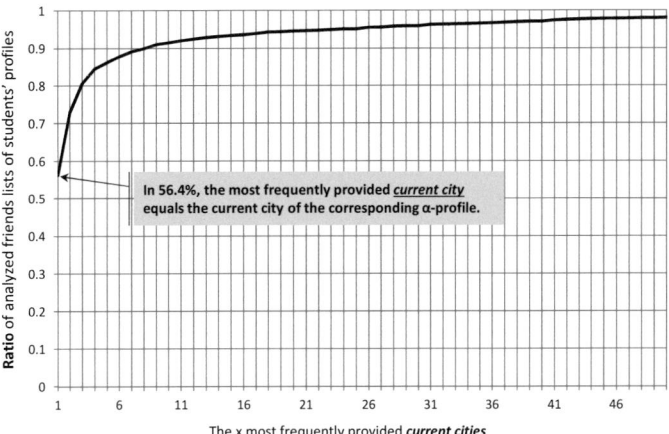

Figure C.5: CDF of analyzed friends lists, in which the most, or rather the second, or the third,... (x-axis) most frequently provided **current city** is equal to the current city of the corresponding $\alpha$-profile (only $\alpha$-profiles of students considered).

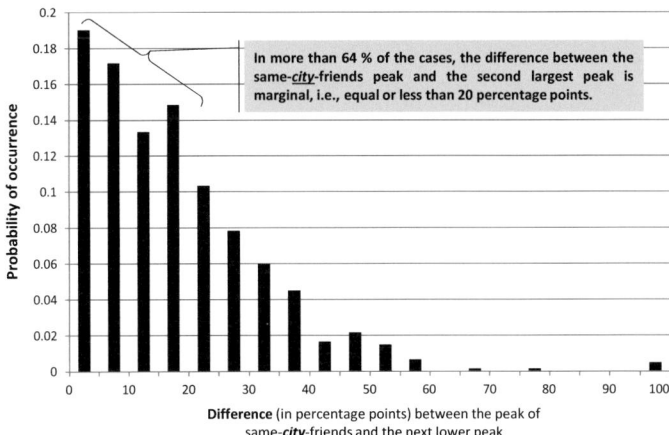

Figure C.6: Probability distribution of the differences between the number of same-city-friends and number of friends that correspond to the second most frequently provided city. The differences are expressed in relative terms w.r.t. the friends list sizes. Only the profiles are considered, in which the same-**city**-friends yield the highest peak (only $\alpha$-profiles of students considered).

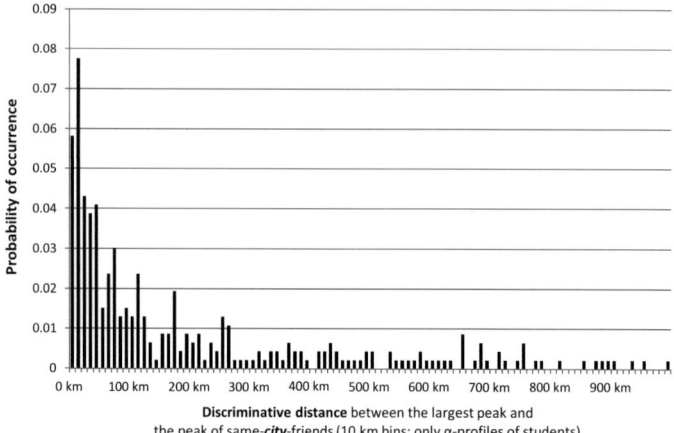

Figure C.7: Probability distribution of the discriminative distances between the most frequently provided **current city** and the current city of the $\alpha$-profile (only $\alpha$-profiles of students considered). Only the profiles are considered, in which the same-city-friends do not yield the highest peak.

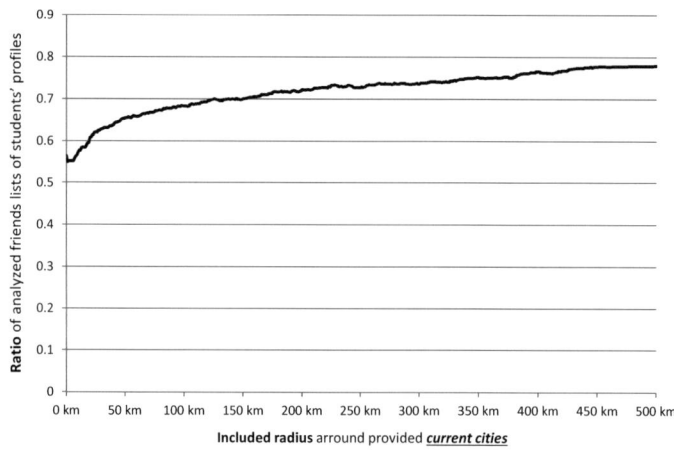

Figure C.8: Ratio of analyzed friends lists, in which a **current city** prediction would be successful if the number of friends in an x km radius around provided current cities is included in the detection of the most frequently provided current city or area, respectively (only $\alpha$-profiles of students considered).

## C.3   Prediction of Students' Hometown

For the results presented in this section, we consider the 803 $\alpha$-profiles of students that publicly provided their *hometown* and a friends list containing, at least, one friend profile that also shared the hometown. The results can be compared to the plots shown in Section C.1 of this appendix. Figure C.9 shows the probability that the most, second most, third most,... frequently provided hometown matches the hometown of the correpsonding $\alpha$-profile. Figure C.10 shows the results of the detailed analysis of potentially successful predictions of the hometown and Figure C.11 the findings regarding the investigation of the discriminative distance of unsuccessful hometown predictions. Figure C.12 again includes a larger radius around provided cities and provides accuracies of respective potential hometown predictions. However, the effects explained by the moving of students from their hometown to another city for studying discussed in Section C.2 are not that obvious in the plots regarding students' hometown. In fact, the results are very similar compared to the results presented in Section C.1, i.e., no significant difference between the analysis of all users' hometowns and those of only students can be detected.

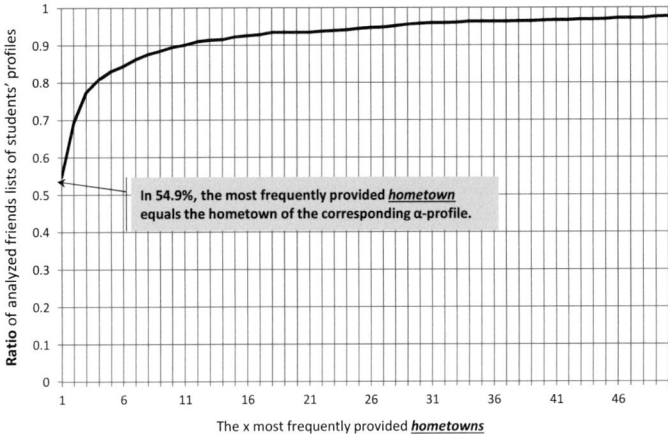

Figure C.9: CDF of analyzed friends lists, in which the most, or rather the second, or the third,... (x-axis) most frequently provided *hometown* is equal to the hometown of the corresponding $\alpha$-profile (only $\alpha$-profiles of students considered).

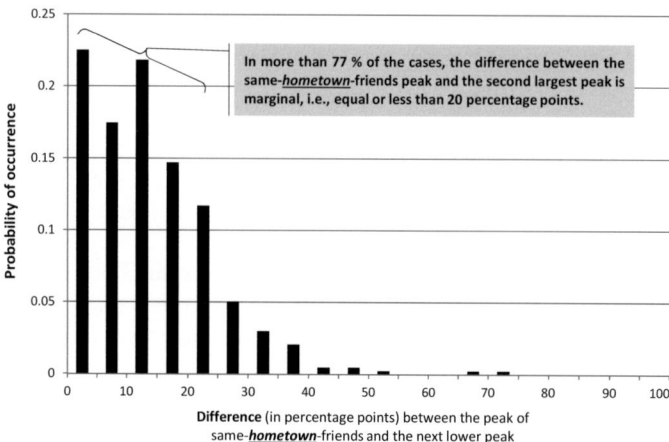

Figure C.10: Probability distribution of the differences between the number of same-hometown-friends and number of friends that correspond to the second most frequently provided city. The differences are expressed in relative terms w.r.t. the friends list sizes. Only the profiles are considered, in which the same-**hometown**-friends yield the highest peak (only $\alpha$-profiles of students considered).

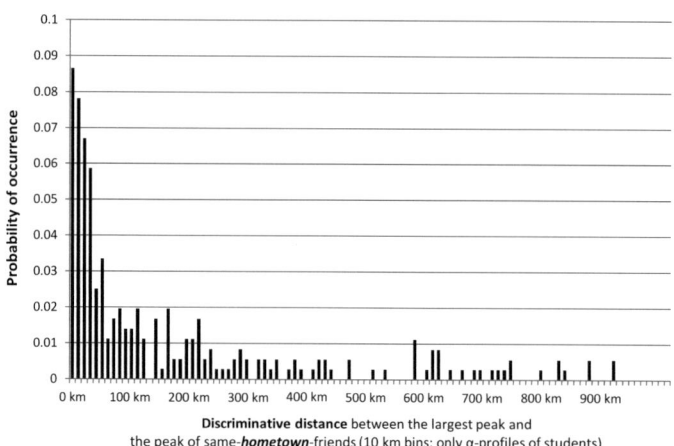

Figure C.11: Probability distribution of the discriminative distances between the most frequently provided **hometown** and the hometown of the $\alpha$-profile (only $\alpha$-profiles of students considered). Only the profiles are considered, in which the same-hometown-friends do not yield the highest peak.

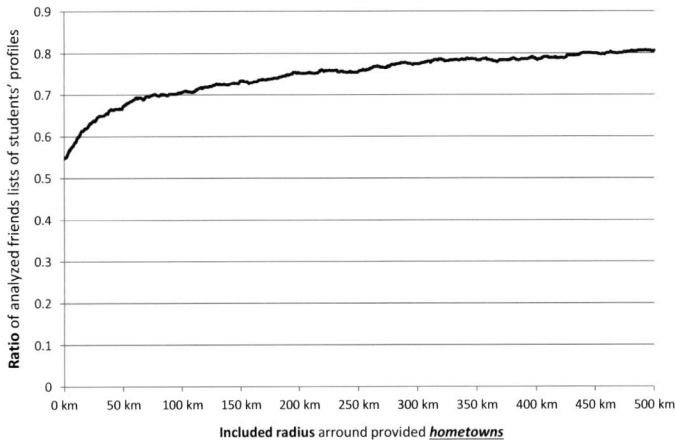

Figure C.12: Ratio of analyzed friends lists, in which a **hometown** prediction would be successful if the number of friends in an x km radius around provided hometowns is included in the detection of the most frequently provided hometown or area, respectively (only $\alpha$-profiles of students considered).

# Bibliography

[AAF11]  Seyed Hossein Ahmadinejad, Mohd Anwar, and Philip W. L. Fong. Inference attacks by third-party extensions to social network systems. In *Proceedings of the IEEE International Conference on Pervasive Computing and Communications Workshops*, PERCOM Workshops, pages 282–287, Seattle, WA, USA, March 2011. IEEE.

[ACF12]  Cuneyt Gurcan Akcora, Barbara Carminati, and Elena Ferrari. Privacy in social networks: How risky is your social graph? In *Proceedings of the 28th IEEE International Conference on Data Engineering*, ICDE, pages 9–19, Washington, DC, USA, April 2012. IEEE.

[Acq04]  Alessandro Acquisti. Privacy in electronic commerce and the economics of immediate gratification. In *Proceedings of the 5th ACM Conference on Electronic Commerce*, EC '04, pages 21–29, New York, NY, USA, May 2004. ACM.

[ASM13]  Haitham S. Al-Sinani and Chris J. Mitchell. Enabling interoperation between shibboleth and information card systems. *Security and Communication Networks*, 6(2):219–229, 2013.

[BBF+06]  Tom Barton, Jim Basney, Tim Freeman, Tom Scavo, Frank Siebenlist, Von Welch, Rachana Ananthakrishnan, Bill Baker, Monte Goode, and Kate Keahey. Identity federation and attribute-based authorization through the globus toolkit, shibboleth, gridshib, and myproxy. In *Proceedings of the 5th Annual PKI R&D Workshop*, Gaithersburg, MD, USA, April 2006. Internet 2.

[BCDF06]  Luca Becchetti, Carlos Castillo, Debora Donato, and Adriano Fazzone. A comparison of sampling techniques for Web characterization. In *Proceedings of the Workshop on Link Analysis: Dynamics and Static of Large Networks*, LinkKDD '06, Philadelphia, PA, USA, August 2006. ACM.

[BDSVM12]  Norbert Blenn, Christian Doerr, Nasireddin Shadravan, and Piet Van Mieghem. How much do your friends know about you?: reconstructing private information from the friendship graph. In *Proceedings of the 5th Workshop on Social Network Systems*, SNS '12, pages 2:1–2:6, Bern, Switzerland, April 2012. ACM.

[BE07]   Danah Boyd and Nicole B. Ellison. Social network sites: Definition, history, and scholarship. *Journal of Computer-Mediated Communication*, 13(1-2):210–230, 2007.

[Bec11]   Christian Beck. Einbindung des Smartphones in eine Single Sign-on (SSO) Architektur mittels QR-Codes (German). Student's thesis, Technische Universität München, 2011.

[BFW10]   Jim Basney, Terry Fleury, and Von Welch. Federated login to TeraGrid. In *Proceedings of the 9th Symposium on Identity and Trust on the Internet*, IDtrust '10, pages 1–11, Gaithersburg, Maryland, USA, April 2010.

[BH11]   Ingmar Baumgart and Fabian Hartmann. Towards secure user-centric networking: Service-oriented and decentralized social networks. In *Proceedings of the 1st International Workshop on Socio-Aware Networked Computing Systems at 5th IEEE International Conference on Self-Adaptive and Self-Organizing Systems*, SaSo'11, Ann Arbor, Michigan, USA, October 2011. IEEE.

[BHI⁺08]   Garrett Brown, Travis Howe, Micheal Ihbe, Atul Prakash, and Kevin Borders. Social networks and context-aware spam. In *Proceedings of the ACM Conference on Computer Supported Cooperative Work*, CSCW '08, pages 403–412, San Diego, CA, USA, November 2008. ACM.

[BKP⁺12]   Sergey Bartunov, Anton Korshunov, Seung-Taek Park, Wonho Ryu, and Hyungdong Lee. Joint link-attribute user identity resolution in online social networks. In *Proceedings of the 6th International ACM Workshop on Social Network Mining and Analysis*, SNA-KDD, Beijing, China, August 2012. ACM.

[RFC1738]   T. Berners-Lee, L. Masinter, and M. McCahill. Uniform Resource Locators (URL). RFC 1738 (Proposed Standard), December 1994. Obsoleted by RFCs 4248, 4266, updated by RFCs 1808, 2368, 2396, 3986, 6196, 6270.

[BLSC09]   Andrew Besmer, Heather Richter Lipford, Mohamed Shehab, and Gorrell Cheek. Social applications: exploring a more secure framework. In *Proceedings of the 5th Symposium on Usable Privacy and Security*, SOUPS '09, pages 2:1–2:10, Mountain View, CA, USA, July 2009. ACM.

[BPL⁺11]   Bibi Berg, Stefanie Pötzsch, Ronald Leenes, Katrin Borcea-Pfitzmann, and Filipe Beato. Privacy in social software. In Jan Camenisch, Simone Fischer-Hübner, and Kai Rannenberg, editors, *Privacy and Identity Management for Life*, pages 33–60. Springer Berlin Heidelberg, 2011.

[BRP05]   Mike Bergmann, Martin Rost, and John Sören Pettersson. Exploring the feasibility of a spatial user interface paradigm for privacy-enhancing technology. In *Proceedings of the 14th International Conference on Information Systems Development*, ISD '05, pages 437–448, Karlstad, Sweden, August 2005. Springer.

[BRS⁺12] Mohamed Bourimi, Ismael Rivera, Simon Scerri, Marcel Heupel, Keith Cortis, and Simon Thiel. Integrating multi-source user data to enhance privacy in social interaction. In *Proceedings of the 13th International Conference on Interaccion Persona-Ordenador*, INTERACCION '12, pages 51:1–51:7, Elche, Spain, October 2012. ACM.

[BSB07] Vittorio Bertocci, Garrett Serack, and Caleb Baker. *Understanding windows cardspace: an introduction to the concepts and challenges of digital identities*. Addison-Wesley Professional, first edition, 2007.

[BSBK09] Leyla Bilge, Thorsten Strufe, Davide Balzarotti, and Engin Kirda. All your contacts are belong to us: automated identity theft attacks on social networks. In *Proceedings of the 18th International Conference on World Wide Web*, WWW '09, pages 551–560, Madrid, Spain, April 2009. ACM.

[BSCGS07] Abhilasha Bhargav-Spantzel, Jan Camenisch, Thomas Gross, and Dieter Sommer. User centricity: A taxonomy and open issues. *J. Comput. Secur.*, 15:493–527, October 2007.

[BSM10] Lars Backstrom, Eric Sun, and Cameron Marlow. Find me if you can: improving geographical prediction with social and spatial proximity. In *Proceedings of the 19th International Conference on World Wide Web*, WWW '10, pages 61–70, Raleigh, NC, USA, April 2010. ACM.

[BVDN12] Faysal Boukayoua, Jan Vossaert, Bart Decker, and Vincent Naessens. Using a smartphone to access personalized web services on a workstation. In Jan Camenisch, Bruno Crispo, Simone Fischer-Hübner, Ronald Leenes, and Giovanni Russello, editors, *Privacy and Identity Management for Life*, volume 375 of *IFIP Advances in Information and Communication Technology*, pages 144–156. Springer Berlin Heidelberg, 2012.

[CAK12] Abdelberi Chaabane, Gergely Acs, and Mohamed A. Kaafar. You are what you like! Information leakage through users' Interests. In *Proceedings of the 19th Annual Network & Distributed System Security Symposium*, NDSS'12, San Diego, CA, USA, February 2012. Internet Society.

[Cam05] Kim Cameron. The laws of identity. Technical report, Microsoft Corporation, 2005.

[CDMF⁺11] Salvatore A. Catanese, Pasquale De Meo, Emilio Ferrara, Giacomo Fiumara, and Alessandro Provetti. Crawling facebook for social network analysis purposes. In *Proceedings of the International Conference on Web Intelligence, Mining and Semantics*, WIMS '11, pages 52:1–52:8, Sogndal, Norway, May 2011. ACM.

[CGNP12]  Sadie Creese, Michael Goldsmith, Jason R. C. Nurse, and Elizabeth Phillips. A data-reachability model for elucidating privacy and security risks related to the use of online social networks. In *Proceedings of the 11th IEEE International Conference on Trust, Security and Privacy in Computing and Communications*, TrustCom '12, pages 1124–1131, Liverpool, UK, June 2012. IEEE.

[CPWF07]  Duen Horng Chau, Shashank Pandit, Samuel Wang, and Christos Faloutsos. Parallel crawling for online social networks. In *Proceedings of the 16th International Conference on World Wide Web*, WWW '07, pages 1283–1284, Banff, Alberta, Canada, May 2007. ACM.

[CRCC07]  Alan Cooper, Robert Reimann, Dave Cronin, and Alan Cooper. *About face 3: the essentials of interaction design*. Wiley Pub, Indianapolis, 3rd edition, 2007.

[CSRH12]  Keith Cortis, Keith Scerri, Keith Rivera, and Keith Handschuh. Discovering semantic equivalence of people behind online profiles. In *Proceedings of the 5th International Workshop on Resource Discovery at 9th Extended Semantic Web Conference*, ESWC 2012, pages 104–118, Heraklion, Greece, May 2012.

[CSS12]  Denzil Correa, Ashish Sureka, and Raghav Sethi. WhACKY ! – what anyone could know about you from Twitter. In *Proceedings of the 10th Annual Conference on Privacy Security and Trust*, PST '12, Paris, France, July 2012.

[DA12]  André Deuker and Andreas Albers. Who cares? content sharing on social networking sites: A grounded theory study. In *Proceedings of the 16th Pacific Asia Conference on Information Systems*, PACIS '12, Hochiminh City, Vietnam, July 2012.

[Deu12]  André Deuker. Friend-to-friend privacy protection on social networking sites: A grounded theory study. In *Proceedings of the 18th Americas Conference on Information Systems*, AMCIS '12, Seattle, Washington, USA, August 2012.

[DHP07]  Catherine Dwyer, Starr R. Hiltz, and Katia Passerini. Trust and privacy concern within social networking sites: A comparison of Facebook and MySpace. In *Proceedings of the 13th Americas Conference on Information Systems*, AMCIS '07, Keystone, Colorado, USA, August 2007.

[DJR12]  Ratan Dey, Zubin Jelveh, and Keith Ross. Facebook users have become much more private: A large-scale study. In *Proceedings of the IEEE International Conference on Pervasive Computing and Communications Workshops*, PERCOM Workshops, pages 346–352, Lugano, Switzerland, March 2012. IEEE.

[DR01]   Pedro Domingos and Matt Richardson. Mining the network value of customers. In *Proceedings of the 7th ACM SIGKDD international conference on Knowledge discovery and data mining*, KDD '01, pages 57–66, San Francisco, CA, USA, August 2001. ACM.

[DRA12]  André Deuker, Christoph Rosenkranz, and Andreas Albers. The usage of individual privacy settings on social networking sites - drawing desired digital images of oneself. In *Proceedings of the 20th European Conference on Information Systems*, ECIS '12, Barcelona, Spain, June 2012.

[Dun93]  Robin Dunbar. Coevolution of neocortex size, group size and language in humans. *Behavioral and Brain Sciences*, 16(4):681–735, 1993.

[Eck08]  Claudia Eckert. *IT-Sicherheit: Konzepte, Verfahren, Protokolle (German)*. Oldenbourg, 2008.

[FE08]   Adrienne Felt and David Evans. Privacy protection for social networking platforms. In *Proceedings of Web 2.0 Security and Privacy*, W2SP '08, Oakland, CA, USA, May 2008.

[RFC2616] R. Fielding, J. Gettys, J. Mogul, H. Frystyk, L. Masinter, P. Leach, and T. Berners-Lee. Hypertext Transfer Protocol – HTTP/1.1. RFC 2616 (Draft Standard), June 1999. Updated by RFCs 2817, 5785, 6266, 6585.

[FHHW11] Simone Fischer-Huebner, Hans Hedbom, and Erik Waestlund. Trust and assurance HCI. In Jan Camenisch, Simone Fischer-Hübner, and Kai Rannenberg, editors, *Privacy and Identity Management for Life*, pages 245–260. Springer Berlin Heidelberg, 2011.

[FK99]   Ian Foster and Carl Kesselman, editors. *The grid: blueprint for a new computing infrastructure*. Morgan Kaufmann Publishers Inc., San Francisco, CA, USA, 1999.

[FL10]   Lujun Fang and Kristen LeFevre. Privacy wizards for social networking sites. In *Proceedings of the 19th International Conference on World Wide Web*, WWW '10, pages 351–360, Raleigh, NC, USA, April 2010. ACM.

[FWCY10] Benjamin C. M. Fung, Ke Wang, Rui Chen, and Philip S. Yu. Privacy-preserving data publishing: A survey of recent developments. *ACM Comput. Surv.*, 42(4):14:1–14:53, June 2010.

[GA05]   Ralph Gross and Alessandro Acquisti. Information revelation and privacy in online social networks. In *Proceedings of the 2005 ACM Workshop on Privacy in the Electronic Society*, WPES'05, pages 71–80, Alexandria, VA, USA, November 2005. ACM.

[GA11]   Daniel Gayo Avello. All liaisons are dangerous when all your friends are known to us. In *Proceedings of the 22nd ACM Conference on Hypertext and Hypermedia*, HT '11, pages 171–180, Eindhoven, Netherlands, June 2011. ACM.

[GGPW07] Ralf Groeper, Christian Grimm, Stefan Piger, and Jan Wiebelitz. An architecture for authorization in grids using shibboleth and voms. In *Proceedings of the 33rd EUROMICRO Conference on Software Engineering and Advanced Applications*, EUROMICRO-SEAA '07, pages 367–374, Lübeck, German, August 2007. IEEE.

[GKBM10] Minas Gjoka, Maciej Kurant, Carter T. Butts, and Athina Markopoulou. Walking in facebook: a case study of unbiased sampling of OSNs. In *Proceedings of the 29th Conference on Information Communications*, IN-FOCOM '10, pages 2498–2506, San Diego, CA, USA, March 2010. IEEE.

[GLP+13] Oana Goga, Howard Lei, Sree Hari Krishnan Parthasarathi, Gerald Friedland, Robin Sommer, and Renata Teixeira. Exploiting innocuous activity for correlating users across sites. In *Proceedings of the 22th International Conference on World Wide Web*, WWW '13, Rio de Janeiro, Brazil, May 2013.

[Gol06] Philippe Golle. Revisiting the uniqueness of simple demographics in the us population. In *Proceedings of the 5th ACM Workshop on Privacy in Electronic Society*, WPES '06, pages 77–80, Alexandria, VA, USA, October 2006. ACM.

[GPV11] Bruno Goncalves, Nicola Perra1, and Alessandro Vespignani. Modeling Users' Activity on Twitter Networks: Validation of Dunbar's Number. *PLoS ONE*, 6(8), August 2011.

[GSMY08] Minas Gjoka, Michael Sirivianos, Athina Markopoulou, and Xiaowei Yang. Poking facebook: characterization of osn applications. In *Proceedings of the 1st Workshop on Online Social Networks*, WOSP '08, pages 31–36, Seattle, WA, USA, August 2008. ACM.

[GTM+12] Neil Zhengqiang Gong, Ameet Talwalkar, Lester Mackey, Ling Huang, Eui Chul Richard Shin, Emil Stefanov, Elaine (Runting) Shi, and Dawn Song. Jointly predicting links and inferring attributes using a social-attribute network (SAN). In *Proceedings of the 6th International ACM Workshop on Social Network Mining and Analysis*, SNA-KDD '12, Beijing, China, August 2012.

[Hughes2005] John Hughes, Scott Cantor, Jeff Hodges, Frederick Hirsch, Prateek Mishra, Rob Philpott, and Eve (Editors) Maler. Profiles for the OASIS Security Assertion Markup Language (SAML) V2.0, 2005.

[HCL06] Jianming He, Wesley W. Chu, and Zhenyu V. Liu. Inferring privacy information from social networks. In *Proceedings of the IEEE International*

*Conference on Intelligence and Security Informatics*, ISI '06, San Diego, CA, USA, May 2006. IEEE.

[HDH10] T. Hoellrigl, J. Dinger, and H. Hartenstein. A consistency model for identity information in distributed systems. In *Proceedings of the 34th Annual Computer Software and Applications Conference*, COMPSAC '10, pages 252–261, Seoul, South Koreo, July 2010. IEEE.

[Hil83] N.J. Hillsdale. *Mental Models*. Erlbaum, 1983.

[HLL11] Gordon Hull, Heather Richter Lipford, and Celine Latulipe. Contextual gaps: privacy issues on facebook. *Ethics and Inf. Technol.*, 13(4):289–302, December 2011.

[HLS⁺09a] Thorsten Höllrigl, Sebastian Labitzke, Frank Schell, Jochen Dinger, Axel Maurer, and Hannes Hartenstein. Identitätsmanagement am KIT - Kurzbeschreibung (Stand: August 2009) (German). Technical Report SCC-TB-2009-2, Karlsruhe Institute of Technology (KIT), Steinbuch Centre for Computing (SCC), Karlsruhe, Germany, August 2009.

[HLS⁺09b] Thorsten Höllrigl, Sebastian Labitzke, Frank Schell, Jochen Dinger, Axel Maurer, and Hannes Hartenstein. KIM-Identitätsmanagement - Projekt-dokumentation (German). Technical Report SCC-TB-2009-1, Karlsruhe Institute of Technology (KIT), Steinbuch Centre for Computing (SCC), Karlsruhe, Germany, August 2009.

[HNS10] Josh Howlett, V. Nordh, and W. Singer. Deliverable DS3.3.1: eduGAIN Service Definition and Policy Initial Draft. Technical report, GÉANT, 2010.

[HPH11] Hans Hedbom, Tobias Pulls, and Marit Hansen. Transparency tools. In Jan Camenisch, Simone Fischer-Hübner, and Kai Rannenberg, editors, *Privacy and Identity Management for Life*, pages 135–143. Springer Berlin Heidelberg, 2011.

[ISO18004] ISO/IEC IS 18004:2000(E): Information technology – Automatic identification and data capture techniques – Bar code symbology – QR Code. International Organization for Standardization, Geneva, Switzerland.

[ISO24760] ISO/IEC IS 24760-1:2011 (E): Information technology – Security techniques – A framework for identity management – Part 1: Terminology and concepts. International Organization for Standardization, Geneva, Switzerland.

[Jac12] Paul Jaccard. The Distribution of the Flora in the Alpine Zone. *New Phytologist*, 11(2):37–50, 1912.

[JIM2009] JIM-STUDIE 2009 – Jugend, Information, (Multi-) Media (German), Medienpädagogischer Forschungsverbund Südwest, http://www.mpfs.de/?id=316 [Last downloaded 2013-05-28], 2009.

[JIM2010] JIM-STUDIE 2010 – Jugend, Information, (Multi-) Media (German), Medienpädagogischer Forschungsverbund Südwest, http://www.mpfs.de/?id=181 [Last downloaded 2013-05-28], 2010.

[JIM2012] JIM-STUDIE 2012 – Jugend, Information, (Multi-) Media (German), Medienpädagogischer Forschungsverbund Südwest, http://www.mpfs.de/?id=527 [Last downloaded 2013-05-28], 2012.

[JK12] Paridhi Jain and Ponnurangam Kumaraguru. Finding nemo: Searching and resolving identities of users across online social networks. *CoRR*, abs/1212.6147, 2012.

[JKJ13] Paridhi Jain, Ponnurangam Kumaraguru, and Anupam Joshi. @i seek 'fb.me': Identifying users across multiple online social networks. In *Proceedings of the 2nd International Workshop on Web of Linked Entities*, WoLE '13, Rio de Janeiro, Brazil, May 2013.

[JKS12] Kazem Jahanbakhsh, Valerie King, and Gholamali C. Shoja. They know where you live! *CoRR*, abs/1202.3504, 2012.

[JM09] Carter Jernigan and Behram F. T. Mistree. Gaydar: Facebook friendships expose sexual orientation. *First Monday*, 14(10), 2009.

[Joi08] Adam N. Joinson. Looking at, looking up or keeping up with people?: motives and use of facebook. In *Proceeding of the 26th annual SIGCHI Conference on Human factors in computing systems*, CHI '08, pages 1027–1036, Florence, Italy, April 2008. ACM.

[KBT⁺10] Christian Kahl, Katja Boettcher, Markus Tschersich, Stephan Heim, and Kai Rannenberg. How to enhance privacy and identity management for mobile communities: Approach and user driven concepts of the PICOS project. In *Proceedings of the 25th IFIP International Information Security Conference Security & Privacy – Silver Linings in the Cloud*, IFIP SEC '10, Brisbane, Australia, September 2010. IFIP.

[KCTR11] Christian Kahl, Stephen Crane, Markus Tschersich, and Kai Rannenberg. Privacy respecting targeted advertising for social networks. In *Proceedings of the 5th IFIP WG 11.2 international conference on Information security theory and practice: security and privacy of mobile devices in wireless communication*, WISTP '11, pages 361–370, Heraklion, Crete, Greece, June 2011. Springer.

[Kem05] Mike Kemp. Insider attacks: Barbarians inside the gates: addressing internal security threats. *Netw. Secur.*, 2005(6):11–13, June 2005.

[KGA08]   Balachander Krishnamurthy, Phillipa Gill, and Martin Arlitt. A few chirps about twitter. In *Proceedings of the 1st Workshop on Online Social Networks*, WOSP '08, pages 19–24, Seattle, WA, USA, August 2008. ACM.

[KHG+08]  Hanna Krasnova, Thomas Hildebrand, Oliver Günther, Alexander Kovrigin, and Aneta Nowobilska. Why participate in an online social network: An empirical analysis. In *Proceedings of the 16th European Conference on Information Systems*, ECIS '08, Ireland, Galway, June 2008.

[Kim12]   Il-Hyun Kim. Analyse von Authentisierungs-Verfahren für Online Accounts. Student's thesis, Eberhard-Karls-Universität Tübingen, 2012.

[KLS11]   Jennifer King, Airi Lampinen, and Alex Smolen. Privacy: is there an app for that? In *Proceedings of the 7th Symposium on Usable Privacy and Security*, SOUPS'11, Pittsburgh, PA, USA, July 2011. ACM.

[KLS+12]  Jens Köhler, Sebastian Labitzke, Michael Simon, Martin Nussbaumer, and Hannes Hartenstein. FACIUS: An easy-to-deploy SAML-based approach to federate non web-based services. In *Proceedings of the 11th IEEE International Conference on Trust, Security and Privacy in Computing and Communications*, TrustCom '12, Liverpool, UK, June 2012. IEEE.

[KMT10]   Maciej Kurant, Athina Markopoulou, and Patrick Thiran. On the bias of BFS (Breadth First Search). In *Proceedings of the 22nd International Teletraffic Congress*, ITC '10, pages 1–8, Amsterdam, Netherlands, September 2010.

[Kri10]   Balachander Krishnamurthy. I know what you will do next summer. *SIGCOMM Comput. Commun. Rev.*, 40:65–70, October 2010.

[KSG13]   Michal Kosinski, David Stillwell, and Thore Graepel. Private traits and attributes are predictable from digital records of human behavior. *Proceedings of the National Academy of Sciences*, 2013.

[KV10]    Hanna Krasnova and Natasha F. Veltri. Privacy calculus on social networking sites: Explorative evidence from Germany and USA. In *Proceedings of the 43rd Hawaii International Conference on System Sciences*, HICSS-43 '10, pages 1–10, Koloa, Kauai, HI, USA, January 2010. IEEE.

[KW08]    Balachander Krishnamurthy and Craig Wills. Characterizing privacy in online social networks. In *Proceedings of the 1st Workshop on Online Social Networks*, WOSP '08, pages 37–42, Seattle, WA, USA, August 2008. ACM.

[KW10a]   Balachander Krishnamurthy and Craig Wills. On the leakage of personally identifiable information via online social networks. *SIGCOMM Comput. Com. Rev.*, 40:112–117, January 2010.

[KW10b] Balachander Krishnamurthy and Craig Wills. Privacy leakage in mobile online social networks. In *Proceedings of the 3rd Conference on Online Social Networks*, WOSN '10, Berkeley, CA, USA, June 2010. USENIX.

[Lab12] Sebastian Labitzke. Who got all of my personal data? enabling users to monitor the proliferation of shared personally identifiable information. In Jan Camenisch, Bruno Crispo, Simone Fischer-Hübner, Ronald Leenes, and Giovanni Russello, editors, *Privacy and Identity Management for Life*, volume 375 of *IFIP Advances in Information and Communication Technology*, pages 116–129. Springer Berlin Heidelberg, 2012.

[LDH11] Sebastian Labitzke, Jochen Dinger, and Hannes Hartenstein. How I and others can link my various social network profiles as a basis to reveal my virtual appearance. In *LNI - Proceedings of the 4th DFN Forum Communication Technologies, GI-Edition*, DFN-Forum '11, pages 123–132, Bonn, Germany, May 2011. DFN.

[Lee61] C. Y. Lee. An algorithm for path connections and its applications. *Electronic Computers, IRE Transactions on*, EC-10(3):346–365, 1961.

[LES07] Cliff A. C. Lampe, Nicole Ellison, and Charles Steinfield. A familiar face(book): profile elements as signals in an online social network. In *Proceedings of the SIGCHI Conference on Human Factors in Computing Systems*, CHI '07, pages 435–444, San Jose, CA, USA, April 2007. ACM.

[LG08] Alberto Leon-Garcia. *Probability, Statistics, and Random Processes For Electrical Engineering*. Prentice Hall, 2008.

[LGK11] Kevin Lewis, Marco Gonzalez, and Jason Kaufman. Social selection and peer influence in an online social network. *Proceedings of the National Academy of Sciences*, 109(1):68–72, 2011.

[LGKM11] Yabing Liu, Krishna P. Gummadi, Balachander Krishnamurthy, and Alan Mislove. Analyzing facebook privacy settings: user expectations vs. reality. In *Proceedings of the 2011 ACM SIGCOMM Conference on Internet Measurement*, IMC '11, pages 61–70, Berlin, Germany, November 2011. ACM.

[LH11] Sebastian Labitzke and Hannes Hartenstein. To whom will all the data flow? Enable users to monitor the proliferation of shared information. In *Proceedings of the Federated Social Web Conference - W3C/PrimeLife Workshop on Social Network Interoperability & Privacy*, FSW '11, Berlin, Germany, June 2011. W3C.

[LHKT09] Jack Lindamood, Raymond Heatherly, Murat Kantarcioglu, and Bhavani Thuraisingham. Inferring private information using social network data. In *Proceedings of the 18th International Conference on World Wide Web*, WWW '09, pages 1145–1146, Madrid, Spain, April 2009. ACM.

[RFC1508] J. Linn. Generic Security Service Application Program Interface. RFC 1508 (Proposed Standard), September 1993. Obsoleted by RFC 2078.

[LL07] Ninghui Li and Tiancheng Li. t-closeness: Privacy beyond k-anonymity and l-diversity. In *Proceedings of the 23rd International Conference on Data Engineering*, ICDE '07, Istanbul, Turkey, April 2007. IEEE.

[LM05] Hugo Liu and Pattie Maes. Interestmap: Harvesting social network profiles for recommendations. In *Proceedings of the Beyond Personalization Workshop*, San Diego, CA, USA, January 2005.

[LNHJ10] Sebastian Labitzke, Martin Nussbaumer, Hannes Hartenstein, and Wilfried Juling. Integriertes Informationsmanagement am KIT: Was bleibt? Was kommt? (German). In Arndt Bode and Rolf Borgeest, editors, *Informationsmanagement in Hochschulen*, pages 35–46. Springer Heidelberg Dodrecht London New York, 2010.

[LSD10] Sebastian Labitzke, Michael Simon, and Jochen Dinger. Integrierter Shibboleth Identity Provider auf Basis verteilter Identitätsdaten (German). In *LNI - Proceedings of the 3th DFN Forum Communication Technologies, GI-Edition*, DFN-Forum '10, pages 73–82, Konstanz, Germany, May 2010. DFN.

[LTH11] Sebastian Labitzke, Irina Taranu, and Hannes Hartenstein. What your friends tell others about you: Low cost linkability of social network profiles. In *Proceedings of the 5th International ACM Workshop on Social Network Mining and Analysis*, SNA-KDD '11, San Diego, CA, USA, August 2011. ACM.

[LWMH13] Sebastian Labitzke, Florian Werling, Jens Mittag, and Hannes Hartenstein. Do online social network friends still threaten my privacy? In *Proceedings of the 3rd ACM Conference on Data and Application Security and Privacy*, CODASPY '13, San Antonio, TX, USA, February 2013. ACM.

[LXH09] Wanying Luo, Qi Xie, and U. Hengartner. FaceCloak: an architecture for user privacy on social networking sites. In *Proceedings of the 12th International Conference on Computational Science and Engineering*, volume 3 of *CSE '09*, pages 26 –33, Vancouver, BC, Canada, August 2009. IEEE.

[Mal05] Eve Maler. Federated identity management. In *Proceedings of the XML Conference*, 2005.

[Mis74] Walter Mischel. Processes in delay of gratification. In *Advances in Experimental Social Psychology*, volume 7. Elsevier, 1974.

[MKG+08]  Alan Mislove, Hema Swetha Koppula, Krishna P. Gummadi, Peter Dr-
          uschel, and Bobby Bhattacharjee. Growth of the flickr social network.
          In *Proceedings of the 1st Workshop on Online Social Networks*, WOSP '08,
          pages 25–30, Seattle, WA, USA, August 2008. ACM.

[MKGV06]  Ashwin Machanavajjhala, Daniel Kifer, Johannes Gehrke, and Muthu-
          ramakrishnan Venkitasubramaniam. L-diversity: privacy beyond k-
          anonymity. In *Proceedings of the 22nd International Conference on Data
          Engineering*, ICDE '06, pages 24–24, Atlanta, GA, USA, April 2006. IEEE.

[MKMT11]  Riccardo Murri, Peter Z. Kunszt, Sergio Maffioletti, and Valery Tschopp.
          Gridcertlib: A single sign-on solution for grid web applications and
          portals. *J. Grid Comput.*, 9(4):441–453, December 2011.

[MM83]    Harriet Nerlove Mischel and Walter Mischel. The development of chil-
          dren's knowledge of self-control strategies. *Child Development*, 54(3):603–
          619, June 1983.

[MMG+07]  Alan Mislove, Massimiliano Marcon, Krishna P Gummadi, Peter Dr-
          uschel, and Bobby Bhattacharjee. Measurement and analysis of online
          social networks. In *Proceedings of the 7th ACM SIGCOMM Conference
          on Internet Measurement*, IMC '07, pages 29–42, San Diego, CA, USA,
          October 2007. ACM.

[Moo59]   Edward F. Moore. The shortest path through a maze. In *Proceedings
          of the International Symposium on the Theory of Switching, and Annals
          of the Computation Laboratory of Harvard University*, pages 285–292.
          Harvard University Press, 1959.

[MSLC01]  Miller McPherson, Lynn Smith-Lovin, and James M Cook. Birds of
          a feather: Homophily in social networks. *Annual Review of Sociology*,
          27(1):415–444, 2001.

[MTW+12]  Anshu Malhotra, Luam Totti, Meira Jr. Wagner, Ponnurangam Ku-
          maraguru, and Virgilio Almeida. Studying user footprints in differ-
          ent online social networks. In *Proceedings of the IEEE/ACM Interna-
          tional Conference on Advances in Social Networks Analysis and Mining*,
          ASONAM '12, pages 1065–1070, Istanbul, Turkey, August 2012. ACM.

[MV09]    Marti Motoyama and George Varghese. I seek you: searching and match-
          ing individuals in social networks. In *Proceedings of the 11th International
          Workshop on Web Information and Data Management*, WIDM '09, pages
          67–75, Hong Kong, China, November 2009. ACM.

[MVGD10]  Alan Mislove, Bimal Viswanath, Krishna P Gummadi, and Peter Dr-
          uschel. You are who you know: inferring user profiles in online social
          networks. In *Proceedings of the third ACM International Conference on*

*Web Search and Data Mining*, WSDM '10, pages 251–260, New York, NY, USA, February 2010. ACM.

[NRG⁺09]  Atif Nazir, Saqib Raza, Dhruv Gupta, Chen-Nee Chuah, and Balachander Krishnamurthy. Network level footprints of facebook applications. In *Proceedings of the 9th ACM SIGCOMM Conference on Internet Measurement*, IMC '09, pages 63–75, Chicago, IL, USA, November 2009. ACM.

[NW01]  Marc Najork and Janet L. Wiener. Breadth-first crawling yields high-quality pages. In *Proceedings of the 10th International Conference on World Wide Web*, WWW '01, pages 114–118, Hong Kong, China, May 2001. ACM.

[ORBL09]  Bernd Oberknapp, Ato Ruppert, Franck Borel, and Jochen Lienhard. From a pile of IP addresses to a clear authentication and authorization with shibboleth. *Serials Journal*, 1:28–32, 2009.

[PCKM11]  Daniele Perito, Claude Castelluccia, MohamedAli Kaafar, and Pere Manils. How unique and traceable are usernames? In Simone Fischer-Hübner and Nicholas Hopper, editors, *Privacy Enhancing Technologies*, volume 6794 of *Lecture Notes in Computer Science*, pages 1–17. Springer Berlin Heidelberg, 2011.

[Rap05]  David Rapp. Mental models: Theoretical issues for visualizations in science education. In John Gilbert, editor, *Visualization in Science Education*, volume 1 of *Models and Modeling in Science Education*, pages 43–60. Springer Netherlands, 2005.

[RCD10]  Elie Raad, Richard Chbeir, and Albert Dipanda. User profile matching in social networks. In *Proceedings of the 13th International Conference on Network-Based Information Systems*, NBiS '10, pages 297–304, Takayama, Japan, September 2010.

[RMN⁺10]  Mary Rundle, Eve Maler, Anthony Nadalin, Drummond Reed, Mary Rundle, and Don Thibeau. The open identity trust framework (oitf) model. Technical report, Open Identity Exchange (OIDX), March 2010.

[Rot92]  Jeffrey Rothfelder. *Privacy for sale: How Computerization Has Made Everyone's Private Life an Open Secret*. Simon & Schuster, August 1992.

[RFC2865]  C. Rigney, S. Willens, A. Rubens, and W. Simpson. Remote Authentication Dial In User Service (RADIUS). RFC 2865 (Draft Standard), June 2000. Updated by RFCs 2868, 3575, 5080.

[RYSG10]  Delip Rao, David Yarowsky, Abhishek Shreevats, and Manaswi Gupta. Classifying latent user attributes in twitter. In *Proceedings of the 2nd*

*International Workshop on Search and Mining User-generated Contents*, SMUC '10, pages 37–44, Toronto, Canada, October 2010. ACM.

[Sam96] Vipin Samar. Unified login with pluggable authentication modules (PAM). In *Proceedings of the 3rd ACM Conference on Computer and Communications Security*, CCS '96, pages 1–10, New Delhi, India, March 1996. ACM.

[SDAN13] Tobias Schreiber, André Deuker, Andreas Albers, and Mickel Neves. The privacy trade-off: App usage on osn. In *Proceedings of the 19th Americas Conference on Information Systems*, AMCIS'13, Chicago, Illinois, USA, August 2013.

[RFC4511] J. Sermersheim. Lightweight Directory Access Protocol (LDAP): The Protocol. RFC 4511 (Proposed Standard), June 2006.

[SGH+11] Simon Scerri, Rafael Gimenez, Fabian Hermann, Mohamed Bourimi, and Simon Thiel. digital.me - towards an integrated personal information sphere. In *Proceedings of the Federated Social Web Conference - W3C/PrimeLife*, FSW '11, Berlin, Germany, June 2011. W3C.

[SGJ+06] David R. Spence, Neil I. Geddes, Jens Jensen, Andrew J. Richards, Matthew J. Viljoen, Andrew Martin, Matthew J. Dovey, Mark Norman, Kang Tang, Anne E. Trefethen, David Wallom, Rob J. Allan, and David J. Meredith. Shibgrid: Shibboleth access for the uk national grid service. In *Proceedings of the 2nd IEEE International Conference on e-Science and Grid Computing*, E-SCIENCE '06, Amsterdam, Netherlands, December 2006. IEEE Computer Society.

[SHH08] Frank Schell, Thorsten Höllrigl, and Hannes Hartenstein. Federated and service-oriented identity management at a university. In *Proceedings of the 14th European University Information Systems*, EUNIS '08, Aarhus, Denmark, June 2008.

[SHH09] Frank Schell, Thorsten Höllrigl, and Hannes Hartenstein. Federated identity management as a basis for integrated information management. *it - Information Technology, Oldenbourg Wissenschaftsverlag*, 51, No. 1:14–23, 2009.

[SKB12] Adam Sadilek, Henry Kautz, and Jeffrey P. Bigham. Finding your friends and following them to where you are. In *Proceedings of the 5th ACM International Conference on Web Search and Data Mining*, WSDM '12, Seattle, WA, USA, February 2012. ACM.

[SKR12] Ahmad Sabouri, Ioannis Krontiris, and Kai Rannenberg. Attribute-based credentials for trust abc4trust. In *9th International Conference on Trust, Privacy & Security in Digital Business*, volume 7449 of *TrustBus'12*, pages 218–219. Springer, 2012.

[SKT09] Johann Schrammel, Christina Köffel, and Manfred Tscheligi. How much do you tell? information disclosure behaviour indifferent types of online communities. In *Proceedings of the 4th International Conference on Communities and Technologies*, C&T '09, pages 275–284, University Park, PA, USA, June 2009. ACM.

[SL08] Katherine Strater and Heather Richter Lipford. Strategies and struggles with privacy in an online social networking community. In *Proceedings of the 22nd British HCI Group Annual Conference on People and Computers: Culture, Creativity, Interaction*, BCS-HCI '08, pages 111–119, Swinton, UK, UK, September 2008. British Computer Society.

[SN93] Nancy Staggers and A. F. Norcio. Mental models: concepts for human-computer interaction research. *International Journal of Man-Machine Studies*, 38(4):587–605, 1993.

[Sol07] Daniel J. Solove. 'I've got nothing to hide' and other misunderstandings of privacy. *San Diego Law Review, GWU Law School Public Law Research Paper*, 44(289), 2007.

[Swe00] Latanya Sweeney. Uniqueness of Simple Demographics in the U.S. Population. Carnegie Mellon University, Laboratory for International Data Privacy, Pittsburgh, PA, USA, 2000. LIDAPWP4.

[Swe02] Latanya Sweeney. k-anonymity: a model for protecting privacy. *International Journal on Uncertainty, Fuzziness and Knowledge-based Systems*, 10 (5):557–570, October 2002.

[SWS+12] Michael Simon, Marcel Waldvogel, Sven Schober, Saher Semaan, Martin Nussbaumer, Tobias Dussa, Sebastian Labitzke (editor), Jacob Becker, Markus Grandpre, Michael Längle, Daniel Scharon, Harald Däubler und Vladimir Nikolov, and Markus Klein. bwIDM: Föderieren auch nicht-webbasierter Dienste auf Basis von SAML (German). In *LNI - Proceedings of the 5th DFN Forum Communication Technologies*, GI-Edition, DFN-Forum '12, Regensburg, Germany, May 2012. DFN.

[SZ88] William Samuelson and Richard Zeckhauser. Status quo bias in decision making. *Journal of Risk and Uncertainty*, 1(1):7–59, March 1988.

[SZD08] Zak Stone, Todd Zickler, and Trevor Darrell. Autotagging facebook: Social network context improves photo annotation. In *Proceedings of CVPR Workshop on Internet Vision*, 2008.

[tbHR34] Aristotle (translation by H. Rackham). *Nicomachean Ethics*. Harvard University Press, original: 350 B.C.E., 1934.

[tbRB68] Plato (translation by R.G. Bury). *Phaedrus (from Plato in Twelve Volumes: Laws, Vol.11)*. Harvard University Press, original: 360 B.C.E., 1968.

[TK73] Amos Tversky and Daniel Kahneman. Availability: A heuristic for judging frequency and probability. *Cognitive Psychology*, 5:207–232, 1973.

[TK74] Amos Tversky and Daniel Kahneman. Judgment under Uncertainty: Heuristics and Biases. *Science*, 185(4157):1124–1131, September 1974.

[TKH⁺11] Markus Tschersich, Christian Kahl, Stephan Heim, Stephen Crane, Katja Böttcher, Ioannis Krontiris, and Kai Rannenberg. Towards privacy-enhanced mobile communities – architecture, concepts and user trials. *Journal of Systems and Software*, 84(11):1947–1960, 2011.

[TLH12] Irina Taranu, Sebastian Labitzke, and Hannes Hartenstein. Zwischen Anonymität und Profiling: Ein technischer Blick auf die Privatsphäre in sozialen Netzwerken (German). In Hannelore Bublitz, Irina Kaldrack, Theo Röhle, and Mirna Zeman, editors, *Automatismen - Selbst-Technologien*, pages 105–129. Wilhelm Fink, 2012.

[TMTM69] Jeffrey Travers, Stanley Milgram, Jeffrey Travers, and Stanley Milgram. An experimental study of the small world problem. *Sociometry*, 32:425–443, 1969.

[TRW09] Mojtaba Torkjazi, Reza Rejaie, and Walter Willinger. Hot today, gone tomorrow: on the migration of MySpace users. In *Proceedings of the 2nd ACM Workshop on Online Social Networks*, WOSN '09, pages 43–48, Barcelona, Spain, August 2009. ACM.

[TS08] Richard H. Thaler and Cass R. Sunstein. *Nudge: Improving Decisions about Health, Wealth, and Happiness*. Yale University Press, 2008.

[TWX⁺11] Cong Tang, Yonggang Wang, Hu Xiong, Tao Yang, Jianbin Hu, Qingni Shen, and Zhong Chen. Need for symmetry: Addressing privacy risks in online social networks. In *Proceedings of the IEEE International Conference on Advanced Information Networking and Applications*, AINA '11, pages 534–541, Biopolis, Singapore, March 2011. IEEE.

[Vel09] Irma Veldman. Matching profiles from social network sites – similarity calculations with social network support. Student's thesis, University of Twente, NL, 2009.

[VHS09] Jan Vosecky, Dan Hong, and Vincent Y. Shen. User identification across multiple social networks. In *Proceedings of the 1st International Conference on Networked Digital Technologies*, NDT '09, pages 360–365, Ostrava, Czech Republic, July 2009. IEEE.

[VTCP12] Massimo Villari, Francesco Tusa, Antonio Celesti, and Antonio Puliafito. How to federate vision clouds through saml/shibboleth authentication. In *Proceedings of the 1st European Conference on Service-Oriented and*

*Cloud Computing*, ESOCC'12, pages 259–274, Bertinoro, Italy, September 2012. Springer Berlin Heidelberg.

[WBKS05] Von Welch, Tom Barton, Kate Keahey, and Frank Siebenlist. Attributes, anonymity, and access: Shibboleth and globus integration to facilitate grid collaboration. In *Proceedings of the 4th Annual PKI R&D Workshop*, Gaithersburg, MD, USA, April 2005. Internet 2.

[WBS+09] Christo Wilson, Bryce Boe, Alessandra Sala, Krishna P. N Puttaswamy, and Ben Y Zhao. User interactions in social networks and their implications. In *Proceedings of the 4th ACM European Conference on Computer systems*, EuroSys '09, pages 205–218, Nuremberg, Germany, March 2009. ACM.

[Wei09] Stefan Weiss. Privacy threat model for data portability in social network applications. *International Journal of Information Management*, 29(4):249–254, 2009.

[Wer12] Florian Werling. Integration of alternative authentication methods into a SAML-based identity and access management implementation. Student's thesis, Karlsruhe Institute of Technology (KIT), 2012.

[WHKK10] Gilbert Wondracek, Thorsten Holz, Engin Kirda, and Christopher Kruegel. A practical attack to de-anonymize social network users. In *Proceedings of the IEEE Symposium on Security and Privacy*, SP '10, pages 223–238, Oakland, CA, USA, May 2010. IEEE.

[Win00] G. Winkler. *Zeit und Recht. Kritische Anmerkungen zur Zeitgebundenheit des Rechts und des Rechtsdenkens (German)*. Springer, 2000.

[WLS+13] Yang Wang, Pedro Giovanni Leon, Kevin Scott, Xiaxuan Chen, Alessandro Acquisti, and Lorrie Faith Cranor. Privacy nudges for social media: An exploratory facebook study. In *Proceedings of the 2nd International Workshop on Privacy and Security in Online Social Media*, PSOSM '13, Rio de Janeiro, Brazil, May 2013.

[WS11] John Watt and Richard O. Sinnott. Supporting federated multi-authority security models. In *Proceedings of the 11th IEEE/ACM International Symposium on Cluster, Cloud and Grid Computing*, CCGRID '11, pages 620–621, Newport Beach, CA, USA, May 2011. IEEE.

[WXG11] Na Wang, Heng Xu, and Jens Grossklags. Third-party apps on facebook: privacy and the illusion of control. In *Proceedings of the 5th ACM Symposium on Computer Human Interaction for Management of Information Technology*, CHIMIT '11, Cambridge, MA, USA, December 2011. ACM.

[XHLZ12] Zhefeng Xiao, Huaping Hu, Bo Liu, and Tian Zhang. Design and implementation of facebook crawler based on interaction simulation. In

*Proceedings of the 1st International Workshop on Trust, Security and Privacy in e-Government, e- Systems & Social Networking, eGSSN '12,* Liverpool, UK, June 2012.

[XZL08]  Wanhong Xu, Xi Zhou, and Lei Li. Inferring privacy information via social relations. In *Proceedings of the 24th IEEE International Conference on Data Engineering Workshops*, ICDEW '08, pages 525–530, Cancún, México, April 2008. IEEE.

[YFB08]  Sarita Yardi, Nick Feamster, and Amy Bruckman. Photo-based authentication using social networks. In *Proceedings of the 1st Workshop on Online Social Networks*, WOSP '08, pages 55–60, Seattle, WA, USA, August 2008. ACM.

[YLL⁺12]  Yuhao Yang, Jonathan Lutes, Fengjun Li, Bo Luo, and Peng Liu. Stalking online: on user privacy in social networks. In *Proceedings of the 2nd ACM conference on Data and Application Security and Privacy*, CODASPY '12, pages 37–48, San Antonio, TX, USA, February 2012. ACM.

[YLW10]  Shaozhi Ye, Juan Lang, and Felix Wu. Crawling online social graphs. In *Proceedings of the 12th International Asia-Pacific Web Conference*, APWEB '10, pages 236–242, Busan, Korea, April 2010. IEEE.

[ZG08]  Elena Zheleva and Lise Getoor. How friendship links and group memberships affect the privacy of individuals in social networks. Technical report, University of Maryland, College Park, 2008.

[ZG09]  Elena Zheleva and Lise Getoor. To join or not to join: the illusion of privacy in social networks with mixed public and private user profiles. In *Proceedings of the 18th International Conference on World Wide Web*, WWW '09, pages 531–540, Madrid, Spain, April 2009. ACM.

[Zim04]  Gerrig Zimbardo. *Psychology and Life.* Pearson, 2004. Translation of the 16th edition (2002), German title: Psychologie.

[ZL09]  Reza Zafarani and Huan Liu. Connecting corresponding identities across communities. In *Proceedings of the 3rd International AAAI Conference on Weblogs and Social Media*, ICWSM '09, San Jose, CA, USA, May 2009. AAAI.

[ZYL⁺10]  Bin B. Zhu, Jeff Yan, Qiujie Li, Chao Yang, Jia Liu, Ning Xu, Meng Yi, and Kaiwei Cai. Attacks and design of image recognition CAPTCHAs. In *Proceedings of the 17th ACM Conference on Computer and Communications Security*, CCS '10, pages 187–200, Chicago, IL, USA, October 2010. ACM.